HISTORIC ORNAMENT

Treatise on

DECORATIVE ART

AND

ARCHITECTURAL ORNAMENT

POTTERY; ENAMELS; IVORIES; METAL - WORK;
FURNITURE; TEXTILE FABRICS; MOSAICS;
GLASS; AND BOOK DECORATION

BY

JAMES WARD

AUTHOR OF "THE PRINCIPLES OF ORNAMENT"

* *

𝔚𝔦𝔱𝔥 𝔗𝔥𝔯𝔢𝔢 𝔥𝔲𝔫𝔡𝔯𝔢𝔡 𝔞𝔫𝔡 𝔖𝔢𝔟𝔢𝔫𝔱𝔢𝔢𝔫 𝔈𝔩𝔩𝔲𝔰𝔱𝔯𝔞𝔱𝔦𝔬𝔫𝔰

LONDON: CHAPMAN AND HALL, LIMITED

1897

PREFACE.

————•————

THIS work is a continuation of the former volume on the subject of Historic Ornament, and treats of the historical development of ornament and decoration as illustrated in furniture, pottery, enamels, ivories, metal work, including goldsmiths', silversmiths', and jewellers' work, textile fabrics, mosaic, glass, and book decoration.

Though each volume may be considered complete in itself as far as it has been possible to consider the subjects therein treated in the dimensions of this work, at the same time the student is respectfully advised to read both volumes, as a few subjects which are necessarily only slightly noticed in the former treatise, particularly those belonging to the Minor Arts, are more fully treated in the present work.

J. WARD.

CONTENTS.

CHAPTER I.

CHAPTER II.

CHAPTER III.

CHAPTER IV.

CHAPTER V.

CHAPTER VI.

CHAPTER VII.

CHAPTER VIII.

CHAPTER IX.

LIST OF ILLUSTRATIONS.

HISTORIC ORNAMENT.

CHAPTER I.

POTTERY.

IN a former volume of this work, under the respective headings, the Pottery of the Prehistoric ages, and of the oldest nations, as Egypt, Assyria, and Phœnicia, has been noticed. The pottery of primitive Greece has also been mentioned, and some illustrations have been given. It is here intended to give a brief outline of the history of Ceramics dating from about the end of the thirteenth century; but to connect this sketch with the notice of Cyprian pottery already given it will be necessary to say something of the Greek, Etruscan, and Roman pottery. Greek vases had been found in great quantities in Etruria before they were found in the islands and colonies of Greece, or to any extent in Athens, and from this circumstance they were wrongly supposed to have been of Etruscan workmanship. The Etruscans imported these vases from Greece during the fifth and sixth centuries B.C., many of which had been placed in their tombs, from where they have been exhumed during the last hundred and fifty years.

The vases found at Athens and other parts of Greece were also, as a rule, found in tombs and burial-places; one class in particular—the Athenian *lekythi*—were made specially to contain the sacred oil or wine and to be afterwards placed in the tomb. These vases are of a long, narrow, and elegant shape, and were decorated with appropriate funeral subjects outlined on a white ground. This white ground is known as *matt*, and is of a dull surface; it is not a glaze, but simply an engobe of clay fired at a very low temperature. The draperies of the figures are occasionally coloured red, brown, pale green, or a bluish tint, and some of them are remarkable for their beauty of drawing and expression of sentiment in the design. They date from B.C. 450 to 350. Greek vases are characterized by their beauty of shape as well as by their refined decoration. Some of the richly decorated ones were given as prizes to the victors in the Olympian games, and it has also been conjectured that some of the terra-cotta vases found in the tombs were designed to represent the costlier metal vases that were offered for prizes at the games held in honour of princes at their death, the coarser terra-cotta vases being used at the death of the common people.

The shapes of the Greek vases vary in the different periods, getting more elegant as they approached the middle period—the fifth and the first half of the fourth century B.C.—and larger in size with the handles more elaborate in the later periods. The principal varieties are known under the following names :—the Amphora, a full-bodied vase with two handles, used for carrying wine ; the Hydria, a wider bodied vase, used for carrying water : it has generally one large and two smaller handles; the Crater, a large wide-mouthed vessel, used for mixing wine and water; the Lebes, a round basin usually placed on the top of a stand or tripod ; the Oinochoè, a ewer-shaped vase, used for pouring out wine ; the Lekythos, a long bottle-shaped vase, used for holding oil ; the Aryballos, for perfumes or oil ; the Cantharos, a two-handled cup on a foot, used for drinking purposes; the Kylix, a shallow cup on a foot, used for drinking wine ; and the Rhyton, or drinking horn, made in the shape of an animal's head or a sphinx.

Greek Ceramic ware, like the Etruscan and Roman, was coated with a scarcely perceptible thin glaze, supposed to be composed of a vitreous alkaline that merely hardened the clay body and left a very faint polish on the surface.

The colouring on the majority of the Greek vases of

the sixth century is a brown or red glaze on which are painted the designs in black ; the markings on the figures and drapery are incised, showing the groundwork, or being sometimes filled in with white, and the faces and limbs usually painted a white colour and fired at a low heat. Sometimes a purple tint was painted over the accessories. Vases of this period have also a white biscuit ground with similar coloured decorations as those of the red ground.

In the fifth century B.C. a change took place in the style of decoration : the figures and accessories are left in the red ground colour of the vase, and the surrounding ground-work is black ; the interior markings are in faint yellow or black, and incised slightly with a tool. This is the period of the best designs and of delicate and correct drawing. Some of the kylixes of this period are exceedingly beauti-ful, and are usually signed with the name of the artist. Some artists' names are Meidias, Polygnotos, Epictelos, Pamphaios, Brygos, Euphronius, &c. It is said that the greatest artists of Greece—Phidias, Polycletus, Apelles, and Myron—furnished designs for the potters.

The Greeks in their vase paintings observed strictly the æsthetic laws of proportion and space division (Figs. 1, 2, 3, 4) as they did in their architecture. The precision of touch which they displayed is remarkable, and the skill in the freehand rendering of their geometric and floral borders, not to speak of their figure-work, is astonishing when we think that if they made a mistake on the absor-bent biscuit ware on which they painted, it could not be altered without showing the defect.

The Levantine island of Samos has been celebrated from the earliest times for its pottery. It has been mentioned by Homer and Herodotus as unparalleled, for its size, in the wealth and artistic qualities of its people. It was renowned for its temples and metal work as well as for pottery. The Temple of Juno—the Heræum—was built in marble, and was of great magnitude—a treasure house of art in itself. The Samians were great traders, and their beautiful red

pottery was carried by their ships to all parts of the known
world.   The clay of which the Samian ware was made was

Fig. 1.—Greek Vase.
Oinochoè.

Fig. 2.—Greek Vase.   Crater.

Fig. 3.—Greek or Etruscan
Ewer.

Fig. 4.—Greek Vase.   Signed
by Nicosthenes.

of a fine red compact earth; the pottery was usually
thicker than that of the other Greek ceramics, and the

decoration was partly modelled and partly incised (Fig. 5). This ware has been found in nearly all parts of Europe, the design of which inclines to the Græco-Roman style, and is doubtless of the variety made during the Roman occupation of the island.

A Græco-Roman vase in terra-cotta is shown at Fig. 6.

Roman pottery and fragments of it have been found in every country that was formerly under the Roman rule, and consists of examples both of a very simple kind and artistic. Great quantities have been found in England, and every year almost brings new examples to light, consisting of vases, lamps, and panels in terra-cotta.

Although the Greeks never quite lost the art of making pottery during the Middle Ages, they did not produce

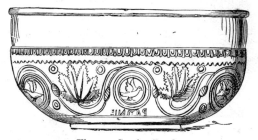

Fig. 5.—Samian Bowl.

much artistic work after A.D. 200, and between this time and the end of the fourteenth century. Artistic pottery as glazed ware was imported into Europe from Damascus through the Arabs or Saracens about this time. Cups from Damascus in glazed pottery were reckoned among the treasures of kings, and it was from Damascus that the Arabs undoubtedly brought the secrets of glazed earthenware to Spain, where they established the potteries that fabricated the famous Hispano-Moresque ware. Before dealing with this ware, it is necessary to note briefly the various kinds of glazed wares anterior to its invention. The process of glazing terra-cotta tiles, bricks, and vessels is of great antiquity. In Egypt, as early as the fourth

dynasty (B.C. 3766—3600), examples of glazed terra-cotta
tiles were in use. Copper has been employed at these
early dates to produce a turquoise blue enamel in Assyria
and Babylon, and tin has been used in the glaze mixture
on the enamelled bricks from the same countries. These
ancient tiles and bricks, therefore, belong to the category of
fayences. The word *fayence*, now of so wide application, is
derived from Faenza, a town in Italy, where enamelled
earthenware, or maiolica,
was manufactured in the
fifteenth century, which
was distinguished by its
fine polished white
enamel. Fayence is a
ware that is distinct from
porcelain; it is a potter's
clay mixed with a marl
of an argillaceous and
calcareous nature and
sand. According to the
composition, and the
degree of heat required
in firing, it is called
"Soft" (*Fayence à pâte
tendre*) and "Hard"
(*Fayence à pâte dure*).

Fig. 6.—Græco-Roman Vase.

English earthenware
made from *pipeclay* is
"soft"; stone ware, Queen's ware, and some other special
wares are hard. Soft wares are unglazed, glazed, and
enamelled. The glazed or *varnished* wares, as we have
seen, were made by the ancient civilized nations, as well as
the coarser terra-cotta or unglazed wares. In medieval and
in modern times enamelled ware, as distinct from merely
glazed or varnished wares, have been made, as well as
porcelain or China ware; the latter is called also Kaolin,
and is a fine white earth in which silex is the chief con-

stituent, which is derived from a decomposition of feldspathic granite.

Vitreous glaze (or glass) is composed of sand or other siliceous matter fused with potash or soda; this is ground and mixed with water, forming a liquid in which the clay biscuit ware is dipped, and afterwards fired, in order to make it impermeable to liquids. Oxide of lead in considerable quantities is added to the vitreous glaze, which increases its fusibility, but still keeping it transparent; this is what is known as a *plumbeous* glaze. This glaze may be coloured yellow by the addition of iron oxide; green by copper oxide; blue by cobalt; and black by manganese. All these coloured glazes were known to the ancients.

A further addition of the oxide of tin to the vitreous or plumbeous transparent glaze, in comparatively small quantities, produces the opaque enamel known as a "stanniferous" or tin glaze. This is the enamelled glaze of the Della Robbia ware, of the Hispano-Moresque, and of the Italian maiolica.

From recent analysis of the enamel on Assyrian tiles and bricks it has been ascertained that the oxide of tin was used by the enamellers of that early time, but not to the same extent as the vitreous glaze.

Persia was the natural inheritor of the art of the ancient land of Mesopotamia, and the beautiful siliceous and probably the stanniferous glaze, and also metallic lustres, have been used in that country from very early times. The Arabs, or Saracens, evidently brought the workmen from the East, and imported many pieces of Damascus ware during the independent Caliphate of the Damascus Caliphs in Cordova in Spain, which lasted from the eighth century to the year 1235, when the Moors drove the Arabs out of Spain. The Arabs (says Riaño) had, as early as the beginning of the twelfth century, if not before, established the industry of metallic-lustred pottery in Spain. Edrisi, the Arab geographer, wrote in 1154, in describing Calatayud in Spain: "Here the gold-coloured pottery is made,

which is exported to all countries." This gold-coloured
pottery is likely to have been similar to the siliceous glazed
ware of the East. The next reference to lustred pottery is
made by Ben Batutah, a celebrated Arab traveller, when
travelling from Tangiers to Granada, and when passing
Malaga (1349-57) he says: "At Malaga the fine golden
pottery is made, which is exported to the furthermost
countries." The golden pottery here referred to is the
tin-glazed Hispano-Moresque. At Manises, in the kingdom of Valencia, the famous lustred pottery *fabriques* or
workshops were in a flourishing state in the fifteenth
century, when Eximenus, in his "Regiment de la cosa
publica," quoted by Riaño, speaking of the excellent things
made in his time at Manises in Valencia, says: "Above
all, the beauty of the gold pottery, so splendidly painted at
Manises, which enamours every one so much that the
Pope, and the cardinals, and the princes of the world
obtain it by special favour, and are astonished that such
excellent and noble works can be made out of the earth."

The same author translates a document he found in the
British Museum, which gives a description of the whole of
the making and preparing of the golden lustre as used at
Manises in 1785: speaking of its composition, the document
runs thus: "Five ingredients enter into the composition of
the gold colour: copper, which is the better the older it is;
silver as old as possible; sulphur, red ochre, and strong
vinegar, which are mixed in the following proportions: of
copper three ounces, of red ochre twelve ounces, of silver
one *peseta* (about a shilling), sulphur three ounces, vinegar a
quart." All these ingredients are fused together, and afterwards ground and diluted with water and the vinegar to
make the gold-coloured glaze or varnish for use in the
decorating of the ware. A woodcut gives a very imperfect
idea of Hispano-Moresque pottery, as the lustre and colour
is everything in the ware; the designs generally are very
simple leaf-work shields and small geometric repetitions.
The beautiful dish (Fig. 7) is one of the finest examples of

the ware made at Murcia in the province of Valencia. The statement of Eximenus regarding the Pope, the cardinals, and princes sending for this ware seems to have been correct, for most of the pieces known have been found or

Fig. 7.—Valencia Dish ; Hispano-Moresque. (S. K. M.)

brought from Italy, to which country the majority of them had evidently been exported.

Besides the lustred ware manufactured in the peninsula in the Middle Ages, the *Azulejos*, or tiles of bright colours, were made in small pieces, and were embedded in the walls to form geometric patterns. This manner of using these tiles was derived from the coloured and geometric Byzantine mosaics, tiles being used in Spain where mosaics would be used in the Eastern Empire; and perhaps the earliest use of them in Spain was in the Alhambra decoration of the fourteenth century. Afterwards the tiles became larger and more complete in their patterns. Terra-cotta figures and ornament, green and white-glazed pottery were also made by the Moors in Spain.

In the sixteenth century Spanish pottery design was of the Italian Renaissance character. Unlike the Moresque work, the designs were shaded and the colours more subdued, but the Moresque design still continued in favour, and to keep its flat treatment and bright effect of colour. The Italian kind of pottery was made at Talavera, at Andujar, and at La Rambla, as well as unglazed porous and coloured ware at the former place, and white unglazed pottery at the latter places. Coarse green and white pottery was made at Toledo in the sixteenth century; a large well-head or brim, with an interlaced Moresque band in relief, from this place is now in the Museum at Kensington.

A bowl of Talavera ware of the eighteenth century, painted in imitation of the Italian maiolica ware, is also in the Museum. The colours used are green, blue, orange, and manganese tint, which are usually found on the Spanish pottery of this period.

The well-known and extensive potteries at Alcora were established by Count Aranda in 1726, where porcelain and pipeclay wares were made with all kinds of designs, mostly imitations of France, Holland, England, and China. Most of the principal painters and modellers at these works were Frenchmen or Germans. The names of the chief artists were Haly, Knipper, Martin, Garces, Ferrer, and Prato. The Duke of Hijar, son of Count Aranda, succeeded his father (1800-1858) in the management of the Alcora potteries. A specimen of this ware is shown in the Rococo plaque (Fig. 8) with the subject of Galatea.

Another celebrated pottery, connected with royalty,

was founded by King Charles III. in 1760 in the gardens of the royal palace of Buen Retiro at Madrid. This King, coming from Naples to inherit the Spanish Crown at the death of his brother Ferdinand, was anxious to establish a similar pottery in Madrid to that which he had previously founded at Capo di Monte, at Naples, so he brought his

Fig. 8.—Earthernware Plaque; Alcora Ware. (S. K. M.

staff of artists, workmen, and director of the works, Boni-celli, over from Italy to Madrid, and established the Buen Retiro works at a great cost. The yearly expenses of these works were £20,000, and all the pottery made was for the exclusive use of the King and Royal Family, and was sent as presents to foreign princes. This was the case for the first thirty years until the death of Charles III. (1798), after which the pottery was allowed to be sold, but at a very high price.

The workmanship of this pottery is good, but there is nothing particularly artistic about it. The designs are in the false taste of the late Italian mixed with Louis Seize incrusted motives. A vase in the Buen Retiro ware is shown at Fig. 9. A room in the royal palace, Madrid, is covered with plaques of this ware.

MAIOLICA.

Before the advent of Maiolica ware in Italy a similar kind of pottery was made in Spain, which had the stanniferous or opaque tin glaze and the golden lustre that belonged to the best examples of Italian maiolica. We refer to the Hispano-Moresque ware. This opaque stanniferous glaze was known to the Arabs

Fig. 9.—Buen Retiro Ware.   (S. K. M.)

of Spain from the end of the thirteenth century, or more than one hundred years before Luca della Robbia (who died in 1430) produced his enamelled earthenware.

The first specimens of Hispano-Moresque pottery were probably made at Malaga, and another important factory was at Valencia. The shape and decoration of the famous Alhambra vase (Fig. 10), one of the earliest specimens of Hispano-Moresque ware (about 1320), clearly points to its Persian origin of design, and was probably made and decorated by a Persian Saracenic artist. It is coloured brown and blue on a yellowish ground, and is decorated with animals and ornament in the Persian manner. It was found about the middle of the sixteenth century, under the pavement of the Alhambra Palace, filled with gold coins.

Fig. 10.—The Alhambra Vase Hispano-Moresque.

Hispano-Moresque ware is of a general yellowish-white colour, with an iridescent metallic lustre similar to the Italian maiolica of the end of the fifteenth and beginning of the sixteenth centuries. The ornamentation is lustrous rather than the ground, and is of a golden copper red to a pale yellow golden tint. It has been divided into three classes: the first has the ornamentation of a copper red colour; the ground is nearly covered by ornament, consisting invariably of birds in the midst of flowers and foliage, resembling Persian pottery. The ware of this class is less perfect in manufacture than that of the golden yellow designs, and is the oldest.   The second class has the colour

Fig. 11.—Hispano-Moresque Vase.   (S. K. M.)

ot a monochrome golden yellow tint, with the ornament of a small geometric character, and Spanish or Moresque

escutcheons. This variety is of Spanish origin of the thirteenth and fourteenth centuries.

The third class has the ornament partly rendered in coloured enamels, and has golden yellow armorial bearings,
interlacings, and foliage. Animals, such as antelopes, sometimes occur. This ware is the carefully executed work of
the fifteenth century. During the first years of the sixteenth

Fig. 12.—Alhambra Tile. (S. K. M.)

century the third class of ware was probably imitated by
the Italians.

The process of the manufacture of lustred earthenware
was introduced into Italy by Arabian or Spanish workmen
from the Balearic Isles.

A beautiful vase of elegant shape with large perforated
handles in Hispano - Moresque, decorated with ivy or
briony leaves and tendrils, is in the Kensington Museum
(Fig. 11).

A curious shaped tile from the Alhambra is shown at
Fig. 12, the decoration of which is purely Saracenic.

Scaliger (1484-1558) tells us that a costly fayence, as beautiful as the pottery of India, was made in his time in the island of Majorca and exported to Italy; he also adds that the name " Maiolica" or Majolica was derived from Majorca.

The island of Majorca was an Arab possession until the year 1230, and no doubt the Arabs had there founded potteries for the production of glazed earthenware.

Towards 1300, as related by Passeri, the Italian potters began to cover a raw clay with a coating of white opaque Sienese earth produced from that territory. This coating of a white opaque substance, called an " engobe," was the ground to which the colours were applied, and which, differing from the older methods hitherto employed in Italy, was a distinct advance in pottery manufacture, and has been considered as the first beginning of Maiolica pottery. Improvements were effected in the use of this engobe or opaque varnish until the time of Luca della Robbia (1355-1430).

DELLA ROBBIA WARE.

It is not known whether the above celebrated artist invented the opaque white stanniferous glaze with which he covered his works, but he was the first to use it successfully in the architectural decoration known as " Della Robbia " ware. He succeeded, however, in colouring his white glaze, thereby greatly enlarging its usefulness for exterior and interior decoration. The colours he obtained were blue, yellow, green, violet, and a copper tint. His sculptured terra-cottas glazed with these colours became objects of great request. He obtained more orders than he could execute himself, and so he employed his two brothers, who were sculptors, to assist him. His nephew Andrea, after himself was the most famous in this kind of work, and produced, like his uncle Luca, groups of figures in panels, single figures, tabernacles, friezes, &c.

Three sons of Andrea, Giovanni, Luca, and Girolamo, worked in the same material, and Girolamo was invited by François Ier to decorate the Château de Madrid with " Della Robbia" ware, representing the " Metamorphoses " of Ovid, which was done at a cost equal to £15,530.

In the Kensington Museum there are many specimens

Fig. 13.—Medallion in Enamelled Earthenware, by Luca della Robbia. (S. K. M.)

of Della Robbia ware, among which are a series of twelve circular medallions in enamelled terra-cotta, representing the twelve months of the year, one of which is illustrated at Fig. 13. The bas-relief of the Virgin and Child (Fig. 14) is likely to be a work of one of the Della Robbia family.

ITALIAN MAIOLICA.

About the year 1450 the Sforzi, the Lords of Pesaro, established at the latter place Maiolica factories, and a decree, dated 1st of April, 1486, was published, granting certain privileges to the ceramists of Pesaro.   The pot-

Fig. 14.—Virgin and Child.   School of Della Robbia.   (S. K. M.)

teries of Urbino, Gubbio, and Castel-Durante were then equally famous with those of Pesaro.   It is generally thought that the use of metallic lustre was first known at Pesaro ; the pearly, the ruby, and the golden lustres appeared at Pesaro and Gubbio before they were known at any other Italian pottery.   The early pieces are decora-

tive dishes, or, as they are called, "bacili," having a
broad border and a deep sunk centre; at the back is a
projecting circular "giretto," pierced with two holes,
which shows that they were intended to be hung up as
decorative objects. Coats of arms, or other devices, occupied the centre; the border usually is simple but well

Fig. 15.—Early Pesaro Dish. (S. K. M.)

designed, showing a mixture of Oriental with Gothic or
Italian forms (Fig. 15). The potteries of Faenza, Forli,
and Caffaggiolo are thought by some to be as early, if
not earlier, in date than those of Pesaro.

In 1444 Federigo, the second Duke of Urbino, built a
castellated palace at Urbino, and gathered around him
men of learning and many artists, and especially encou-

raged the manufacture of maiolica. His son, Guido-
baldi I., succeeded him in 1482, and he also was a great
patron of the ceramic arts. The ware made in Italy during
this time—the latter half of the fifteenth century—was
known under the name of " mezza-maiolica," this ware
differing from tin-glazed or true maiolica in its glaze in its
having a lead or plumbeous glaze; but in common with
the true maiolica, the mezza-maiolica is also a lustred ware,
having a peculiar iridescent lustre, derived from the lead
used as a glaze. This lustred ware was therefore made
anterior to the tin-glazed dishes and other objects, and
chiefly at Pesaro and Gubbio. The lustre was obtained on
a glaze of oxide of lead and glass by the use of certain
metallic oxides, and the art of making it was probably
learnt from the potters of the island of Majorca, where the
making of the Hispano-Moresque ware was well known.

The Italian writer Passeri states that the tin-glazed
ware or true maiolica was made at Pesaro in 1500, and
that the process was introduced from Tuscany. A better
ground for the reception of the colours used in the decoration was afforded by the new enamel, but it did not
entirely supersede the manufacture of the mezza-maiolica,
as a great deal of the latter ware still continued to be
made of a brilliant metallic lustre at the fabriques of
Pesaro and Gubbio. At Castel-Durante, Urbino, and
Diruta were other famous botegas or fabriques where the
lustred ware was made, but none were so celebrated as
that of Maestro Giorgio at Gubbio. It was at this famous
botega that the best of all the golden and ruby metallic
lustres were produced. The ruby lustre particularly seemed
to be a monopoly of the Gubbio workshops, for it is
known that many of the Italian factories sent their pieces
to Maestro Giorgio at Gubbio to have the ruby and the
gold lustre added as a finish to parts of the designs.

Maiolica was made at Venice in the sixteenth century,
also at Forli, Diruta, Siena, Caffaggiolo, and Faenza, where
much early work of great beauty in design was produced.

We shall only have space to describe a few of the most important products of Italian maiolica.

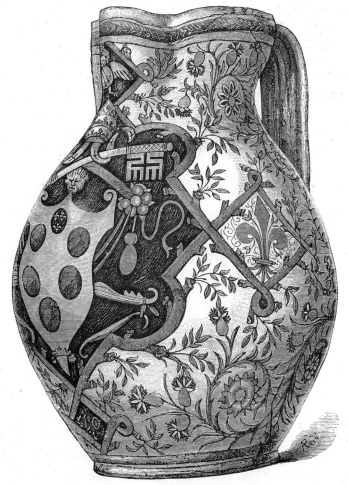

Fig. 16.—Pitcher; Caffaggiolo Maiolica. (S. K. M.)

An early method of decorating maiolica pottery is known as "sgraffitto-work," in which the patterns are scratched or incised into the ground: this was a favourite method of

executing outdoor plaster decoration in Italy. It consists
in laying on a ground of coloured clay or plaster on another
coating of a different colour, and while this second coating
is moderately soft, the pattern or design is incised or
" scratched " down to the first coating or ground, which,
being of a different colour, reveals itself, and thus forms the
pattern. In both pottery and plaster decoration sgraffitto
work is usually accompanied by modelling in relief, such
as representations of leaves, flowers, and fruit in bas-relief

Fig. 17.—Sgraffitto Maiolica. (S. K. M.)

bands, or medallions of figures and animals, in high relief.
After the ware is incised it is glazed with a translucent lead
glaze, variegated with green and yellow colouring over the
white engobe (Fig. 17). The sgraffitto pottery of Italy is
either of Lombardic or Venetian origin, as appears from
the usual Gothic character of the designs.

The wares of Caffaggiolo are distinguished by a purely
white glaze, with masses of a rich cobalt blue used as
portions of the groundwork for the ornament; sometimes

green and purple are used with the blue, and at other times a bright orange yellow and a copper green or an Indian red. Caffaggiolo, Faenza, and Forli wares have much resemblance to each other. The pitcher (Fig. 16), with the arms of the Medici family, belongs probably to the Caffaggiolo school, and is a work of the early years of the sixteenth century.

Fig. 18.—Maiolica Plate; Caffaggiolo Ware (?). (S. K. M.)

The tazza (Fig. 19) is another example of this ware. The fine plate (Fig. 18) is thought to be a work from the same botega, and the subject is supposed to represent Raphael and the Fornarina.

The plate (Fig. 15) is an example of the mezzo-maiolica ware, and is anterior to the date 1500. The more beautiful one (Fig. 20) is a work dating from the first years of the sixteenth century, at the time when the stanniferous glaze was coming into use. Both these plates are supposed to be from the Pesaro fabriques. They may have been made as wedding presents from the bridegroom to the bride, and are portrait dishes, with an inscription on the ribbon, with the name of the bride, or some endearing motto.

These plates are known as "amatorri" pieces. The colours used in the Pesaro maiolica are yellow, green, manganese, black, and cobalt blue, and have what is known as the "madreperla" lustre, which has a beautiful

Fig. 19.—Plateau or Tazza ; Caffaggiolo Ware.

changing effect in colour. The outlines are manganese, and the flesh left white in the best pieces. The finest work executed in Pesaro came from the fabrique of Lanfranco in the years 1540-45.

The products of the Sienese potteries are worthy of being ranked with the best works of Pesaro and Caffaggiolo, to which they are closely allied.

There is a fine pavement of tiles in the Kensington Museum from the Petrucci Palace at Siena, dated 1509. Benedetto is the name of an artist of the Sienese school, who painted in maiolica, from whose hand most of the best Siena maiolica has come; the drug pot (Fig. 21) and the two plates (Figs. 22 and 23) are works of his. On the drug pot, tiles, and some large dishes, grotesques were very much used as ornament, and in colour, yellow, orange, and particularly black grounds, were used in the Siena production.

The maiolica wares of Gubbio are the most celebrated

Fig. 20.—Pesaro Portrait Dish (about 1500). (S. K. M.)

in all Italy, as regards their richness and beauty of colouring; this, of course, was due mostly to the beautiful effects gained by the unique ruby and gold lustres used at this fabrique. The name of one man, Maestro Giorgio Andreoli, as the chief artist, is connected with the Gubbio ware. He was a native of Pavia, and came of a noble family. He finally established himself at Gubbio, where

he was made a "castellano" of that city in 1498, and
enjoyed the patronage of the Dukes of Urbino.   He was a

Fig. 21.—Drug Pot; Siena.
(S. K. M.)

Fig. 22.—Siena Plate.   (S. K. M.)

Fig. 23.— Siena Plate.   (S. K. M.)

modeller as well as a painter of maiolica, and is said to
have executed some altar-pieces in relief before coming to

Gubbio. In the Kensington Museum there is a bas-relief of St. Sebastian which is supposed on good authority to be a work of his hand; it is coloured with the gold and ruby lustres.

A circular dish or "bacile" of lustred ware (Fig. 24), with the subject of two mailed horsemen in the centre,

Fig. 24.—Lustred Dish; Gubbio Ware. (S. K. M.)

and a border of foliated ornament, is a work of the Gubbio fabrique, but is an earlier work than the time of Mᵒ· Giorgio.

The embossed vase in copper lustre (Fig. 25) is a very beautiful example of the stanniferous glaze and ruby copper lustre. The design is well adapted to show the "reflets" of the lustre by the variety of form on its embossed surfaces.   This work is ascribed to the same artist who executed the previous example.

The tazza (Fig. 26), with the subject, "The Stream of Life," after Robetta, is one of Giorgio's best figure pieces. Though not very good in figure draughtsmanship, it is excellent in colour, and is cleverly heightened with ruby lustre.   This and another plaque in Kensington Museum, representing the "Three Graces" after Raphael, are

Fig. 25.—Vase in Copper-ruby Lustre; Gubbio.   (S. K. M.)

amongst if not the best of Giorgio's work: for colour and richness of lustre, and for clearness and perfection of the enamel glaze, they are the best works in Italian maiolica that we possess.   The date of both is probably 1525.

A work by Giorgio is shown at Fig. 27.   This is a highly decorative tazza in the best manner of Giorgio, who was very clever at this kind of design.   The groundwork of this piece is blue, parts of the decoration are green, and other parts ruby, while all of the decoration is lustred. The back of this piece is covered with a yellow lead glaze, which seems to be the case with many examples of maiolica. Probably it was done for economical reasons. We close the list of illustrations of Gubbio ware with that of a dish, "Fruttiera" (Fig. 28). The design is simple and very good for showing the beauties of the ruby and gold

Fig. 26.—The Stream of Life; Tazza by M⁰· Giorgio.

lustres. It is embossed, and has been made from a mould, and is an unsurpassed example of the famous Gubbio lustre. Mr. Fortnum thinks that Giorgio obtained the secret of the ruby lustre from an artist that formerly worked at the Gubbio fabrique, and that he did not invent it, and also that all the similar lustred ware was produced at Gubbio, the wares of Urbino, Castel-Durante, and of

other fabriques having been sent to Gubbio to get the
final lustre added to them.

Another artist who executed many important works at
the Gubbio botega signs his productions with the letter N.
Some think that this is meant for a signature of M°· Cencio,
a son of Giorgio who succeeded his father at the fabrique.
Another name that appears on some of this ware is M.

Fig. 27.—Tazza by Giorgio.   (S. K. M.)

Prestino. It is known that Giorgio signed his name on
many pieces that were painted by other artists or by his
pupils.

A beautiful specimen of Castel-Durante ware is the
plate (Fig. 29) with a deep centre—"tondino"—which has
a border of cupids, foliage, and medallions on a dark
blue ground. The centre has cupids, and the sides of the

centre painted with solid white ornaments on a low white ground. It is probably the work of the artist Giovanni Maria (1508).

The vase (Fig. 30) is a richly decorated specimen of the same ware; the grotesque masks and arabesques are vigorously drawn, and the ornament generally is a good example of that used on the Castel-Durante ware. This vase has been used as a drug pot, and was made at the botega of Sebastiano di Marforio. Giuseppe Raffaelli in his "Memorie" (1846) says that the manufacture of glazed

Fig. 28.—Embossed Fruit Dish; Gubbio. (S. K. M.)

pottery as an art began when Monsignor Durante built a "castello" on the Metauro at Correto in the year 1284, and the names of potteries are recorded that were in existence in 1364 to 1440. The year 1490 began a period of great activity in the Castel-Durante fabriques, and we hear of many artists who were Durantine maiolica painters going to various parts of Europe and establishing works in pottery. Tesio and Gatti went to Corfu in 1530, and taught the art in the Ionian Islands; Francesco de Vasaro went to Venice, where he was eminently successful in deve-

loping the Venetian phase of maiolica; others went to
Nevers and Lyons, in France, and one to Antwerp. The
artist who styled himself "Francesco" of Urbino, and who
also worked at Perugia, sometimes signed his works
"Durantino." Vasari, in his "Lives of the Painters,"
speaks of Battista Franco of Venice, a clever painter and

Fig. 29.—Castel-Durante Maiolica. (S. K. M.)

designer, as having been employed by the Duke of Urbino,
Guidobaldo II., in 1540, to design subjects for the excellent
ceramic painters of Castel-Durante. The death of Duke
Francisco Maria II. (1631) put an end practically to the
maiolica industry of the place; the trade generally then
declined, and the artists were forced to emigrate.

Urbino is a city celebrated in the art and literature of

Italy in the Renaissance period, and her dukes rivalled the Medici family of Florence in the patronage and encouragement of art, science, and literature. The names of the Urbino maiolica artists have been fortunately well preserved. Those of Nicola da Urbino, Guido Fontana, and his more famous son Orazio, also another son, Camillo,

Fig. 30.—Drug Pot ; Castel-Durante Ware. (S. K. M.)

the versatile artists in "Majoliche istoriate," and Francesco Xanto, may be mentioned as the most important.

To the first-named artist, Nicola, is ascribed the earliest authentic works from the potteries of Urbino, the celebrated service of maiolica, painted probably between the years 1490 and 1519, for Isabella d'Este, wife of the Marquis of

VOL. II.   D

Mantua, and known as the Gonzaga-Este service. Two fine plates of this service are in the British Museum. They have the arms of Gonzaga impaling those of Este on a shield, and one of them has the painted subjects of Apollo and Daphne, and Apollo and the Python, while the other has a representation of a troop of horse soldiers entering a city. The figures are delicately and carefully outlined and the colouring is brilliant.

Orazio Fontana was the most celebrated of the family of that name. His best work was done from 1540 to 1560, and he was the artist proprietor of a botega at Urbino, from whence came many of the finest works ever made in that city, not only as regards their artistic qualities but in the beauty and finish of the maiolica ware. The "istoriati" panels, or figure subjects (usually mythological) which were copies or adaptations of engraved designs by Italian painters, were the work of Orazio himself, and the grotesques probably from the hand of his brother or some other artist.

The pilgrim bottle (Fig. 31) is from the botega of Orazio Fontana, but the grotesques on it are supposed to have been painted by his brother Camillo. One artist named Gironimo was very clever at this grotesque, or "Raphael-esque" work as it is sometimes called—not from the great Raphael Sanzio, but from the artist Raphael dal Colle, who introduced this grotesque design among other work of his for the decoration of the Pesaro ware, in the duchy of Urbino. These grotesques were afterwards called "Urbino arabesques" and were of a different character to the grotesques of the Gubbio ware, which may be seen by comparing the dish of Urbino ware signed by Gironimo (Fig. 32) with Fig. 27.

There is a circular dish of Urbino ware in the Museum at Kensington on which is painted the subject of the marriage of Alexander with Roxana, from an engraving by Marc Antonio Raimondi, after Raphael's design. This work is signed by Francesco Xanto (1533), a prolific and somewhat

careless artist who took great liberties with the designs he
adapted, like most of the maiolica painters. The colouring of this dish is very rich : the colours generally of the
Urbino school were green, yellow, and blue, and a predo-
minance of orange on a light or white ground.

Fig. 31.—Pilgrim Bottle; Urbino Ware. (S. K. M.)

Faenza pottery is among the oldest in Italy, but little is
known of the early artists or potteries. Many pieces of
doubtful origin have been classed as Faentine, but without
any positive proof.

In the Cluny Museum in Paris there are a pair of pharmacy jars or vases, one of which bears the inscription "Faenza," and the other is dated 1500, their excellence proving that good work was done at Faenza at this date, or perhaps much earlier. The pottery works called the

Fig. 32.—Urbino Dish, with "Urbino Arabesques."　(S. K. M.)

Casa Pirota was the principal establishment for the production of maiolica at Faenza.

Many works from this pottery are in the Kensington Museum, and they seem generally to be the work of one hand, but there is no record of the artist. He painted a certain kind of grotesque, and figures of boys on plates of

a wide border. The colours are a light blue on a dark blue ground, the light blue heightened with touches of white, and shaded with a brownish yellow. This style is known as "sopra azzuro" and is very characteristic of the unknown painter's work (Fig. 33).

A fine tazza in the same museum by the Faentine artist who signs himself as F. R. has the painted subject "the Gathering of the Manna," after Raphael.

The colours used are strong and rich yellows, blues, greens, orange, and purple tints. This work is much

Fig. 33.—Faenza Plate.   (S. K. M.)

superior to that of another Faentine artist who used the same initials. An oblong panel or plaque in the Kensington Collection, $9\frac{3}{4}$ inches in height by 8 inches in width, has a painting of the Resurrection after a design by Melozzo de Forli, signed with a monogram consisting of T and B. It is a maiolica work of the highest rank, carefully executed yet with perfect freedom of touch—for carefulness of execution in pottery painting very often implies hardness—and pleasing combinations of blues, yellows, greens, and golden browns, with little touches of red. Mr. Fortnum thinks it

was painted by the same artist that executed the famous
service of maiolica of which seventeen pieces are in the
Museo Correr at Venice. The tazza at Fig. 34 is ascribed
to the Faenza fabriques. It is as much Gothic as Italian
in design, which is the case sometimes in Northern Italian
art, and it has been found also that the "istoriati" maiolica of Faenza has more of its subjects from the engravings
of German artists' works, such as Dürer, Martin Schon, and

Fig. 34.— Faenza Maiolica.   (S. K. M.)

others, than the pottery of any other Italian fabrique.
Maiolica has been fabricated at many other places in Italy,
such as Diruta, Forli, Rimini, Padua, Ferrara, Genoa, and
Venice, but space prevents us here from giving any de-
scriptive notice of them, further than the mention of the
Venetian botegas where many important examples came
from during the sixteenth century. The Venetian dishes
of this time were covered with ingenious and elaborate
designs of interlacing ornament, foliage, birds, masks,

with tyings of ribbons or drapery (Fig. 35). The colour of
the enamelled surface is white slightly tinted with zaffre
blue. A low-toned blue colour was employed for the orna-

Fig. 35.—Venetian Dish. (S. K. M.)

ment, which was outlined and shaded with a darker blue
and heightened with white.

PERSIAN, DAMASCUS, AND RHODIAN WARES.

The artistic pottery and tiles of Persia, though forming a
large variety, may nearly all be brought under the desig-

nation of siliceous or glass-glazed wares, the tin glaze
being only met with occasionally in some Persian and
Damascus examples, where an unusually white surface
was required.   All the glazed wares of Persia are highly
baked, and are mostly of a semi-translucent character.

There is the fine copper, ruby, and brown lustred ware,

Fig. 36.— Persian Lustred Ware.

which has sometimes a white and at others a blue ground.
The plate (Fig. 36) is an example of this ware.   The design
on this ware is in the pure Persian character.

Another kind, and by far the most numerous, are the
wares of a coarse porcelain variety, not only made in imitation of Chinese porcelain, but decorated to imitate the
Chinese ware, the ornament being sometimes mixed with
Arabian forms; the colour a bright blue on a white

ground, and the Chinese marks or signatures being copied as well (Figs. 37 and 38).

Fig. 37.—Flower Vase, Persian, with Chinese decoration.

In the reign of the Persian Shah Abbas the Great (A.D. 1586-1628) the route for travellers and merchants from China to Europe lay across Persia, and many objects of merchandise were imported from China to Persia, including great quantities of Chinese porcelain, many examples of which were purchased in Persia that are now in our museums, as well as specimens in abundance of the imitated Chinese variety.

The beautiful enamelled earthenware tiles were made

Fig. 38.—Persian Water-bottle ; imitated Chinese decoration.

with and without the metallic lustre in the days of, and anterior to the reign of, Shah Abbas, but since his time the art has declined, and nothing but a coarse and inartistic pottery has been made in recent times. As a rule

the excellence of Persian pottery, like wine, is augmented
in proportion to its age.

The picturesque wall tile (Fig. 39) was found in the

Fig. 39.—Persian Tile; Seventeenth Century.

ruins of the palace of Shah Abbas II. (1642-1666), near
Ispahan. It has a blue ground with white embossed
decorations and black pencillings, and is lustred.

Wall tiles have been in use in Persia from a very early date. Some of them are beautiful in colour, having usually a deep lapis-lazuli blue ground or white. Sometimes the design is complete on one tile, but generally a whole tile has only a portion of the pattern, many tiles being required to make up the complete pattern (Fig. 40). The tiles are made to fit into all kinds of spaces, according to the shape of the wall, and these arrangements have usually a border design.

The lustred tiles are of an older date than the Persian

Fig. 40.—Persian Wall Decoration.

fayence fine ware, or imitated Chinese porcelain. The body composition of the tiles resembles that of the old bricks that are found in great quantities in the ruinous mounds of Rhages (Rhé), where also many fragments of tiles have been found, and some remains of potters' kilns, proving that Rhages must have been the centre of extensive pottery works. Another class of Persian ware has a thin, hard, and nearly translucent paste, which is decorated by having pierced holes filled in with transparent glaze. It is creamy white in colour, and has foliated ornament in blue or brown. This has been called Gombion Ware.

One variety of decoration on a late seventeenth-century Persian bowl is shown at Fig. 41. This is a good example of the late floral ornament.

Damascus ware has generally been classified as Persian,

Fig. 41.— Blue Persian Bowl; Seventeenth Century. (S. K. M.)

but in many points it is different from the latter. It is better in colour and design. Some examples have a smooth even glaze, and are coloured with a fine quality of

cobalt blue, turquoise green, and a dull lilac or purple intermixed with white portions of the design evenly distributed. The ornament is less florid and the fayence is of
an older date than the majority of Persian examples. The
"Damas" cups or vases have always been highly prized

Fig. 42.—Rhodian Ware.

for their beauty, and the wall tiles from Damascus are the
most beautiful of all Oriental tiles.

Rhodian or Lindus tiles and pottery have been also
classified as Persian, but again this ware is quite distinct
from Persian or Damascus wares. Rhodian pottery is
coarser than the two former varieties, and the decoration
is brighter and more strongly marked. The ornament is
of a very conventional character, and in colour it is charac-

terised by having a red opaque pigment used in spots and patches, and sometimes in bands, but always raised or embossed.

The plates shown in Figs. 42 and 43 are examples of Rhodian ware.

The island of Sicily was conquered by the Saracens in

Fig. 43.—Rhodian Dish.

A.D. 827, and about the thirteenth and fourteenth centuries potteries of glazed wares had been established by the latter.

Some examples of their work of these periods have decorations of animals, figures, birds, and also mock Saracenic inscriptions like the Siculo-Arabian textiles of the same and later periods (Fig. 44).

Anatolian ware is a later variety that is akin to the

Persian wares, but somewhat coarser and of a duller surface. This ware is small in size, and the colouring is
usually gay on light grounds. The tiles from Anatolia are

Fig. 44.—Vase, Siculo-Arabian Ware ; Fourteenth Century.

less inventive in their ornament and rougher in execution
than the Damascus or Rhodian.

The decoration of Turkish tiles and Turkish ornament
generally is of the Saracenic kind, but has neither the

beauty nor the invention of the other varieties of Persian. There are no plant nor animal forms in the Turkish variety of Saracenic ornament; it is more allied to the Egyptian Saracenic, but lacks the ingenuity of the latter. The colour is harsh and crude. It is seen at its best in the tomb mosque of Soliman the Great at Constantinople (Fig. 45), built in 1544.

The decoration of the palace of the Seraglio and of the

Fig. 45.—Ornament from the Cupola of the Mosque of Soliman the Great, Constantinople.

"Sultanin Valide" consists of beautiful tiles that were brought from Persia to Constantinople.

FRENCH POTTERY.

The art of the potter flourished in Gaul before the time of the Romans, but this early pottery was of a coarse kind, used mostly for domestic purposes, and of an unglazed variety (*poteries mates*). The use of a vitreous glaze was common in France as early as the thirteenth century, and in a grave that had the date of 1120, in the Abbey of Jumièges, two small broken vases were found covered with a yellowish lead glaze. We are informed by an old French chronicler that "On fait des godets à Beauvais." A *godet* was a goblet or cup of glazed fayence, with a wide mouth, and often had a cover, and was usually silver-mounted. Beauvais was noted in the thirteenth and fourteenth centuries for its glazed pottery.

It has been mentioned before that the Italian artist, Girolamo della Robbia, introduced the famous enamelled earthenware invented by his grand-uncle, Luca della Robbia, into France, when he came by invitation of Francis I. to decorate the exterior of the Château de Madrid, in the Bois de Boulogne, and the Pesaro maiolica painter, Francesco, also settled and worked in France; but apparently little came of these attempts to naturalise Italian pottery on French soil, except that the art must have been spread in some degree by the workmen, and by French artists who would naturally have assisted the Italians, and the traditions left by the latter must have helped considerably to influence the subsequent fabrication of enamelled earthenware.

OIRON WARE.

To take our subject in a chronological order, the wares of Oiron, or "Henri-Deux ware," as the name they are better known by, must be noticed first.

Until a recent date the origin of this was only guessed at, but the late M. Benjamin Fillon by his researches has cleared up the mystery. It appears now that the invention of this scarce and unique ware was due to Hélène de Hangest, Dame de Boissy, the widow lady of Gouffier, who was formerly governor to Francis I. This lady established the pottery in 1564 in the Château of Oiron, near

Thouars; and, being gifted with strong artistic tastes, conducted the work with great success, assisted by two skilful collaborateurs, François Charpentier and Jehan Bernart. The former was the modeller, and the latter—Bernart—was her librarian, and the artist who designed and adapted the stamped ornament which is so characteristic of this ware. This ornament is copied from the bookbindings of the period, and seems to have been stamped in colour on the Oiron ware with tools similar to

Fig. 46.—Tazza, Henri-Deux Ware. (S. K. M.)

those used in the bookbinding craft. The vase or tazza (Fig. 46) is a fine example of this ware of the earlier period, showing the stamped decoration. The ornament is identical with the peculiar Italo-Saracenic style of the Grolier and contemporary bookbindings.

The decoration is of a dark brown colour, sometimes heightened with pink, on an ivory-coloured ground.

Another and later class of this ware has modelled decorations in high relief. The colouring and technical skill

Fig. 47.—Candlestick, Henri-Deux Ware.   (S. K. M.)

generally was also improved, as may be seen in the profusion of small figures, masks, and festoons that were added
to the candlesticks and vases after the earlier period, but

these additions were not always improvements in the general design. The colouring is also of a greater variety : ochre, green and blue, and sometimes gold, was added in small quantities.

The celebrated candlestick (Fig. 47) is one of the best examples in which modelled ornament is a feature. It is

Fig. 48.—Oiron Ewer and Tazza. (S. K. M.)

now in the Kensington Museum, where there are various fine specimens of Oiron ware.

This candlestick shows the Italian Renaissance influence very strongly, and probably owes much to the art of Cellini, as seen in his metal-work designs. The ewer and tazza betray also his influence (Fig. 48).

The saltcellar (Fig. 49) is a restrained piece of architectural design and is altogether a very fine piece of work.

It is said by some that there are eighty pieces of this ware in existence, and others that there are only fifty-three genuine pieces. The early examples bear the emblems of

Fig. 49.—Oiron or Henri-Deux Saltcellar. (S. K. M.)

Francis I., and the later ones those of Henry II. and Diana of Poitiers. The paste used in this ware is a white pipe-clay, and is covered with a thin glaze.

PALISSY WARE.

Bernard Palissy was one of the most remarkable men who practised the art of the potter in France or in any other country. He was born about the year 1510, but his birthplace is not exactly known. He worked in his younger days and up to the period of his middle age at surveying, glass-making, portrait painting, and was also

well skilled in natural sciences, but was not brought up to
the trade of a potter.

It was in the year 1542, at Saintes, that in order to increase his slender means he took to the making of earthenware. In writing his life he says: "It is now more than
five-and-twenty years that a cup was shown to me of
fashioned and enamelled clay, and of such beauty, that from
that day I began to struggle with my own thoughts, and
hence, heedless of my having no knowledge of the different
kinds of argillaceous earth, I tried to discover the art of
making enamel, like a man groping in the dark."

So he struggled on for fifteen years, with starvation and
death often at his door, until at last he mastered his art,
and produced ultimately, as he says, "those vessels of
intermixed colours, after the manner of jasper."

The particular jasper enamel invented by Palissy is a
deep rich glaze of a green and brownish variegated
character. He made many "rustic pieces" as dishes,
plates, and plaques, on which he admirably arranged
reptiles, fishes, frogs, shells, insects of various kinds, fruits,
leaves, acorns, &c., modelled in relief and covered with the
jasper glaze.

Most of these dishes were elliptical in shape and had
broad rims (Fig. 50).

He decorated a "grotto" with his famous pottery at the
Château of Ecouen for his patron the Constable de Mont-
morency, and similar grottoes at the Tuileries, and at
Reux, in Normandy, for Catherine de' Medici. Palissy
made other forms of pottery besides his rustic pieces, such
as ewers, bottles, hunting flasks, and dishes, ornamented
with figures and other work. It is likely that the figure
work was executed by his sons or relatives, Nicholas and
Mathurin Palissy, who worked for Catherine de' Medici on
the Tuileries grotto. Many of the Palissy wares are similar
in design to the *étains* and pewter works of Briot and of other
artists, as Prieur, Rosso, Gauthier, and Primaticcio. Open-
work baskets and dishes and other modelled works were

covered with the jasper glaze. Of the invention of the
latter Palissy does not seem to have communicated the
secret to his successors, for after his death the jasper glaze
was imitated, but without much success, as appears evident
from some specimens that are now in existence which were
made from his moulds.

Palissy was nearly all his life engaged in lecturing on
scientific and other subjects, and in the work of proselytism

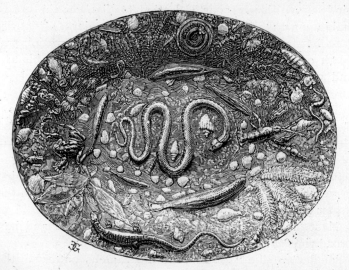

Fig. 50.—Rustic Dish, with Reptiles and Fishes ; Palissy Ware.   (S. K. M.)

for the Reformed Church of which he was a member, being
in prison more than once on account of his religious ideas,
and eventually died in the Bastille Prison in poverty in
1590 at the age of eighty.

As efforts of decorative design the encrusted wares of
Palissy cannot be placed in a high rank of decorative art,
but the art of France would be considerably poorer without
the genius of Palissy, an artist of whom any nation might
be justly proud.

NEVERS, ROUEN, AND MOUSTIERS WARES.

We have mentioned before that some maiolica artists and workmen came from Italy in the sixteenth century to Nevers and Lyons and there set up potteries. One of these

Fig. 51.—Pilgrim's Bottle, Nevers Ware.   (S. K. M.)

artists, named Scipio Gambin, worked at Nevers, under the patronage of the Duc de Nivernais.

The maiolica productions at Nevers were in imitation of the Urbino, Castel-Durante, and Faenza wares, but the colours were inferior, probably owing to the poorer glaze

used by the French potters. The subjects of the decoration
were at first similar to the "istoriati" decoration of the
Urbino ware, and were compositions from Ovid's "Metamorphoses" (Fig. 51) or from the Bible. Later on the
potters of Nevers imitated the shapes of Oriental pottery
with French decorations (Fig. 52).

Fig. 52.—Vase, Nevers Ware.

In 1608 two Italians—the brothers Conrade—came from
Genoa to Nevers, and were probably the successors of
Gambin: the ware made by them was decorated with a
mixture of Chinese and Italian ornament, and the colouring
was blue, manganese, brown, and white.

In 1632 a Frenchman named Pierre Custode and his
sons established a pottery at the sign of "The Ostrich"

at Nevers. To them is ascribed the beautiful Persian blue-coloured pottery decorated with naturalistic flowers and birds in solid white with yellow heightenings, the shape and decoration being Chinese in character. The blue glaze peculiar to Nevers pottery of this period is very fine, and has been imitated by French and foreign potters, but without success.

Fig. 53.—Pilgrim's Bottle, Nevers Ware. (S. K. M.)

The great importation of Chinese porcelain into Europe in the seventeenth century and at the beginning of the eighteenth had a strong influence on the art of the Nevers pottery, and many pieces exist on which Chinese designs almost pure were copied in a blue *Camaïen* (monochrome), or in a harmonious mixture of blue and purple-black manganese, the latter colour being a mixture of the blue with manganese. In the eighteenth century the style of design was debased and very much degraded, and the pottery became coarse and heavy.

ROUEN WARE.—A much better class of pottery both in manufacture and design is the famous Rouen ware, made in the town of that name in Normandy. In the year 1644

Fig. 54.— Plateau, Rouen Ware. (S. K. M.)

Edme Poterat obtained a licence to make and sell fayence in the province of Normandy.

This monopoly did not last long, for we find that in 1673 his son, Louis Poterat, obtained another licence, and from that time a new development takes place in the ornament that is so characteristic of Rouen ware. The greater part of this ornament is composed of a scallop form of setting out, with alternating compositions of ornamental flowers, called *lambrequins*, and baskets of ornamental flowers that

Fig. 55.—Tray, Rouen Ware.   (S.K.M.)

repeat at intervals around the border of plates or trays; light pendentives and wreaths of artificial flowers are painted in a lighter tone, and occur between the richer lambrequins (Fig. 54). Richly ornamented coats-of-arms, or baskets of flowers and cornucopias, occupy the centres (Fig. 55).   The beautiful plate in the Kensington Museum (Fig. 56) is unique in Rouen ware in having *amorini*, or cupids, in the centre.   All of the foregoing examples are painted in blue of different shades on the white enamel, or sometimes on yellow ochre grounds.   Indian red colour

Fig. 56.—Plateau, Rouen Ware.   (S. K. M.)

and a warm reddish yellow is sometimes also used.   The ornament is pseudo-Chinese, and is a Norman development of Oriental forms with some Italian influences which are reminiscences of the decoration brought by the Conrade brothers from Genoa to Nevers.

Some of the Rouen ware is decorated with a ray forma-

tion on which the ornament is painted on a light or dark
ground. This is known as the *style rayonnant.* The drawing
of these patterns is always very careful and correct, the latter
often being copies of the printed decoration of the books
of that period. Later on the decoration became of a freer
type, with bouquets of artificial flowers, and in the eighteenth century the *Rocaille* or Rococo element began to
creep in, and the Rouen ware developed from the camaïen
blue style of decoration to a polychrome style.

The Chinese element in design became everywhere in the

Fig. 57.—Dish, Rouen Ware. (S. K. M.)

ascendant, not only in late Rouen ware, but in the pottery
of every country in Europe, and remains more or less in the
work of to-day. Some of the late Rouen ware is not so
bizarre in its decoration as many other French and
European styles of the same period. Fig. 57 shows the
Chinese influence, but is in better taste than the majority
of contemporary designs.

As a style decays the colour as a rule becomes more
gaudy, which applies to Rouen ware as to other varieties
of fayence. The "Cornucopia pattern" belongs to the

decadence period : this is full of unrestrained liberty both in form and colour. It ought to be mentioned that Louis Poterat, of Rouen, first discovered the secret of making the Chinese soft porcelain *(pâte tendre)* in France. Several pieces of this Rouen porcelain are preserved in the Museums at Sèvres and at Limoges.

The Rouen School of Decoration has influenced modern pottery designers in France, Germany, Holland, and England, more than any other school; but unfortunately they all copied its later defects with greater zeal than in taking lessons from its earlier excellencies.

Rouen ware was imitated in the Sinceny pottery, but this pottery was made by some workmen who had formerly belonged to Rouen, and established themselves at Sinceny in 1713, and copied the Rouen ware so closely that the copies have often been mistaken for the latter ware.

At Paris, St. Cloud, Quimper, and Lille, imitations of Rouen ware have been attempted with success. The St. Cloud pottery is of a slatey blue colour. The pottery of Lille is a close imitation of Rouen ware, as the plate (Fig. 58) clearly shows.

MOUSTIERS, in the south of France, was an important centre for enamelled pottery works, where a style of decoration was used that was a mixture of the Italian Urbino and the School of Rouen, the borders of the plates having the Rouen lambrequins, and the centres having figure subjects and landscapes, or, as in the later work, grotesques and ornament after the French artists, Callot and Berain.

The colour was in shades of a deep blue (Fig. 59).

Pierre Clérissy (1728) was the name of the first artist and also of his nephew, who continued the works after him in Moustiers.

Polychrome decoration became common at a later date, when some Moustiers workmen, who had been to the Alcora potteries in Spain, introduced the Spanish style of colouring, then in great fashion, which consisted of bright orange yellow, light green, and blue outlines. The later

Moustiers ware is decorated with festoons and ovals with figures or busts painted in them.

MARSEILLES fayence is of a delicate and pure enamel, and is painted with flowers, shell fish, and insects, &c., which as a rule are thrown on or disposed in an irregular sort of way. Much of the decoration was Chinese or

Fig. 58.—Plate, Lille Ware.

Rouen imitations, and little landscapes painted in red camaïen; gold was sometimes used in the stalks of the flowers.

STRASBURG pottery, though classed as French, owed a good deal of its process of manufacture and general character to German methods of manipulation and decorative processes, as German potters were mostly employed in the works.

VOL. II.   F

The great difference was in the mode of decoration, the latter being applied on the fired surface of the enamel in the Strasburg wares; whereas in the wares of the other French potteries that have just been considered the decoration was applied to the unbaked and conse-

Fig. 59.—Plate, with Stag Hunt; Moustiers Ware.

quently absorbent ground. The latter was the more artistic method, and the former, or German method, allowed a wider range of the artist's palette, and admitted of greater delicacy of execution, but was more harsh in effect, and did not incorporate the colours with the enamel in a way that an absorbent ground or unbaked enamel would do.

The name of Charles Hannong is connected with an

early pottery of Strasburg, which was mostly a manufactory of earthenware stoves. This pottery was founded in
1709. In 1721 Hannong and a German porcelain worker,
who was taken into partnership by the former, began to
make porcelain, but after a short existence under the sons
of Hannong this pottery was closed.

Statuettes, clocks, dinner and dessert services were made
in Strasburg glazed earthenware, with modelled and painted

Fig. 60.—Plate, Strasburg Ware.

decoration. The colouring and decoration was of the pre-
valent Rococo, bright and clear; flowers of all kinds, and
Chinese pictures, were imitated mostly on white grounds
(Fig. 60).

FRENCH PORCELAIN.

The desire to imitate the porcelain ware of China led to
the discovery of the soft paste *(pâte tendre)*. The names
" *porcelaine de France* " and " *Sèvres porcelain* " have also
been given to it. As previously mentioned, it was made at
Rouen in 1690, at St. Cloud in 1698, and at Lille in 1711,
but in all these cases in a small and tentative way.

The composition of the paste in the French soft porcelain is described by MM. Gasnault and Garnier in their handbook of "French Pottery" as follows : "The paste was composed of the sand of Fontainebleau, saltpetre, sea salt, soda (*soude d'Alicante*), alum, gypsum, or parings of alabaster; all these elements were mixed together and placed in an oven in a layer of considerable thickness, where, after being baked for at least fifty hours, they formed a perfectly white frit, or vitrefied paste. The frit was mixed with Argenteuil marl in the proportion of nine pounds of frit to three pounds of marl, &c."

The glaze is described as consisting of "the sand of Fontainebleau, litharge, salts of soda, Bougival silex or gun-flint, and potash." All these were ground and melted together, and afterwards the vitreous mass was re-ground in water and thus formed the glaze.

The soft paste is much superior for artistic works owing to the glaze incorporating with the colours in a perfect manner, rendering them equally brilliant with the enamel, but this is not the case with the hard or natural kaolin, as the glaze on this does not blend completely with the colours of the decoration. The soft paste porcelain is, however, too porous for articles of domestic use, and can be tested by its being easily scratched by a knife.

The Marquis Orry de Fulvey made an attempt to establish the soft paste porcelain works at Vincennes in 1741, but this was not a success. It was established again under new conditions in 1745, and after many experiments some important vases were made decorated with flowers in relief. The manufactory was reorganized again and removed to Sèvres, near Paris, in the year 1756. The products of the Sèvres works at this time were the fine vases with the *bleu de roi*, or *bleu de Sèvres*, and the lovely *rose Pompadour* colours, and numerous fancy articles, as heads of canes, buttons, snuff-boxes, needle-cases, also table services, &c. Many artists were employed to paint the flower and figure decorations; the latter were painted after the designs of Boucher, Vanloo, and others.

The soft paste porcelain was made from about 1700 to 1770. Some of the finest soft paste Sèvres porcelain may be seen in the Jones Collection at South Kensington, of which there are nearly sixty examples. The vase (Fig. 61) has a dark blue ground. The clock of Sèvres porcelain (Fig. 62) is a beautiful and unique example that was made especially for Marie Antoinette. The clock is mounted in ormoulu by Gouthière, and is in his best style of work.

The egg-shaped vase (Fig. 63) has a blue ground and is decorated with subject of Cupid and Psyche.

The artists Falconet, Clodion, La Rue, and Bachelier modelled and designed many of the statuettes, plaques, and vases for the Sèvres manufactory.

Cabinets and tables of the Louis Seize period were often inlaid with painted plaques of Sèvres ware, and have ormoulu mountings. This kind of furniture is exceedingly refined in design and workmanship, and reflects in a high degree the Pompadour and Du Barry period of French taste.

Fig. 61.—Sèvres Vase; Jones Collection. (S. K. M.)

In 1768 beds of kaolin clay were found in France at St. Yrieix, near Limoges. Maquer, a chemist attached to the Sèvres factory, in 1769 submitted for the king's (Louis XVI.) inspection at the

Fig. 62.—Sèvres Porcelain Clock ; Jones Collection.   (S. K. M.)

Château of Versailles sixty pieces of the new *hard porcelain*
made from this native clay.

Fig. 63.—Sèvres Vase, dark blue; Jones Collection. (S. K. M.)

During the time of the French Revolution the manufactory was in a critical state of existence, but was still kept

in a working state. In the year 1800 Alexandre Brongniart was appointed director, a post he held for forty-seven years—and after his appointment the manufacture of soft porcelain ceased.

In his time the manufactory was in a state of great prosperity, and the science he brought to bear on the manufacturing processes was of immense importance. Vases over seven feet in height were produced, and the pieces which were made were ornamented with trophies and battle scenes that glorified the events in the reign of Napoleon I.

In the reign of Louis Philippe the artists Fragonard, Chenavard, Clerget, and Julienne introduced a new style of Renaissance decoration and design, but this was of a heavy and overloaded order that was not exactly suited to the character of porcelain.

About the middle of the present century Louis Robert, the chief painter at Sèvres, introduced the novelty of *coloured pastes*, which was to develop later into the *pâte-sur-pâte* process, so successfully practised by the talented M. Solon, who has executed so much of this beautiful work for Minton's in England. The process of Louis Robert consisted in the use of porcelain paste coloured with oxides. A *barbotine* or *slip* was made of this composition and paintings were executed with it in slight relief, the white paste being used chiefly on a coloured ground, the modelling or light and shade being regulated according to the thickness of the semi-transparent material employed. When finished this kind of work has a cameo-like effect.

GERMAN POTTERY.

German stoneware was manufactured at an early date, and in the countries bordering upon the Rhine the industry must have been in an active state in the fifteenth and sixteenth centuries, judging from the plentiful examples of the different varieties of the ware formerly known as " Grès Flamands " or " Grès de Flandres," but now classified under their proper German origins. In the sixteenth century this ware was carried in great quantities from Raeren, from Frechen and Sieburg, near Cologne, and from Greuzhausen, near Coblentz, down the Rhine to Leyden and the Low Countries.

The brown stoneware of Raeren—which formerly belonged to the ancient Duchy of Limbourg—was especially in great request in Flanders. This brown ware was of a spherical or cylindrical shape, divided by a central broad band, with decorations of figure subjects, shields, masks, arms, &c.; the neck is also decorated with shields and bosses, and the foot with rings and guilloche ornament.

Some good specimens of blue stoneware—called the "blue of Leipzig"—were also made at Raeren.

Fig. 64.—Delft Vase.

At Frechen, near Cologne, the celebrated "Greybeards" or "Bellarmines" were first made, that were imported and imitated so much in England during the reign of James I. (see Fig. 73). They were decorated with the head of an old man with a long beard, and sometimes also with armorial bearings or figure subjects.

The Sieburg stoneware was a cream-coloured ware, richly decorated in relief, and chiefly consisted of long narrow drinking tankards with metal covers, called "Pokals."

At Greuzhausen and at Höhr were manufactured small jugs called "*cruches*," also saltcellars, inkstands, and braziers were made in grey stoneware decorated in parts with the rich "blue of Leipzig" and with various relief ornaments.

In the end of the seventeenth century and beginning of the eighteenth at Creussen, in Bavaria, tankards or drinking mugs were made of a round shape with covers, and decorated with figures of the Apostles in relief, and coloured in bright crude colours that look like oil painting : they are known as "Apostel Kruges," or Apostle mugs.

At Nuremberg, tiles, pipes, and stoves were manufactured in glazed brown or green stoneware, and at the same place a celebrated potter named Augustin Hirschvogel made different kinds of ware in tin-glazed enamel, who with his family preserved for a long time the secret in Germany of this particular glaze.

Delft, a town in Holland, was renowned in the seventeenth century for its extensive manufacture of the fayence known as " Delft." The potteries of Delft were established in the early years of the century, and towards the end upwards of thirty potteries were in full working order. The genuine delft ware is of a fine hard paste, has a beautiful and clear smooth enamel, and is decorated with almost every kind of subject, chiefly in a blue camaïen.

Attempts at polychrome decoration are very rare, but a red colour has been often used. The style of design and shapes were generally imitations of Chinese, Japanese, and Dresden wares (Fig. 64). Almost every class and shape of the usual pottery objects were manufactured, and some plates and vases were of very great dimensions.

German Porcelain.

The Portuguese introduced China porcelain into Europe, and for a long time the potters sought to imitate it, but without much success, until the true kaolin was discovered by Böttger, about 1709. At Aue, Schneeberg, and in the year 1715, a pottery for the manufacture of hard porcelain was established at Meissen, by Augustus II., Elector of Saxony and King of Poland, with Böttger as director.

This porcelain, after it had been brought to a considerable degree of perfection, turned out a great success in its similarity to the Chinese composition of body, but in spite of all precautions to keep the making and the nature of the clay secret, the knowledge leaked out, and in a short time

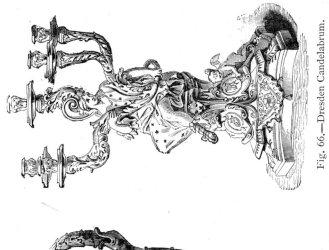

Fig. 66.—Dresden Candelabrum.

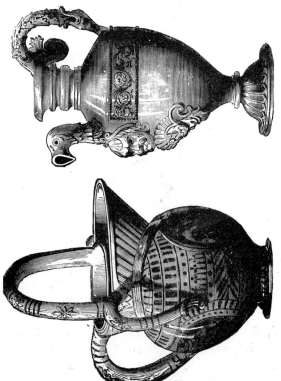

Fig. 65.—German Stoneware.

after we find that hard porcelain was made in many parts
of Germany and Austria.

Like most of the wares made at other potteries at this

Fig. 67.—Dresden Vase; Jones Collection.   (S. K. M.)

period, the Dresden porcelain was at first an imitation of
Chinese in shape and decoration. Almost every kind of
articles were made at Dresden, such as candelabra, statuettes, modelled flowers, vases, services, &c., on which were

painted with great delicacy, flowers, landscapes, and figures on grounds of different rich colours (Figs. 66 and 67).

ENGLISH POTTERY.

Ancient British pottery has been found in the barrows and burial mounds in the form of incense cups, drinking and food vessels, and cinerary urns. These have all been made of clays that were found usually on the spot, and are either sun-dried or imperfectly burnt.

The drinking vessels were tall and cylindrical in form, and the incense cups were wider in the centre than at either end. The urns and food vessels have a similarity of shape, being globular, with or without a neck. The decoration is of the simplest description, such as chevrons, or zigzags, and straight-lined patterns produced by scratching with a stick, or the impressions of a rope tied around the vessel while the clay was soft.

The Romans made pottery in Britain from native clay, and also imported much of the Samian ware. The Roman wares of British manufacture are known as Castor, Up-church, and New Forest wares; they are generally of very good shapes, and are decorated with slips, dots, bosses, and indentations, and are unglazed or slightly glazed (Fig. 68).

The Romano-British urn in the illustration has a slight yellow glaze. The pottery made by the Anglo-Saxons is of the same type and pattern as that made by the Saxons on the Continent. It is rough and inartistic in shape, except in some specimens that were made in the south of England, where an imitation of Roman and probably Norman pottery was attempted.

We do not meet much Saxon pottery in England of any importance until we come to the twelfth or thirteenth centuries, when some of the best efforts in tile making and decoration are seen in the beautiful floor-tiles of the early Gothic period. Many examples of these tiles have been preserved in the British and other Museums, and some are still *in situ* in Westminster Abbey, Malvern, Ely, and Gloucester Cathedrals, and Chertsey Abbey. The designs are often heraldic in character (Fig. 69), and consist of geometrical, floral, animal, and architectural forms. Badges, shields, and texts are also found as decorations, and sometimes the human figure is also represented. The earliest are of one colour, or two, as a yellow or a dull red, and the later ones have several colours. They are generally called " encaustic" tiles.

Fig. 68.—Romano-British Urn, with Slip Decoration. (B. M.)

Slip wares were made extensively at Wrotham in Kent as early as 1650, and at Staffordshire, Derby, and other places in England even earlier than this date. Many of them are of quaint and uncouth forms, and are generally covered with a rich green, brown, or yellow glaze, made from copper, manganese, or iron oxides. Curious two-handled, three or four-handled mugs or *tygs* used for handing round drinks, posset cups or pots, plates, dishes, candlesticks, jugs, and piggins were made in these wares, and decorated with " slip," which is a mixture of clay and water used in the thickness of cream, and which is dropped

or trailed from a tube or spouted vessel, on the surface of
the ware, forming the decoration according to the fancy of
the designer.   The colour of the slip varied from light to
dark (Fig. 70).

Fig. 69.—Encaustic Tile, from Monmouth Priory.   (B. M.)

The dish of Toft's ware (Fig. 71) is a specimen of the
slip decoration, date about 1660.   Toft was a potter who
had his kiln at Tinker's Clough, near Newcastle in Staf-

fordshire. His work is decorated with coloured slip on a
common red clay, with a wash of white or pipe clay, upon
which the decoration was laid in red slip; darker tints
were used for the outlines, and sometimes white dots. The
lead glaze used gave a yellow tint to the white clay
coating.

Marbled and combed wares, &c., were made in the seventeenth and eighteenth centuries, in which different coloured

Fig. 70.—Tyg of Wrotham Ware.

bodies were mixed in the paste to form a mottled, marbled,
or variegated appearance.

Lambeth has been noted for its potteries from about
1660. Lambeth delft comprised such objects as wine jars,
candlesticks, posset pots. The ware is of a pale buff tint;
the paste is covered with a white tin-glaze or enamel, and
a lead glaze over the decoration. Some plates have figure
subjects and floriated borders, which seem to be imitations of Italian majolica (Fig. 72). The names of
Griffith and Morgan appear as Lambeth potters in the
eighteenth century; and the present "Stiff's" pottery

was founded in 1751. The most noted pottery now in London is the manufactory of Messrs. Doulton—"The Lambeth Pottery"—founded in 1811, whose original and beautiful work is so well known to everybody in the present day.

In Staffordshire pictorial delft ware was made in Wil-

Fig. 71.—Dish of Slip Ware; by Thomas Toft. (S. K. M.)

liam III. and Queen Anne's time, but was of a coarser kind and less pure in the enamel than Lambeth delft.

Stoneware of an extremely hard and translucent kind was made by John Dwight at Fulham, about 1670. He made grey stoneware jugs, flasks, statuettes, and busts. The busts and statuettes were of great excellence. The jugs and tankards were made in imitation of the German "Grès"—the so-called "Grès de Flandres." These were called in England "Bellarmines," "longbeards," or "greybeards," by way of mockery of the Cardinal Robert Bellarmine, who was unpopular with the Protestant party in the reign of James I. (Fig. 73).

Fig. 72.—Dish of Lambeth Delft.   (B. M.)

Salt-glazed stoneware is still made at the present time at the Fulham works, which are now in possession of Mr. C. J. C. Bailey.

The salt-glazed white stoneware of Staffordshire was made from 1690 till after 1800. The introduction of the salt glaze ware in Staffordshire is ascribed to the celebrated potter John Philip Elers and his brother David. They are likely to have been Dutchmen who had also worked in the potteries of Nuremberg, and had brought with them the knowledge of the salt-glaze process to Staffordshire, together with the style and ornamentation of the Holland stonewares. Dwight of Fulham made salt-glazed wares before the time that the Elers settled at Bradwell in Staffordshire (1690-1710). John Elers made a revolution in the style of working the English pottery by turning his ware in the lathe instead of the exclusive use of the potter's wheel. The Elers made a red unglazed stoneware chiefly for teapots, cups, saucers, milk jugs, chocolate pots, besides other salt-glazed wares.

The salt-glazed ware is one of the hardest wares known, and is almost a porcelain in composition. The glaze gives a slighty uneven surface to the ware, which comes from the manner in which the wares receive the glaze. The pieces are not dipped in a glaze mixture, but when the kiln has reached a very high temperature common salt is thrown into the kiln; the soda

Fig. 73.—Bellarmine, Fulham Stone Ware.

is liberated from the salt by the action of the heat, and coming in contact with the silica of the stoneware clay, forms with it a silicate of soda, which is really a glass glaze. The composition of the ware is, generally speaking, clay and fine sand. Astbury, the potter, in 1720 used what is considered the best composition—grey clay and ground flint instead of sand. The colour is drab, or sometimes has a dull cream-coloured covering.

The colour of the old Staffordshire ware is drab, with small white applied ornaments that were previously cast

from moulds of brass or stoneware. Coloured enamels
have also been very much used for decorating later work.
The ornaments are single roses, may blossoms, *fleur-de-lis*,
spirals, small interlacings, birds, figures, straight or wavy

Fig. 74.—Jar, White Stoneware of Staffordshire.　(S. K. M.)

lines, &c., all generally very sharp and clear cut (Figs.
74, 75).

The potter John Astbury worked for the Elers, and after
finding out as many secrets as he could from them, he left
them and started a pottery of his own in Staffordshire. He
used a wider range of clays and colours than those used by
the Elers, and had more variety also in the decoration of his

ware, which consisted of such ornaments as harps, crowns, stags, lions, and heraldic designs.

Brown stoneware was made at Nottingham during the whole of the eighteenth century, and was of a bright rich

Fig. 75.—White Salt-glazed Ware of Staffordshire. (S. K. M.)

colour; the material was thin and well fabricated. Besides the ordinary shaped jugs, puzzle-jugs and mugs in the shape of bears with movable heads were made, that were used in the beerhouses of the last century.

Bristol and Liverpool were famous for their delft-ware

during the last century. Richard, Frank, and Joseph Flower are names of potters who had delft works in Bristol.

In Liverpool bowls with pictures of ships, arms, and landscape decoration were made of delft. Tiles on which were printed transfer decorations were also made of Liverpool delft by Sadler and Green, the inventors. These tiles were about five inches square, were printed in black or red, and were used for lining stoves and fireplaces. Theatrical characters and portraits of celebrities were the usual subjects. Wedgwood and other Staffordshire potteries sent their wares to Liverpool to get transfers printed on them.

Wedgwood ware is one of the most technically perfect productions that has been invented. The colouring is quiet and refined, and the decorations—following the classic ideals of the period—are severe and rather cold, but the workmanship is of such a perfection and delicacy that is seldom found in the ceramic products of any other manufactory.

Josiah Wedgwood came of a family of potters. He was born in 1730, and died in 1795. He was the youngest son of Thomas Wedgwood, a potter of Burslem, who died in 1739, and after his death Josiah left school and was bound apprentice to his brother Thomas, who succeeded his father in the pottery. Josiah concentrated his energies to the designing and modelling of pottery ornaments and to the invention of new paste compositions and glazes. Later on he sought to imitate in appearance and composition the precious stones of agate, onyx, jasper, &c.

After his apprenticeship was over he joined partnership with Harrison, of Stoke, and afterwards with Wheildon, of Fenton, but these associations did not last long, and in 1759 he started business in a small way at Burslem, where he executed many works, and by degrees perfected the cream-coloured ware which is known by the name of "Queen's ware." In the year 1776 he took into partnership Mr. Thomas Bentley, a Liverpool merchant of artistic tastes, who attended chiefly to the production of the decorative wares of the firm. This partnership lasted until the death of Bentley in 1780. It was in 1769 that Wedgwood removed his works and went also to live at his new house at Etruria, where he founded and named this village. He took his sons John, Josiah, and Thomas into partnership, and also his nephew Thomas Byerley in 1790. Five years after this date he died.

The products of the Wedgwood manufacture—which may be found more fully described in Professor Church's excellent book on " English Earthenware," to which we are indebted for many particulars on English pottery and for some of the illustrations—are thus classified :—

" 1. *Cream-coloured ware*, or ' Queen's ware,' comprises dinner and dessert services, tea and coffee sets. Cream-coloured, saffron, and straw-coloured, with well-painted designs of conventional foliage and flowers, and later work with transfer engraving in red or black, printed by Sadler and Green, of Liverpool.

" 2. *Egyptian black*, or basalt ware, owing its colour chiefly to iron. Seals, plaques, life-size busts, medallion portraits, and vases. Black tea and coffee sets decorated with coloured enamels and gilding (Fig. 76).

" 3. *Red ware*, or *Rosso Antico*, used for cameo reliefs.

" 4. White semi-porcelain or fine stoneware. This ware was composed of one of Wedgwood's improved bodies.

" 5. *Variegated ware* is of two kinds, one a cream-coloured body, marbled, mottled, or spangled with divers colours upon the surface and under the glaze; the other an improved kind of agate ware, in which the bands, twists, and strips constituted the entire substance of the vessel.

" 6. *Jasper ware.* The body of this ware was the material in which the chief triumphs of Wedgwood were wrought. Outwardly it resembled the finest of his white terra-cotta and semi-porcelain bodies, but in chemical and physical properties it differed notably from them. There are seven

colours in the Jasper body besides the white Jasper, but
the solid Jasper is of a blue tint. The seven colours are :—

Fig. 76.—Lamp, Black Egyptian Ware.

blue of various tints, lilac, pink, sage-green, olive-green,
yellow, and black."
    Plaques, tablets, large portraits, and other medallions,

cameos, intaglios, vases, statuettes, pedestals, flower-pots, &c., are objects and vessels that were made in Jasper ware.

Flaxman collaborated with Wedgwood in making many designs for his work. The beautiful pedestal shown at

Fig. 77.—Pedestal in Green and White Jasper, Wedgwood Ware. (S. K. M.)

Fig. 77 is from a design by Flaxman, and is made in green and white Jasper.

Other names of artists who designed or modelled for Wedgwood are Hackwood, Stubbs, Bacon, Webber, Devere, Angelini, Dalmazzoni, &c. An influence on some of his work was due to his studying and copying the celebrated

Portland Vase, which was lent to him for this purpose for more than three years by the Duke of Portland.

English Porcelain.

Porcelain was first made in England about the year 1745. The best period of the manufacture dates from 1750 to 1780, though some of the oldest factories have survived to the present day. English porcelain, or as it is better known as "China" ware, was made at Chelsea, Bow, Derby, Worcester, Plymouth, Bristol, and in Staffordshire. Some of the best porcelain from these places does not yield in beauty to the finest of Sèvres ware.

The Chelsea porcelain works were first under a Mr. Charles Gouyn, and it appears that Nicolas Sprimont was his successor, who was originally a goldsmith in Soho, and who was probably of Flemish origin.

Chelsea ware is remarkable for its deep rich claret-coloured grounds. This colour was first used on the Chelsea porcelain in 1759. Turquoise-blue, pea-green, and Mazarine-blue were also, though in a lesser degree, peculiar to Chelsea ware. The early pieces are without gilding, which is more of a distinguishing mark of the later productions. The paste, the enamel, the colour, and technique are all perfect in their way, but the art and design of the objects do not by any means equal the workmanship; this was of course due to the false taste of the period, when the rococo element in design was fashionable everywhere (Fig. 78). Vases, statuettes, scent bottles, compotiers, bowls, cups, saucers, animals, birds, fruit, and flowers were made by Sprimont in an extravagant style of design.

In 1769 William Duesbury, of the Derby porcelain works, purchased the Chelsea manufactory, and six years later he acquired the Bow porcelain works. A less extravagant style of design and decoration characterized the Chelsea-Derby productions, a specimen of which is seen in the cooper's bowl, Fig. 79.

The Bow China factory was owned by two partners, Weatherby and Crowther, in 1750; the former died in 1762, and the latter failed in the business in 1763. Duesbury, of

Fig. 78.—Chelsea Vase; Jones Collection. (S. K. M.)

Derby, bought up the Bow works in 1776, when he removed the moulds and models. Chelsea and Bow ware are very similar in design and appearance, and consequently a difficulty exists in classifying doubtful pieces. There are a

great many examples of Bow porcelain in the Schreiber
gift in the South Kensington Museum, and Professor
Church is of the opinion that they are mostly authentic

Fig. 79.—Bowl of Chelsea-Derby Porcelain.

specimens. The Chinese-shaped vase with the rococo and
Louis-Seize decorations is a typical example of the Bow
porcelain (Fig. 80).

The date of founding of the Derby porcelain works is not exactly known, except that certain pieces of Derby ware have been advertised for auction " after the finest Dresden models " in 1756 and up to 1770, proving that the works

Fig. 80.—Bow Porcelain Vase. (S. K. M.)

must have been going on during these periods. According to Professor Church, William Duesbury, the first of that name, was connected with the Derby works in 1756, and died in 1786. He was succeeded by his son of the same name, who took into partnership Michael Kean in 1795.

This W. Duesbury died in 1796. The works were carried on by another William Duesbury until the year 1815, when they passed into the hands of Robert Bloor, who carried the manufactory on until 1848, when it ceased. Locher, a manager of Bloor's, started another factory after this which

Fig. 81.—Derby Statuette.

still exists to-day. The Derby coloured porcelain statuettes are imitated more or less from Dresden ware, even to the Dresden marks of the crossed swords (Fig. 81), which marks are copied by a great many porcelain manufacturers. The cup and saucer (Fig. 82) is a specimen of early Crown Derby. The borders are deep blue and the festoons pink.

Some of the names of the painters who were engaged at the Crown Derby works are:—F. Duvivier (1769), P. Stephan (1770), R. Askew (1772), J. J. Spengler (1790), and W. J. Coffee (1791). Askew was a clever figure painter. Deep blues, reds, and greens, with lavish gilding, and ornament of a very conventional character, are found on some of the late Derby cups, saucers, and plates.

WORCESTER porcelain was first made by a company consisting of fifteen shareholders, formed in the year 1751

Fig. 82.—Crown Derby Covered Cup and Saucer.

by Dr. Wall and Mr. W. Davis, the inventors. The name given to the early ware was the "Tonquin porcelain of Worcester." These works have been going almost without interruption under different names of proprietors until the present day.

Vases and other objects in Worcester porcelain of the early period were decided imitations of Chinese and Japanese wares, but at the same time they were dignified examples both as to form and decoration compared with the meaningless rococo designs of Chelsea and Bow.

The vase (Fig. 83), in the Schreiber Collection, is Oriental in form and decoration, but has a restrained

Fig. 83.—Worcester Vase. (S. K. M.)

character of its own that is not usually met with in the contemporary wares of the period.

The vases are the chief glory of Worcester ware; in colour they are exceedingly rich, having grounds of " gros bleu," turquoise, pea-green, maroon, and a fine shade of yellow; gold is also used in modified proportions.

We have mentioned before the mode of decoration by transfer printing adopted by Janssen on the Battersea enamels and by Sadler and Green on the Liverpool delft; this style of decoration was extensively employed by the Worcester decorators for the fillings of the panels with landscapes and rustic figures, after engravings by Watteau, Gainsborough, and others.

Dresden and Sèvres wares were imitated at Worcester, and it is generally thought that when this was done—during the period 1768-1783—the Worcester ware was at its best. This was the middle period, and towards the time that ended about the beginning of this century the designs became laboured, and lavish use of gold rendered the work vulgar and showy.

Josiah and Richard Holdship and R. Handcock are names of some of the principal artists of the early and middle period. Donaldson, Neale, and Foggo were names of enamellers who worked at the Worcester pottery. A curious design in this ware of a tobacco-pipe bowl (Fig. 84) is in the Schreiber Collection.

PLYMOUTH porcelain manufactory was established by William Cookworthy (1705-80), who was the first to discover in England the real China clay or kaolin, about the year 1755. Cookworthy had a good knowledge of chemistry, and was a wholesale chemist and druggist. He found both the China clay and China stone at Tregonning Hill and at two other places in Cornwall. A patent was granted to him in 1768 for the manufacture of porcelain, and the firm of " Cookworthy and Co." established itself at Coxside, Plymouth. A French ceramic artist named Sequoi was engaged to superintend the works. The Plymouth works were not of long duration, for shortly afterwards they were removed to Bristol, and Richard Champion, of

Bristol, obtained a licence from Cookworthy to make the
Plymouth porcelain, and bought the entire rights from the
latter in 1773.　From this date until 1781 Champion
owned the Castle Green works at Bristol which formerly
belonged to Cookworthy.　Statuettes, vases, rustic pieces,
teapots, cups and saucers, &c., were made in both Ply-

Fig. 84.—Bowl of Tobacco-pipe, Worcester Ware.

mouth and Bristol china, many of them being imitations
of Sèvres and Oriental wares.

In Staffordshire many porcelain works are still in existence that began in the last century or early in this, such
as Longton Hall, New Hall, Spode, Wedgwood, and
Minton, but space prevents us from giving any details
of their work.　Liverpool, Lowestoft, Coalport, Swansea,
Nantgarw, and Rockingham may be mentioned as other
places where English porcelain was made.

Chinese Porcelain.

The manufacture of porcelain in China, according to their own accounts, dates for more than two hundred years before the Christian era. The composition of Chinese porcelain is of two elements: one, the infusible argillaceous earth or clay called kaolin; and the other the " pe-tun-tse," which is feldspar slightly altered, a micaceous mineral and quartz or silica, which is fusible. The latter is used with or without other mixtures to form a glaze for hard porcelain. Other materials are sometimes used in the glaze, but, unlike the enamel of earthenware, tin or lead is not used.

Fig. 85.—Chinese Vase.

The Chinese made their porcelain in different degrees of translucency. The kind made especially for the Emperor's use, such as cups, saucers, and rice plates of a ruby-red tint, are very thin and almost transparent.

The porcelain coloured in turquoise blue, violet, sea-green, and celadon are of the oldest varieties made. Yellow, the colour of Ming dynasty, is a common colour in Chinese porcelain.

The Chinese decorated their vases sometimes without much regard to the spacing or divisions of body, neck, or foot (Fig. 85). Landscapes, dragons, fanciful kylins,

dogs, and lions, as well as nearly all kinds of natural
objects were used by them as decoration. Conventional

Fig. 86.—Oriental Porcelain ; Chinese, with French Ormolu Mounting.
(S. K. M.)

renderings of flowers and foliage and geometric ornament
are often used in a judicious sense.

Peculiar shapes of vases, such as the square, hexagonal, and octagonal forms, are found very frequent in Oriental ware. The vase (Fig. 86), from the Jones Collection, is a less extravagant example of Chinese porcelain than usual; the egg-shaped body is, however, the only Oriental part of the vase.

JAPANESE ware is more interesting and more varied in

Fig. 87.—Japanese Ancient Vase; *circa* B.C. 640.

design, though not so gaudy in appearance as the Chinese, owing to the higher sense of artistic feeling and individuality of the Japanese artists. The art, as seen in the ceramic productions as well as in most other things of Japanese art and design, was originally borrowed from the older nation of China and from the Coreans. From their keen sense of beauty, and also greater artistic power, the art products of the Japanese are superior to those of China.

The first glazed pottery made in Japan is supposed to date from the year 1230—this was made at Seto by Tôshiro, who had learnt the art in China, and the first porcelain just before the year 1513, for the maker of this early Japanese porcelain—Shonsui, a Chinese potter—had returned to China in that year.

Fig. 88.—Incense-Burner, Satsuma Ware; *circa* 1720.

Pottery of an inferior kind was made anterior to the Christian era, but probably the oldest known was made by the people who occupied the country before the present Japanese. The ancient vase (Fig. 87) is an example of this early ware. It is of a coarse kind of earthenware, baked or fired in a hole in the ground, over which and around the vessel was built a wood fire.

Japanese wares are of three kinds: the common stone-

Fig. 89.—Incense-Burner, Arita Ware; *circa* 1710.

ware ornamented with scratched lines and glazed; a crackled glazed ware with painted decorations; and the porcelain. The porcelain of Japan is first baked to the biscuit state, then the colours of the decoration are applied, and the piece is afterwards glazed, and is again fired at a greater heat. The gilding or enamel colours that may be required are put on afterwards, when a third firing at a lower temperature is necessary. The Japanese porcelain paste does not stand the firing so well as the Chinese, and consequently the pieces are often twisted and altered in shape.

The factories of Hizen are among the very oldest and are still in working order in Japan. Old Hizen ware is decorated with blue paintings.

The pottery and porcelain of Seto manufacture is highly esteemed, and the name of *Setomono* has been given by the Japanese to their porcelain ware.

The Kutani ware is a coarse porcelain, known also under the name of Kaga ware; the pieces with a red ground and gold ornamentation are highly valued. It is also glazed with deep green, light purple, and yellow colours.

Fig. 90.—Pierced Glazed Water-bottle, from Madura. (B.)

One of the most famous and costliest Japanese wares is the old Satsuma, which was first made by the Corean potters who settled in the village of Nawashirogawa, in the province of Satsuma, about 1600. This ware is of a dark cream colour, with a crackled glaze, and is decorated with red, green, and gold outlined ornament (Fig. 88)

A specimen of the Hizen potteries porcelain, Arita ware, is illustrated at Fig. 89, of an incense-burner. It is painted in bright colours of red, green, pale blue, and has some gilding. It is decorated with hares or rabbits and waves in the panels and dragons on the cover.

INDIAN POTTERY.

The making of pottery is universal throughout India. The unglazed wares are made everywhere, and of various colours. Red glazed pottery is made at Dinapur, gilt pottery at Amroha and in Rajputana; black and silver pottery at Azimghar in the north-west, and at Surujgarrah

Fig. 91.—Glazed Pottery of Sindh. (B.)

in Bengal; painted pottery at Kota, the unglazed pierced variety at Madura, and the celebrated glazed pottery made at Sindh and in the Punjaub.

It may be said that in general the pottery of India is good in shape, colour, and decoration, the latter never violating its purpose, nor distracting the eye from the shape of the vessel. The designs are very simple, and repeating, perhaps to monotony in many cases; but the painted pottery decoration, by reason of its broad and direct application, although the ornament is very simple in character, is better, and less monotonous, for instance,

than the Indian wood-carving decoration. The designs
take the form of panels of flower and leaf ornament
placed side by side, bands of guilloches, chevrons,
running ornament, and lines, the knop-and-flower pattern,
and a panel filling or an all-over decoration consisting of
diapered flowers, leaves, or stars. The elegant shaped
water bottle from Madura (Fig. 90) is pierced so that the

Fig. 92.—Glazed Pottery of Sindh. (B.)

air may circulate round the inner porous bowl. This ware
is coloured a dark green or a golden brown glaze.

The Sindh glazed pottery is beautiful, though very simple
in colour and decoration. The colours are mostly blue of
two or three shades, turquoise greens, and creamy whites,
and sometimes the glaze is purple, golden brown, or
yellow. Many of the vases are bulbous or oviform in shape,
with wide necks and bottoms, and are decorated with the

Sventi, or daisy-like flower (Fig. 91), or the lotus (Fig. 92).

The enamelled tile from Sindh (Fig. 93) has a knop-

Fig. 93.—Enamelled Tile, from Sindh. (B.)

and-flower decoration, the larger flower having the character of an iris, and, at the same time, something of the lotus flower in its composition.

CHAPTER II.

ENAMELS.

ENAMELLING is the art of applying a vitreous material to an object, as decoration, to the surface of which it is made to adhere by heat. Metals are the usual foundations to which enamels are applied, but stone, earthenware, and glass may be enamelled. When one speaks of "an enamel" we understand it to mean a metal that is ornamented by a vitreous decoration fused and fixed to the metal surface by heat. There are three principal kinds of enamels: the "embedded or encrusted," the "translucent upon relief," and the "painted." Some enamelled objects have a mixture of two methods.

The embedded or so-called encrusted kind has two varieties, which are best known under their French names, the *Cloisonné* and the *Champlevé*. When floated in a transparent state over a bas-relief, showing the chased details below, it is *translucent*, or, as it is called by the French, *émaux de basse-taille*. The *painted* is a later variety developed by the school of Limoges.

The Cloisonné is the oldest variety; it is that in which the Greek or Byzantine enamels are made, and also the Chinese. In this method of enamelling the plate or metal foundation which is to receive the enamel is first cut to the required shape, and a little rim of gold ribbon soldered around it.

The design is formed by narrow strips of gold ribbon or filigree, fastened to the foundation by a strong gum or cement, and bent to form the lines of the design. The cells thus formed are filled in with the enamel in a fine powdered state, or in a paste, the vitreous materials of the selected enamel having previously been tried, as to their colour and time required for perfect and equal fusion.

The piece is then placed in a furnace or "muffle," sufficiently open so that the progress of the fusing can be watched while firing, and withdrawn when perfectly fused. As the enamel generally sinks lower than the walls of the cells after fusion, it is necessary to add a second thin coating, or sometimes more, and to re-fire it in order to fill all the cavities. After this the work will require grinding down and polishing to level the surface and restore the brilliancy of the colours that may be slightly deadened by the cooling of the enamel.

The materials of enamel colours are metallic oxides. These colours are finely pulverized, washed, and mixed with vitreous compounds, called fluxes, which are easily fusible, and in melting impart an extra brilliancy to the colours, and form with them by fusion the almost imperishable substance of enamel.

The Champlevé enamels are made in the same way as the Cloisonné, with this exception, that instead of the thin gold ribbons or filigree work forming the design, the walls of the cells that compose the design and separate the enamel colours in the Champlevé variety are formed by the hollowing out of the thick metal—usually copper— and leaving the design to be formed out of the thin partitions that are left standing. The cavities are filled with the enamel mixtures and fused as in the Cloisonné method.

On account of the articles being small, and also being mostly made on a gold foundation, they were more likely to have been stolen or melted down, and this accounts in a great measure for the scarcity of Cloisonné enamels in our collections. The Champlevé, on the other hand, being generally enamels on copper or brass, that from the cheapness of those materials, larger vessels and other objects were extensively made, and from both size and lesser value of the materials they were more likely to have escaped the melting-pot.

When the foundation of the Champlevé enamels was copper, the lines of this metal that formed the design would be gilt with an amalgam of melted gold and mercury, and the piece re-fired at a lower temperature, in order not to injure or disturb the enamel surface.

"Translucent" enamel upon reliefs known as *de basse taille* is the art of enamelling reliefs of silver or gold that have previously been chased or engraved with the design required. The enamel is laid on in various degrees of thickness, according to the strength of shading or depth of tone required. The transparent varieties of enamels are selected for these works, and opaque varieties avoided.

"Painted" enamels were suggested by the translucent enamels upon reliefs. The extensive demand for the latter variety, and the great number executed, gave rise to the invention of using enamel colours as in oil-painting; that is, instead of engraving the subject or design previously on the metal, the method of expressing with the brush the drawing and the light and shade with the enamel colours direct was resorted to, on grounds specially prepared upon copper surfaces. Labarte believes that the modification in the art of glass painting introduced in the fourteenth century had the effect of causing enamel painters to experiment in painting with the enamel colours direct, as in painting on glass.

About this time the method of painting on glass was introduced, which formerly was decorated by simply using the pieces of *stained* or coloured glass as in mosaic work, the only difference between the superficial glass painting and the painting in enamels being that in the latter the opaque enamel colours are used instead of the transparent as in glass painting. It was, however, a considerable time from the introduction of painting on enamels before any good specimens of the art were executed.

Among the earliest specimens of Cloisonné enamels was the golden altar given to the cathedral of Sta. Sophia at Constantinople by Justinian.

This altar was dismantled and divided amongst the Crusaders at the taking of Constantinople in 1204. The next important works in date are the gold altar of Ambrose at Milan, made by Volvinius in 825; the votive crown of

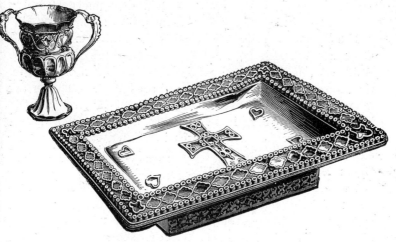

Fig. 94.—Altar Tray and Chalice, Cloisonné Enamel; Sixth Century (?).

St. Mark, Venice, 886-911; the Limburg reliquary made for Basil II. (the Macedonian), 976; and the famous altar, the Pala d'Oro, in St. Mark's, Venice, 976-1105, made at Constantinople, and brought from there to Venice by order of the Doge Ordelafo Faliero. This altar had precious stones added to it and was enlarged in 1209 and in 1345. If the crown of Charlemagne (Fig. 96) was used at his coronation it would make the date of the four enamelled gold plates with the figures of Solomon, David, and Our Lord between two seraphim and Esaias and

Hezekiah, anterior to the year A.D. 800, when he was crowned. These enamels are enclosed in filigree bands and sunk into the metal in the Greek manner.

The sword of Charlemagne, made in the ninth century, has the golden scabbard inlaid with filagree Cloisonné enamels. Both the sword and crown are in the Imperial treasury at Vienna.

The gold altar tray and chalice (Fig. 94) were found near Gourdon, in the Department of the Haute-Saône. The altar tray has a cross in the centre, and lozenge and trefoil ornaments of Cloisonné garnet-coloured enamels. Greek coins of the sixth century were found with it.

The Byzantine reliquary (Fig. 95) is another example of Cloisonné work.

At Cologne, in the cathedral, is the shrine of the Magi that contains the skulls of the " Three Kings." This is a magnificent reliquary made by the order of the Archbishop Philip von Heinsberg in two storeys, both of which have a series of arcades with figures in each. It is also an example of enamelled work in which the Cloisonné and Champlevé processes may be seen.

The first authentic or dated specimens of Champlevé enamels belong to the twelfth century, though some specimens are likely of an earlier date. Some crosses and other works of the dates 1041-1054 show a mixture of the two embedded varieties of enamels.

It is probable that the Rhenish Provinces of Germany were the first places where Champlevé enamels were extensively made; but almost simultaneously in the twelfth century there arose an active centre of work in this method in Limoges, the future great seat of the enamel industry.

The German variety may be distinguished from the French by the greater number of colours employed : there is a difficulty in deciding which of the two is the earlier.

The Abbé Suger, when building the Abbey of St. Denis, brought enamellers from Loraine, near the Rhine, to make an enamelled cross, which they completed between 1143 and 1147. A portable altar, and a cruciform reliquary with a dome, in the treasury at Hanover, are early

Fig. 95.—Byzantine Reliquary, Cloisonné Enamel; Tenth Century.

examples of the German school. One of these portable altars in enamel, of the German school, thirteenth century, is shown at Fig. 98. The earliest Champlevé enamel of the Limoges school is that of the monument to Geoffrey

Plantagenet, who died in 1151. It is now in the Museum
of Le Mans (Fig. 97).

At Limoges towards the end of the twelfth century
Champlevé enamels were made in great numbers. Two
specimens of this date are in the Cluny Museum in Paris:
one has the subject of the adoration of the Magi, and the

Fig. 96.—Crown of Charlemagne.

other St. Stephen with St. Nicholas, both having Limousin
legends. In the same museum are Champlevé enamels as
book-covers of the Gospels, croziers, plaques, and "gemel-
lions." The latter is the name given to certain hand-basins
used for religious purposes. In the Louvre is an example of
Champlevé enamel—a ciborium of the fourteenth century.
This is a vessel in which the Host is kept. Another

Fig. 97.—Champlevé Enamel of Geoffrey Plantagenet.

vessel used for similar purposes is the *pyx*. Both are small round boxes in which the sacred wafers were kept, and were used for carrying the sacrament to the sick. Ciboria were also in the forms of doves or little towers suspended over the altar. They were kept in little cupboards on either side of the altar, and at later periods the name "ciborium" was applied to the tabernacles having architectural pretensions erected over the altar, and which had a canopy or curtain used as a covering. These tabernacles became shrines of great size and beauty in the fifteenth and sixteenth centuries, and were carved in wood

Fig. 98.—Portable Altar; German, Thirteenth Century. (S. K. M.)

as that in Nuremberg by Adam Kraft, or were stone erections of great dimensions with sculptured figures as decorations, the doors of which were often made in gold and enamelled. Fig. 423 (previous volume) is an example of a fifteenth-century tabernacle with a gilt metal door.

When Justinian rebuilt Sta. Sophia he placed in it a ciborium or tabernacle of great splendour. Ciboria are now changed into what are known as *baldacchinos*.

In the Kensington and British Museums are many examples of Champlevé enamels, both German and Limoges, such as book-covers, croziers, pricket candlesticks, châsses, chefs, reliquaries, paxes, crosses, and nuptial caskets, &c. Most of them have blue grounds, with light bluish-grey and dark blue or green ornaments, and are usually enamelled on copper. Some of the reliquaries or châsses have gilt figures in high relief. From the eleventh to the fourteenth centuries is the date of these enamels.

In the latter end of the thirteenth and in the fourteenth centuries enamels became simplified in execution ; the figures were mostly incised and gilt, and the background a level coating of enamel—generally of a blue colour. (Fig. 100.)

Fig. 99 is a Limoges enamelled châsse or shrine of the twelfth century, and is in the British Museum.

The Italians did not make Champlevé enamels; but they worked in the Cloisonné process from the eleventh to the fifteenth centuries, as we know from examples, and from the work, "Diversarum Artium Schedula," written by the learned monk Theophilus, in the twelfth century, wherein he describes very minutely the whole process of making Cloisonné enamels, according to the methods of the Tuscan enamellers of his time.

As regards the antiquity of the art of enamelling on

Fig. 99.—Châsse in Champlevé Enamel; Twelfth Century. (B. M.)

metal, it is generally agreed by learned authorities in the matter that before the art was known at Constantinople or in the workshops of Greece, it was practised by the "barbarians" of Western Europe in the Gallo-Roman period. We apologize for quoting here the oft-repeated passage from Philostratus, the Greek who established himself at Rome in the early part of the third century at the request of the Empress Julia, wife of Septimus Severus. In his "Treatise upon Images" he says: "It is said that

the barbarians living near the ocean pour colours upon
heated brass, so that these adhere and become like stone,
and preserve the design represented."

This passage proves at any rate in Greece and in Italy
enamelling on metal was an unknown art in the third
century, the time in which this Greek writer lived, and
sufficient examples exactly answering his description have
been found in Gaul and in Britain, in Roman burial-
places and in caves, all bearing evidences of belonging

Fig. 100.—Champlevé Enamel ; French, Fourteenth Century.

to this period. The Celtic objects in vitreous enamel are
on bronze or copper, and prove that enamelling was an art
carried on in the Roman Provinces of Gaul and Britain,
which was unknown in Italy at that time.

The beautiful vessel at Fig. 101, found in a Roman
sepulchre in the Bartlow Hills, in Essex, is a fine example
of this early enamel. Other existing specimens of the
Gallo-Roman period are in the Museum at Poitiers, in the
Imperial Library, Paris, and in the Museums of London.
From the Gallo-Roman period until the eleventh century

most of the arts were at a low ebb, owing to the devas-
tating wars and invasions that spread all over Europe;
the art of enamelling had been almost lost, and had quite
died out in France and Germany, but is likely to have
still been practised in Ireland, where no doubt the art of
the goldsmith and the enameller in conjunction had
flourished less disturbed than in France or England. We
have existing remains of pure Irish Celtic work that date

Fig. 101.—Enamelled Vase, found in Essex in 1834, since partially destroyed
by fire. Diameter, 4¾ inches.

from the ninth and probably earlier centuries, and are of
unsurpassed workmanship. Chalices, books of the Gospels, croziers, reliquaries, brooches, jewellery, &c., more or
less enamelled, were made in the ninth century, and some
earlier. Ireland had a school of living art when in the
ninth and tenth centuries the rest of Christendom was
sitting wrapped in chaotic gloominess, idly awaiting the
supposed end of the world, in A.D. 1000. As regards our

present subject, we must notice as coming under the head of enamels that beautiful Irish relic known as the Ardagh Chalice. (Fig. 102.) The body of the cup is silver with about one-third or one-fourth of copper alloy. It is a wonderful mixture of metals, there being gold, silver, copper, bronze, brass, and lead ; and an iron bolt secures the stem and bowl together. The ornaments are belts, and the handles, to which are fastened the beautifully designed and worked interlacings of Celtic ornament, of

Fig. 102.—The Ardagh Chalice ; Irish Celtic Work.   Height, 7 inches.

which each little panel is different; it is said that forty distinct varieties in the designs can be traced, consisting of interlaced bands of Celtic twistings, knots, and arabesques: each compartment of the principal belt of ornament is divided by a boss, or enamelled bead, of which there are twelve. The handles are composed of enamels and filigree work similar to the work of the belt, but different in design, with blue glass or paste bosses. The two larger circular ornaments on the sides are composed of gold filigree with a central enamelled boss. The four settings of these ornaments had two pieces of blue glass paste and two pieces of amber, which have fallen out.

The stem is composed of bronze metal gilt, and is richly chased with interlaced ornaments. The circular foot is ornamented with gold and bronze plaques alternating on the outer rim ; the bronze divisions are enamelled.

The inside, or under the foot of the cup, is divided into a series of circular divisions around a central crystal, composed of amber and bronze, gold filigree, amber, bronze, and translucent green enamels respectively. In some of the enamels were embedded small portions or grains of gold while the enamel was in fusion. There is a chiselled inscription on the plain surface of the bowl consisting of the names of the Apostles. The workmanship of this exquisite chalice is infinitely superior to the Byzantine work of the same period.

A detailed and exhaustive description of this chalice is given in Miss Stokes's " Early Christian Art in Ireland," from which our illustration is taken.

Going back to the ninth century, we have the ring of King Ethelwulf, bearing his name, which is of Saxon workmanship. It was found in Hampshire, and is made of gold and blue-black enamel. Another ring, that of Alfred the Great, was found at Athelney in Somersetshire, the place where Alfred retired to in 878. It is of gold, wrought in filigree and chased. The face is of rock crystal, and the design is in filigree fastened to the gold plate and enamelled in the Byzantine manner. Round the edge is the inscription (translated), " Alfred ordered me to be made."

Enamelled disks, fibulæ, finger rings, and other articles of personal adornment have been found in England of the Anglo-Saxon period, mostly having a bronze foundation for the enamel.

Documents are preserved at Oxford proving that Limoges enamellers were brought over to England in the thirteenth century to execute effigies, tombs, and other work in

enamels. Master John, a native of Limoges, was employed
to construct the tomb and recumbent figure of Walter de
Merton, Bishop of Rochester. This work was destroyed
at the period of the Reformation. There still exists, however, some of the Limoges work of that date in the effigy
of William de Valence, who died in 1129. This tomb is in
Westminster Abbey.

The enamels known as *émaux de plique à jour*, are a
kind of Cloisonné work in which there was no background,
the enamel being in variety transparent, in imitation of
precious stones, and set between the Cloisons or network
of gold. The beautiful specimen (Fig. 103) is a cup with
a cover, and with architectural features; it is now in
South Kensington Museum.

Translucent enamels upon relief date from the period
when Art in Italy was beginning to throw off the stiff-
ness and angularity of Byzantine traditions. This was
towards the end of the thirteenth century, in the early dawn
of the Renaissance.

Freedom in sculpture and painting brought with it a
desire to treat enamels in the same freedom, and so we find
that engraving on silver and gold, and placing carefully
the various powdered enamels in their proper proportions
over the engraved surfaces, produced an entirely new and
splendid effect; besides, it required more artistic skill to
execute this kind of enamelling, and consequently the
best artists of the Renaissance were not only goldsmiths,
painters, sculptors, and architects, but executed important
works in enamels as well. The method was one that could
be described as a link between the art of the painter and
the goldsmith, and no doubt the demand for enamelled
altars, and religious vessels of all kinds, both sacred and
secular, in the fourteenth and fifteenth centuries, was the
cause of producing many artists that subsequently rose to
great eminence. For instance, among others may be mentioned Francisco Francia, the celebrated painter who lived
in the fifteenth century, who was originally a goldsmith,

and as Vasari says, he excelled everybody of his time as an engraver on metals and as an enameller on silver. There is a fine oil-painting by him in the National Gallery of London, on which he has signed himself as "Francia the Goldsmith." Many names of eminent Italians artists

Fig. 103.—Cup of Translucent Enamel. (S. K. M.)

might be given who executed works in enamel in the translucent process: Nicolas Pisano and John his pupil, who executed an altar for Bishop Gubertini of Arezzo in translucent enamel on silver in 1286. Agostino and Agnolo were pupils of John, and helped him at this altar.

Forzore, the son of Spinello of Arezzo, is mentioned by Vasari as a famous enameller. Pollaiuolo is another great name in the Italian art of the goldsmith and enameller. He was also a celebrated modeller and sculptor who had helped Ghiberti in the ornamental work of his gates of the Baptistery of St. John. He died in 1498. Many other celebrated names could be mentioned, but the greatest of all, both as a goldsmith and as an enameller, was Benvenuto Cellini (1500-1570), whose work is well known, and who tells us himself, in his "Treatise on the Goldsmith's Art," so much about the method of enamelling in his time. The celebrated ewer, called "The Cellini Ewer," is a masterpiece of jeweller's work, and is attributed to Cellini. The body of the ewer is composed of two oval slices of brown sardonyx, carved with radiating ribs in relief. These slices are fastened in an ornamental frame of gold, richly worked. A female figure sits on the top front curve of the body under the lip. The neck, lip, stem with dragons, and other parts of the framework, are enamelled in the translucent method.

A book-cover in the Kensington Museum, of very fine workmanship, with several small figure compositions enamelled on gold, is attributed to Cellini. Works by him in jewellery, vases, salt-cellars, &c., are preserved in various museums on the Continent. Cellini spent five years in France, ending the year 1540, where he executed some works for Francis I., notably the fine salt-cellar now at Vienna.

The art of enamelling on reliefs was introduced to France by Italian artists during the early years of the fourteenth century, and about the same time to Flanders. We read of a manufactory of this kind of enamelling as having existed in 1317 at Montpellier, the seat of the royal Mint.

"Painted enamels," as we have seen, were suggested by the translucent enamels on relief. Painted enamels were first made at Limoges, and also brought to great perfection at the same place. Any painted enamels found in Italy are Limoges enamels or the work of Limousin artists. The fifteenth century was the period during which the painted enamels were brought to perfection. In the earlier part of the century the enamel was applied directly to the plate of metal and united to it by fusion; but later, towards the middle of the century, a ground of translucent enamel coating was laid on the metal, over the engraved outline of the design, and on this transparent flux the colours were applied. The outlines of the design, which appeared through the transparent coating, were then covered over with a dark-coloured enamel; the various parts, such as draperies, background, and sky, were then laid in with thick coatings of enamel; the spaces left for the flesh tints were filled in with black or violet enamel; and the modelling of the flesh was obtained by layers of white enamel in varying degrees of thickness, leaving the darker violet parts for shade or shadows, and thicker layers represented the highest lights. Thus, all the flesh tints in enamels of this period are slightly brownish or violet in hue.

The other parts of the design were left without shadow, or sometimes the highest points in the hair or draperies would have little fine touches of gold pencillings, in order to bring out some kind of relief. Imitations of precious stones or jewellery on the dresses were brought out in translucent bits of enamel.

An entire change in the process is seen in the Limoges painted enamels of the sixteenth century. The plate of metal was covered with a layer of black or some very dark-coloured enamel, and the design carefully outlined in white. The whole work was then modelled up with white, laid on in varying thicknesses, so as to produce an effect of light and shade called *grisaille* (grey), the flesh tints being slightly higher in relief than the other parts, and a flesh-coloured enamel being always employed. Fine touchings of white and gold were added to finish off the work.

To make a coloured enamel of the grisaille work it was

only necessary to add a thin transparent coating of coloured enamel.

Some splendid effects of a translucent character were obtained in the enamels of this period by the use of gold and silver leaf (*paillon*) fixed on the enamel ground behind the draperies and other accessories, and sometimes on the backgrounds. Over this leaf of shining metal transparent enamels were painted. Armour, imitation jewellery, and other accessories were rendered by this means of a rich and dazzling brilliancy. In the Kensington Collection many examples of this kind of enamelling may be seen.

One work amongst others is an oval plaque of the sixteenth-century Limoges enamel, which has a representation of a warrior on horseback, and has portions of the armour in translucent enamel. The horse is white, and the groundwork dark. It is one of the best works of the Courtois family.

The enamel painters of Limoges had many methods and secrets in the exercise of their art, and, as a rule, kept them in their families. Generally speaking, we find many enamellers of the same name and family, and their works bear also a strong family likeness, both in subject, colour, and methods.

The greatest name amongst these Limoges artists is Léonard Limousin. This surname was bestowed on him by Francis I. to distinguish him from Leonardo da Vinci. Léonard Limousin was the chief enameller to this monarch, and worked at his art between the years of 1532-74. Léonard in his early works copied his subjects from engravings of the German school of artists, but at a later period, owing to the influence of the Italian artists that were brought to the Court of Francis I., he adopted the subjects of Raphael and the Italian masters. He also improved at this period in his colour and drawing. Some of his best works are those that he painted in the year 1553 for the Sainte-Chapelle by order of Henry II., which consist of two magnificent frames of pictures in enamel, now in the Louvre, and which are acknowledged as his masterpieces. He also excelled in portraits, among which from his hand are those of the Duke de Guise, the Constable de Montmorenci, and that of Catherine de' Medici in her mourning robes, taken after the death of Henry II. A full-length portrait of Henry II. is preserved in the Louvre, executed by Léonard. The monarch is represented in the character of St. Thomas, and is painted on a white enamel ground, as several other works by this artist are similarly executed. This style of work looks, however, too much like majolica painting, and was not persevered in to any great extent. Léonard was noted for some good original work, both in oils and enamel; but, generally speaking, the Limoges enamellers were fond of copying subjects from German, Italian, and French engravers, who engraved many works after the great painters of these countries. The German engravers were known under the name of the "Petits-Maîtres," many of whom were pupils or imitators of Albert Dürer. Some of the more important were Heinrich Aldegrever, Hans Sebald Behan, Virgilis Solis, Theodore de Bry, Jean Collaert, Albrecht Altdorfen, and Georg Pens. Two celebrated French engravers who supplied many designs for the Limoges enamellers were Étienne de Laulne, known also as Stephanus, and Pierre Woeiriot, the former a copper-plate and the latter a wood engraver. The Courtois and Raymond enamels have many subjects from the designs of Étienne de Laulne. Another engraver, Marc Antonio Raimondi, of the Italian school (1500-1540), supplied copies of the works of Raphael to the Limousin enamellers, and also to the Italian majolica painters. This engraver was the most celebrated of his time. He was a pupil at first of "Francia the Goldsmith," learnt much from Albert Dürer and Lucas van Leyden, and was the engraver of many of the works of Raphael, which he executed in what is known as his Roman method.

In the British Museum there is the enamel of the twelve Sibyls of Léonard Limousin, painted about 1550.

Another well-known name is that of Pierre Raymond. He painted chiefly in grisaille, or in camaïeu, and not often in colour. His works date from 1534 to 1572 (Figs. 104 and 105).

The Pénicaud family (*circa* 1540) consists of four enamel painters of this name—Jean Pénicaud, the elder, Jean Pénicaud, junior, Pierre Pénicaud, and N. Pénicaud.

The elder Pénicaud was a good draughtsman, and often employed "paillon" to get the rich colouring in which he

Fig. 104.—Portion of a Salt-cellar, by Pierre Raymond.

excelled. He executed portraits of Luther and Erasmus, which are signed with his initials.

The Courtois or Courteys family was another celebrated family of painters on enamel. Pierre Courtois was the eldest (*circa* 1550). He painted some of the largest enamels ever executed. These were large oval panels measuring 66 inches in height by 40 inches in width, on which were painted the subjects of the cardinal virtues and heathen divinities, and which formerly decorated the façade of the Château de Madrid, built by Francis I. and

Henry II. They are signed and dated 1559. In his larger works Pierre Courtois does not show himself so good in his draughtsmanship as in his smaller enamels.

Jean Courtois (*circa* 1560) was a prolific enameller. His work is characterized by a profusion of arabesque ornament of the period of Henry II. His flesh tints and other parts of his compositions are generally highly coloured, the flesh having a salmon-coloured tint.

Another member of this family signs his work I. D. C. His principal figures are usually hammered out in relief, and his work is of a high finish.

Jean Court (*circa* 1555) was also known under his other surname of "Vigier." He was formerly confounded with Jean Courtois, but his work is different from the latter's. His drawing is better, and his colouring not so strong but more natural than that of Jean Courtois.

Suzaune Court, as she signed herself, was an enameller of the school of Jean Courtois.

Martial Raymond (*circa* 1590) was an artist of considerable power, and a goldsmith, who worked at the end of the sixteenth century. His work is usually heightened with gold, and he used "paillon" very much.

Fig. 105.—Vase; Painted Enamel, by Pierre Raymond.

Jean Limousin (*circa* 1625), and François Limousin (1633), were enamellers who carried out the traditions of the Limoges school in a worthy manner during the early part of the seventeenth century.

The former passes for the son of Léonard Limousin, and was supposed, from the fleur-de-lis that always appears between his initials on his works, to have been the director of the royal manufactory at Limoges, as his predecessor Léonard was in the reign of Francis I. Jean Limousin executed some beautiful enamels, in which the translucent birds, arabesques, and small figures were treated with rare delicacy.

In the reign of Louis XIV. (1643-1715) Jaques Nouailher introduced a new kind of enamel, which consisted of modelling in relief on copper with a white enamel paste, and afterwards covering it with a transparent coloured enamel.

Pierre Nouailher was another enameller of this family who was noted for his correctness of drawing.

The school of Limoges of this date exhibits a greater correctness of drawing, accompanied with a marked diminution of good colouring ; the enamels of the seventeenth century show a decline of that splendour of colouring which characterized the former century. This was owing to the abandonment of the silver and gold " paillon " backgrounds, and to the exclusive use of the brush alone in the enamels of this period.

The process of painting with a preparation of opaque enamel colours on a gold ground direct, without previously using the heretofore black ground for the purposes of getting the shadows, is ascribed to Toutin (1632). This was the first step to the decadence of enamelling, as the system of Toutin was restricted to the production of portraits in miniature, and in course of time nothing else was done but miniatures. Many artists in the period of this decadence executed good work, amongst which may be mentioned the names of Gribelin, a fellow-worker with Toutin, Dubié, Morlière of Orleans, and Vacquer of Blois. The latter were pupils of Toutin.

Chartier, Petitot, and Bordier were three other noted miniature painters on enamel. The latter two worked in conjunction, and lived for some years in England, until the death of Charles I., when they returned to the Court of Louis XIV., and there painted the portraits in miniature of the principal people of the time.

The art of enamelling was carried on in Spain, in Italy,

and in some parts of Germany during the sixteenth and seventeenth centuries, but not to the same extent as in France. Such articles as crosses, crucifixes, rosaries, pendants, ewers, medallions, perfume bottles, rings, badges, small panels with figure subjects, and numerous small objects, particularly in jewellery, were made in enamels in these centuries throughout Europe.

In the seventeenth century, in England, a good deal of enamelling was done at Battersea, and at Bilston in Staffordshire. A kind of coarse enamel was made in England at that time on cast iron and on brass. The cavities were cast to receive the enamel. There are some candlesticks and fire-dogs in existence that are made in this way.

Stephen T. Janssen had his enamel works at York House, Battersea, in the years 1750-5. After this time the English practice of enamel-making died out. Kensington and the British Museums contain many specimens of Battersea enamel (Fig. 106). Snuff and tobacco boxes, scent-bottles, candlesticks, small dishes, crests, labels of wine-bottles, and minia-

Fig. 106.—Battersea Enamel.
(S. K. M.)

tures are the principal articles of Battersea enamel. The decorations are chiefly small flowers and ornament on light-coloured or white grounds enclosing pastoral subjects. Some have prints of calendars, and other black and white subjects, printed by transferring. In the British Museum there are two large oval medallions with the portraits of George III. and Queen Charlotte, painted by the English enameller W. H. Craft.

ENAMELS OF THE COUNTRIES OF THE EAST.

China, India, and Persia have been famed from early times for their exquisite productions in enamels. Japan also has made, and continues to make, enamels of great beauty. The older or Cloisonné method is mostly in favour with the natives of the East, and very little Champlevé work is executed. Although enamelling is an old art in China, yet Chinese enamels are rare that have been executed before the fifteenth century. In the Ming dynasty, under the Emperor King-tai (1450-7), enamel working was in its highest state of excellence.

The designs on the enamelled vases are pretty much the same as on all their other works, such as textiles, embroideries, and porcelain. In fact, a Chinese enamelled vase is as a rule very similar in shape, colour, and decoration to a porcelain one of the same country, and sometimes the likeness is so great as to demand a close inspection to determine which is enamel and which porcelain.

The Chinese used as a rule light colours in their enamel grounds : light turquoise blue, light olive green, or a bright yellow ground; the latter colour was mostly used in the painted enamels of the Thsing dynasty, yellow being the national colour of this dynasty. The general type of the design is made up of such things as a very crooked tree or branch, decorated with large clusters of flowers and foliage, slightly conventional in drawing; sometimes with birds and butterflies, or with dragons ; some vases have one large dragon occupying the greater part of the field.

The colouring is generally very bright, the ground light and brilliant ; the flowers may be red, deep blue, pansy-violet, golden yellow, or white. The foliage is usually of a crude emerald green type. Borders of conventional cloud forms or other geometric forms surround the panels, or form belts to the fields of the ornamental compositions.

Religious vases, altar furniture, perfume-burners, candle-sticks, lamps, screens, and table-tops are some of the articles in Chinese enamels made invariably in the Cloisonné manner.

The Chinese also make a species of enamel that has no metal foundation, which consists of a cloisonnage of net-work in which the enamel is skilfully fused between the divisions, and is of a semi-translucent character.

Japanese enamels are more modern than the Chinese, old pieces of Japanese being extremely rare. The enamels of Japan are darker in the ground colour than the Chinese, being generally of a dark olive green, or of a warm neutral grey tint. Some very large vases, braziers, and large dishes are made by the Japanese. These wonderful people are extremely clever in the use of the enamellers' lamp and the blowpipe, for the purpose of fusing the enamel in sections, as the large pieces they made could not possibly be fired entire. The Chinese excel in the painting of enamels, but the Japanese do not seem to cul-tivate this art to any great extent.

Indian enamels are characterized by their extreme brilliance and splendour of colouring, in which qualities they excel the enamels of all other countries. The native enamellers work in the translucent, Cloisonné, and Champ-levé processes, and the methods and secrets of their craft are kept in their families. Greens of the peacock and emerald hues, coral and ruby reds, torquoise and sapphire blues are the favourite Indian enamel colours.

The celebrated Jaipur enamels are of the Champlevé kind. In Cashmere and in the Punjaub jewellery is made of gemmed gold and enamels (Fig 107). The Queen and the Prince of Wales possess many articles that are masterpieces of Indian enamelling. The Haka stand lent by the Queen to the Indian Museum is a splendid speci-men of translucent painted enamel in green and blue, of the Mongol period (Fig. 108).

A large plate of Jaipur enamel, said to be the largest

ever made, was presented to the Prince of Wales. A
unique and beautiful specimen of the same kind of enamel

Fig. 107.—Necklace ; Punjaub. (B.)

is the Kalamdan, or pen-and-ink stand in the shape of an
Indian gondola (Fig. 109).

The stern is formed of a peacock's head and body, the tail of which decorates in brilliant enamels the underneath part of the boat.

Fig. 108.—Enamelled Haka Stand; Mongol Period. (B.)

The canopy of the ink receptacle has green, blue, coral, and ruby enamels laid on a gold foundation.

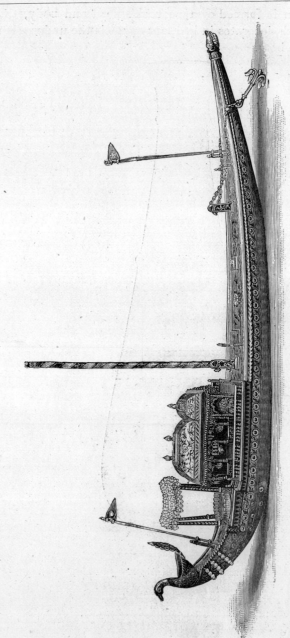

Fig. 109.—Enamelled Pen-and-Ink Stand ; Jaipur.   (B.)

The vase, or Sarai (Fig. 110) in possession of Lady Wyatt is a fine example of Cashmere enamel, on which the shawl pattern may be seen.

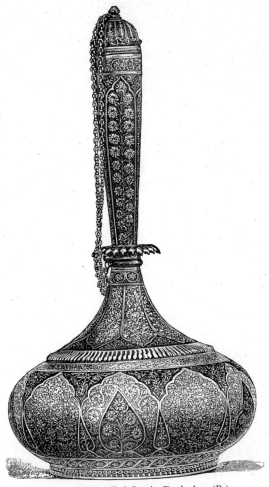

Fig. 110.—Enamelled Sarai; Punjaub. (B.)

A kind of enamel is made at Pertabghar in Rajputana, which consists in covering a plate of burnished gold with a rich green enamel, and placing on the surface while it is hot thin plates of gold ornaments, which are fastened to the enamel by heat; afterwards these gold plates are engraved elaborately with incised lines, so as to bring out the design. Sometimes the enamel itself is engraved, and an easily fused gold amalgam is rubbed into the incised lines, and fused to form the decoration.

Persian enamels are applied mostly to the heads of "Kalians," or tobacco water-pipes, jewellery, and coffee-cup holders. The foundations are gold or copper. A large tray enamelled on copper on both sides is in the Kensington Museum. It is decorated with flowers of various colours on a white ground, and has an Armenian inscription with the date A.D. 1776, and comes from Ispahan. In most Persian enamels the grounds are usually of a white or light tint, with brightly coloured flowers as decoration.

CHAPTER III.

IVORY CARVINGS.

IN the former part of this work we have noticed the ivory carvings of the ancient world, and it is proposed in the following pages to give an outline of ivory carvings of the Middle Ages and of the comparatively modern periods.

One of the oldest and most important works in ivory carving of the sixth century is the celebrated Chair of St. Maximinian, now preserved in the metropolitan church of Ravenna. It is entirely overlaid with plates of ivory, and has five upright panels in the front and below the seat which are carved with figure subjects. The legs and back are overlaid with ivory plates, carved with animals, foliage, and figures, and on the rail in front of the seat is carved the Archbishop's monogram. It is altogether a very fine and rich piece of Romanesque work.

Very important works in ivory were executed in the time of the Roman Empire, in the nature of " Consulare " diptychs and triptychs. These Consular diptychs were originally made of wood or ivory, and were hinged tablets that folded over each other, the outside surfaces being carved elaborately, with a portrait or figure of the Consul or chief magistrate of the province in the centre, the inside surfaces being used for writing purposes. These consulares were also called "pugillares" from being portable objects that could be carried conveniently in the hand or *fist*. They were usually made as presents to be given to important people of distant provinces, or to very intimate friends of the Consuls. After the adoption of the Christian religion by the Roman Empire it was the custom of the Consuls to send these consulares in the form of a diptych or triptych, as a present to the bishop of a church in his province, to show his patronage and good-will, and they were usually placed on the altar of the church, in order that the congregation should see them and remember the giver in their prayers. This custom led to the making of the diptychs (*two-leaved*) and the trip-tychs (*three-leaved*), for the purpose of the altar decorations, and usually on the plain inner leaves were inscribed the names of the newly baptized (*neophytes*) Christians, bene-factors to the church, dignitaries of the same, and Christian martyrs. The use of these led to the later magnificent painted and carved altars of the triptych order in Chris-tian churches. During the persecution by the iconoclastic Emperors of the Eastern Empire a great number of these triptychs were made in wood and in ivory of Greek work-manship, carved or painted on the interior faces with representations of saints and sacred personages. These were used as portable altars, and were carried about the person of those who used to pray before them in secret. Many of them were also of a good size, and became later important objects that were placed above or near the "prie-dieus" in private rooms or chapels. The smaller pugillares, and larger ecclesiastical diptychs were used in later times to form the coverings of costly illuminated books, and it is owing to this use of them that so many have been preserved to our day.

Byzantine sculpture and ivory carvings of the eleventh and twelfth centuries were invested with the same severe and solemn character that was the distinguishing feature of the ceiling and wall mosaics of the same period. The figures were long and attenuated, the draperies very stiff and angular and arranged in parallel folds, which, with the German phase of Christian art, developed later into a

still more angular and rocky character. In France, on the
other hand, in the thirteenth century there arose a splendid
and original school of sculpture, entirely native, whose

Fig. 111.—Coronation of the Virgin; Ivory Carving relieved with Colours and
Gold; Thirteenth-Century French. (Jacquemart.)

richest efforts culminated in such masterly achievements as
the figure sculpture of the cathedrals of Rheims, Chartres,
and Amiens.

Small statuettes in ivory were made in great quantities
in the Middle Ages, and as an example of the French
school of ivory carving of this period there is an exceedingly fine representation of the "Coronation of the Virgin"
(Fig. 111) in the Louvre. In this work the figure of Christ
has the dress and lineaments of Philip III. (the Bold), the
son of St. Louis, and that of the Virgin is personified as
Mary, his Queen, daughter of Henry III. (the Debonnaire),
Duke of Lorraine and Brabant. This example dates from

Fig. 112.—Image Painter; Fifteenth Century.

about 1274, and is certainly one of the most perfectly
finished works of French sculpture of that time.

Colour and rich decoration were seen very much on the
sculpture of the Middle Ages, for we find traces of it in
the mediæval tombs, effigies, and all kinds of statuary.

Some of the ancient diptychs had both ground and
figures coloured and perhaps gilt. Coloured and gilded
statues and reliefs were common in Germany and France,
and are so to-day in those of the Roman and Greek
Christian churches.

The dresses of the figures are semé (sown) all over with fleurs-de-lis and very rich diapers in gold and silver, on rich red, blue, and white grounds. Statuary painting was a profession in the Middle Ages. The illustration (Fig. 112), from a French fifteenth - century manuscript, shows an image painter at work.

Returning to the ivory plaques or diptychs, the illustration at Fig. 113 is that of the most perfect and most beautiful specimen of antique ivory carving that we have any knowledge of. It is now in the Kensington Museum, and represents the figure of a young girl, or Bacchante, with a younger girl attending her. The figure has a well-designed arrangement of drapery hanging in graceful folds. She stands at an altar, and is in the act of making an offering. A vigorously carved oak-tree with 'acorns and foliage occupies the left top of the panel, and a border of a Greek character surrounds it. The corresponding half of this plaque is in the

Fig. 113.—Leaf of a Roman Diptych. (S. K. M.)

Cluny Museum in Paris. It was found at the bottom of a well at Montier-en-Der, and is much injured. The latter half shows the figure of a female standing at an altar, and

holding in her hands inverted flaming torches. These
famous plaques, which measure nearly 12 inches by 5, are
supposed to have formed the doors of a large shrine or
châsse that was brought from Rome in the days of Childeric.
They are supposed to be Roman work of the sixth or
seventh century, though some think the work is earlier:
they are undoubtedly executed by a Greek artist. There
are many specimens of consular diptychs in the museums
of London, Liverpool, and the Continent. The earliest
dates from about A.D. 250, and the latest about A.D. 540.
The Roman Consuls continued for nearly one thousand
years: the last Consul of Constantinople was Basilius
(A.D. 541), and the last Consul of Rome was Paulinus
(A.D. 536).

There is a large plaque of ivory in the British Museum
which measures 16 inches by nearly 6 inches in width—
the largest known—on which is carved the figure of an
archangel holding in one hand a globe and in the other a
long staff. He stands on the top of a flight of steps under
a round arch supported by Corinthian pillars. Its date is
uncertain, but is probably of the seventh century; it is
grandly designed and of excellent workmanship (Fig. 114).

A work of the same or slightly earlier period is the
beautiful ivory vase (Fig. 115), which has well propor-
tioned horizontal divisions and well-designed ornamentation. The style of design suggests a copy from metal
work.

Triptychs, as we have seen, were used above and behind
the altar tables, and were at first portable, so that they
could be carried away after the service was ended; but
later they became the "retables," fixed altars, or "rere-
doses," and were carved or painted, or were partly executed
in both ways.

Many objects of secular art, and articles that the wealthy
could afford to use in every-day life, were made in ivory
during the Middle Ages, such as book-covers, toilet-combs,
mirror-cases, chessmen, horns, hilts of knives, swords, and

daggers, caskets, small coffers, &c., in addition to the
objects required for use in religious ceremonies, as pyxes,
croziers, crucifixes, crosses, and taus, the latter being an

Fig. 114.—Ivory Carving with
Archangel. (B. M.)

Fig. 115.—Ivory Vase ; Roman,
Seventh Century. (B. M.)

early form of the pastoral staff. The pastoral staffs of
ivory are not very common, and most examples known
belong to the thirteenth century.

VOL. II.   L

The woodcut (Fig. 116) of the pastoral staff shows the

Fig. 116.—Pastoral Staff; German, Thirteenth Century.   (S. K. M.)

subject of the Crucifixion on one side and the Virgin and
Child with attendant angels on the other.   It is German

work of the thirteenth century, and is now in the Cathedral of Metz.

An older specimen of the pastoral staff, which Mr. Maskell thinks is English work, is carved in bone with

Fig. 117.—Pastoral Staff; Bone Carving, English ; Twelfth Century.

interlacing scrolls, and has a grotesque and serpent forming the crook decorations (Fig. 117).

In the fourteenth century ivory carvings were in great demand, judging from the great number of the various ivories of that date which have been preserved.

Belonging to this period are the beautiful ivory hunting horns called "oliphants" (from elephant) that were much used by kings and nobles in hunting, and were sometimes mounted in gold.

The ivory carvings known as pierced or "open-work" are usually of very fine and delicate workmanship. The illustration (Fig. 118) shows two compartments of a larger plaque in the Kensington Museum, the full size of the originals that have sacred figures under Gothic canopies of

Fig. 118.—Ivory Carving; Fourteenth Century Pierced Work. (S. K. M.)

fourteenth-century work. It is not known exactly to what country they belong, as ivory carvings as a rule are undated and unsigned, but the woodcut (Fig. 119) represents an undoubted piece of English work. It is one leaf of a diptych made for Grandison, Bishop of Exeter.

Few names of artists, as ivory carvers, have come down to us from the Middle Ages. One named Jean Lebraellier was the carver to Charles V. of France; Jehan Nicolle is another who has signed his name on an ivory pax in the

British Museum. Henry des Grès was a "pignier" or carver of combs (1391). Héliot has dated work of 1392.

Fig. 119.—Ivory Diptych; English Work; Fourteenth Century. (S. K. M.)

Henry de Senlis, "tabletier," plaque carver of 1454, and Philip Daniel, "pignier" and "tabletier" (1484), in Paris.

The top of a Moorish casket from Spain, with Saracenic engraved ornament of the eleventh century, is shown at

Fig. 120, and a beautiful casket from Italy, carved and engraved in bone, is illustrated at Fig. 121. This is fourteenth-century work. Caskets and coffers made of slabs of

Fig. 120.—Lid of Ivory Cabinet ; Spanish ; Eleventh Century. (S. K. M.)

bone, carved and inlaid with figure subjects and armorial bearings, were made extensively in Italy at this period, and used as marriage coffers.

Combs and mirror cases were naturally objects that

Fig. 121.—Coffer in Bone Carving and Engraved Work ; Italian ; Fourteenth Century. (S. K. M.)

received much attention at the hands of the carver in ivory. A beautiful comb in the British Museum (Fig. 122) belongs to the eleventh century, the central scroll-work of which is very rich and ornate.

Ceremonial combs, with finely carved ornamentation, have been found in tombs of bishops, and many are preserved in churches that date from the sixth to the fifteenth centuries. The mirror case, Fig. 123, is a beautiful example

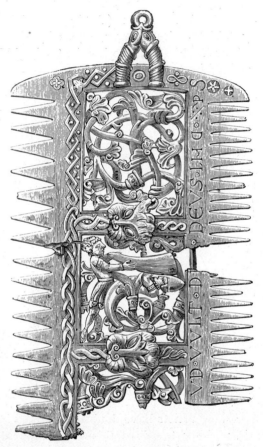

Fig. 122.—Ivory Comb ; Eleventh Century.

of fourteenth-century work. It has the carved subject of the " Siege of the Castle of Love "—a favourite subject for mirror case decoration—and four lions forming the corners to the circular ring.

In reference to the ivory carver Héliot, mentioned above, Jacquemart quotes—when speaking of his work, the oratory of carved ivory tablets in the Cluny Museum that belonged to the Duchess of Burgundy—" Accounts of Amiot Arnant from 1392 to 1393. Paid 500 livres to Berthelot Héliot, ' varlet de chambre ' of the duke (Philip the Bold), for two large ivory tablets with images, one of which is the ' Passion of Our Lord,' and the other the ' Life of Monsieur

Fig. 123.—Ivory Mirror Case.   (S. K. M.)

Saint Jean-Baptiste,' which he has sold for the Carthusians."

Many celebrated artists have doubtless worked in ivory, but there is nothing to prove this except the supposed hand-work of the artists.   Michelangelo is credited with working in ivory ; Cellini, Donatello, Agostino, Carracci, and other famous names in Italian art have been mentioned as ivory carvers ; and in the seventeenth century a celebrated ivory carver named Copé, but better known as Fiamingo, who was Flemish by birth.   He made many basins, ewers, tankards, and carved figures of children in bas-relief. Fiamingo worked and lived in Rome at the end of the sixteenth and during the first ten years of the seventeenth centuries. He died in 1610. His work, like that of many other artists of this period, was greatly influenced by the style of Rubens, and a strongly marked realism in the manner of treating allegorical subjects was the prevailing taste in painting and carving. Very fine tankards in ivory, and basins, were carved by Fiamingo with bacchanalian scenes in a realistic manner. The tankard from the Jones Collection (Fig. 124) is believed to be the work of Fiamingo. It is a Flemish ivory mounted in silver-gilt work of good design. The body of the tankard is spiritedly carved with the figures of a nymph and satyr dancing, Silenus, and some children carrying grapes.

Another Flemish artist in ivory was Francis von Bossuit, who spent a great part of his life in Rome, and whose figure carvings are of great value. Alessandro Algardi was an Italian artist of the seventeenth century, who carved the ivory bas-relief of St. Leo going out to meet Attila, now in St. Peter's at Rome, and also a very fine bust of Cosimo II. de' Medici. One of the best ivory carvers that ever lived was François Duquesnoy, known better as François Flamand (1594-1644); he was a native of Brussels, and went to Rome when a young man for the purpose of study. He supported himself in his *wanderjahr* period by carving little figures in ivory and wood. In the Cluny Museum and in the Louvre some groups, and bas-reliefs of females and children, may be seen, executed by Flamand, that are full of roundness and life, boldly conceived and extremely graceful.

We have noticed how plentiful the ivory carvings were of the fourteenth century period; but at the end of that century ivory sculpture fell in abeyance, which lasted during almost the whole of the fifteenth and sixteenth centuries. This was due to the very great impulse given to wood carving by the French, and even more so by the

Fig. 124.—Ivory Tankard, Silver-gilt Mounted ; Flemish ; Seventeenth Century.
(S. K. M.)

German wood sculptors. Large wooden altar-pieces, or
"retables," came into fashion, and also minute wooden

portraits and statuettes, which for a long period superseded ivory carvings; and in Germany a good deal of
carving was executed in "Speckstein" or Soapstone, a
kind of drab-coloured lithographic stone that was not difficult to work. Albert Dürer and Lucas Cranach carved
some very fine works in Speckstein. At the beginning of
the seventeenth century ivory carving became again in
great request.

The Germans carried the arts of ivory and miniature
wood carving, as they did the larger style of wood
carving, to great perfection ; in fact to an astonishing
degree of dexterity, that would compare with Chinese or
Japanese carving, but lacking in the restrained artistic
power of the latter nation's productions. All kinds of
astonishing creations are preserved in the museums of subjects such as little ivory carvings of skeletons in company
with groups of female figures, miniature hunchbacks, and
beggars with diamonds for buttons on their dresses. Leo
Pronner, of Nuremberg, carved on a cherry-stone a hundred heads, that required the aid of a magnifying glass to
see the expressions, and later Simon Troger, of the same
city, produced many marvels in ivory figures with brown
wood dresses and other accessories in wood.

Many good ivories have been the work of Spanish
carvers, and as a rule they are tinted or coloured.

Nearly all the carvings in ivory that we have noticed
have been statuettes, reliefs, or objects in which the
human figure predominates.

As a matter of fact there are very few ivories of any
artistic value in which the human figure is not the most
important part of the composition, purely ornamental work
being very rare. Even in Saracenic work, where the figure
and animal representations are not found, the amount of
carved ivory work is limited, and the specimens are very
scarce.

In an ancient Coptic church in Cairo there is a massive
partition or screen of ebony, in which is a central door and

two side panels. This screen has a rich display of inlaid ivory carved with arabesques, and has ivory crosses in high relief. The screen is believed by Mr. Butler—the

author of "The Ancient Coptic Churches of Egypt"—to be a work of the tenth century, and also to be the model on which the ivory carving of the mosques was founded.

The ivory carvings in Saracenic work are usually found as carved or chased panels, with arabesque designs, and surrounded with geometric linear framing (Fig. 125).

The best of this type of work was executed in the fourteenth century. Objects made of ivory alone are very rare in Saracenic art. The illustration given of an ivory ink-horn is unique in this material, but ink-horns of the same shape are common that have been made in copper and brass.

Fig. 125.—Carved Ivory Panels of a Pulpit Door; Saracenic. (S. K. M.)

Figure and animal carvings of Saracenic or Moorish design have been made in Spain, and in some other countries under the rule of the Saracens, but are not found in the Egyptian Saracenic.

China has always been prolific in the production of ivory

carvings. There are numerous statuettes of Confucius, Cheoü-lao, the god of old age, of the Buddhist female divinity Kouan-in, and of other divinities. Necklaces, pierced plaques for waist-belt decoration, and the *su-chus* or rosaries, all are carved with a certain archaic quality and quaintness, but of a minute and unsurpassed dexterity of workmanship.

The Chinese ivory fans of pierced work are beautiful and as delicate as lace-work. Examples of these are very common.

The pen-cases called *pitongs* are beautiful objects, carved

Fig. 126.—Ivory Ink-Horn ; Saracenic. (S. K. M.)

with dragons, flowers, and quaint figures in toy-like houses and gardens.

The " puzzle balls " are amongst the most wonderful of the Chinese carvings in ivory, where quite a number of loose balls of lessening sizes are contained within each other, and are all carved out of a solid ball of ivory. The outer surfaces of each ball are also carved with elaborate ornamentation. The method of cutting out these balls consists in boring a number of holes at regulated distances on the surface to a measured depth of the thickness of each outer shell, and then to cut around the circumference of each hole with a steel tool made with a bent end to suit the concentric curve of the sphere, and turned until each shell is freed from its next smaller ball. The Chinese puzzle balls are not very perfect examples of accurate turning, as the ornamentation conceals the rough workmanship in a great degree, but still they are marvels of skill and patience.

The Japanese carvings in ivory are better in an artistic sense than the Chinese, and exhibit the same surprising beauty of finish and minuteness of detail. All kinds of little cases for pens, jewels, powders and perfumes ; little divinities, small caskets and cabinets put together with plaques of slabs of carved ivory, gilt and coloured with lacquers, and also encrusted with lapis-lazuli, mother-of-pearl, and precious stones. There is also the most wonderful little ivory figure and groups of animal carvings called *netsukes.* These in many instances are works of the highest order. Many of them are meant as embodied jokes, puns, or satires. Some consist of groups of real or sham cripples, beggars with monkeys on their backs, wrestlers, boxers, all kinds of domestic scenes, warriors on foot and on horseback ; other subjects full of dignity and grace, and animal groups carved as no other people in the world can do. These netsukes are used not only as ornaments that are treasured for their own sakes, but also as dress-fasteners and as articles of personal adornment by the better classes in Japan.

Many other uses for ivory carvings are found by the Japanese, such as handles of swords and daggers, and some of their beautiful lacquered panels have encrusted eagles and other birds beautifully carved, and perched on the branches of trees, the latter being made from mother-of-pearl, and sometimes the flowers, foliage, and fruit of tinted ivory minutely chased.

India is famed for its extremely elaborate ivory carvings. The elaborated richness of Oriental ornament is seen in the ivory carvings of India more than in almost any other material except the goldsmiths' work ; but this may be more excused in such precious materials as ivory, gold, or hand-made laces, where it is quite legitimate to give to the ornament that necessary character of elaborate detail which always adds to the preciousness of the material.

Sometimes the carved ivory cabinets from India have Biblical subjects in the panels, which proves them to be works made to the order of the European missionaries, by native artists.

The ivory jewel casket with gold mountings (Fig. 127) is thoroughly Hindu in design and execution. Deified

Fig. 127.—Ivory Casket with Gold Clasp and Hinge; Indian. (Jacquemart.)

females with outstretched arms form a natural palanquin for the seated figure of an Indian divinity; other figures act as palanquin bearers, and the intervening spaces are richly filled with characteristic foliage and fruit.

Ivory carving is so extensively carried on throughout India that it would be difficult to say in what part of the

country it was not done.   In some districts ivory carving
in certain articles is done to the exclusion of others.
Bison horn is carved at Ratnagiri.

Tortoiseshell is plentifully used for carving in Bombay.
The Hindoos, like the Chinese, carve fans in a wonderfully
delicate manner.   Ivory bracelets, little elephants with all
their trappings, tigers, oxen, gondolas, fully-rigged ships,
hunting scenes, gods and goddesses, &c., are all made in
ivory throughout India.

CHAPTER IV.

METAL WORK.

GOLD, SILVER, BRONZE, PEWTER, AND IRON.

THE early Egyptian, Assyrian, Phœnician, and Primitive Grecian metal work has been noticed under the historic sketch of the art of these nations in the former volume.

We read in the Bible of the great magnificence of Solomon's Temple, especially in the extreme richness and wealth of the gold, silver, and brazen vessels, utensils, and architectural decorations, in which the precious metals were used in the solid or plated manner on capitals, pillars, doors, seats, thrones, and on the decorations of the Ark; but no remains of all this magnificence have survived the wrecks of time or the greed and spoliation of the conquerors of Jerusalem.

The sculptured decorations of the Arch of Titus at Rome afford us the only tangible testimony as to the kind or shapes of the tables, vessels, and seven-branched candlesticks which were carried off by the Romans after the sacking of Jerusalem, A.D. 73. The workmanship and design of these objects were probably a mixture of Egyptian and Assyrian forms, passing through the hands of the probable Phœnician artificers.

Some of the earliest goldsmiths' work that possesses a real artistic value consists of personal ornaments, such as wreaths, earrings, brooches, and diadems of Etruscan workmanship. Much of this work was made very thin, in plates or scales joined together, and was generally designed for funeral uses. Articles of personal adornment

were very rich and beautifully made, having the usual
character of Greek design (Figs. 128, 129).

Fig. 128.—Gold Brooch and Earrings set with Garnets; Etruscan.   (J.)

The Etruscans were greatly skilled in the making of all

Fig. 129.—Head of Bacchus, part of Necklace; Etruscan Jewellery.   (J.)

kinds of gold, silver, and bronze vessels, jewellery, cups,
goblets, and articles of domestic use (Fig. 130). A remark-

able bronze of a monster or chimæra was found at Arezzo, in Italy, in 1534, which no doubt was a representation of an Etruscan deity (Fig. 131). The art of the Etruscans was strongly imbued with a decided Oriental character of mysteriousness.

We have noticed before the gold and other metal work of primitive Greece that was found by Dr. Schliemann at Mycenæ and on the site of ancient Troy. Most of this work was in beaten and inlaid metals, but in later periods the arts of soldering grains and plates of gold, and fine wire drawing for delicate filigree work were well known. Minute grains of gold that had the appearance of frosted work were in reality soldered to the plate. Statues were made in gold, but more often were plated. Chryselephantine statues were common in the best days of Greek art, as those of Athene and Jupiter by Phidias, and the statue of Bacchus in his temple at Athens.

Crœsus made offerings of gold and silver vessels to the shrine of Delphi, and both he

Fig. 130.—Etruscan Bronze Vessel.

and Darius had images of their wives made in gold by Greek artists. Very few examples of Greek goldsmiths' art have come down to us, for owing to the valuable nature of the material, nearly all such work has been, in the course of time, pillaged and melted down by the barbarians or conquerors, and it is only in a few isolated cases such valuables have been preserved by being buried or hidden purposely in the earth, and in late years have been brought to light.   We are, therefore, indebted to the ancient historians for most of our knowledge concerning the goldsmithery of Greece and Rome.

Some very valuable finds have been brought to light, such as that of the Hildesheim treasures (Fig. 132), and the articles of bronze found at Herculaneum and Pompeii give a good idea of the richness and beauty of the metal work of ancient Greece and Rome.   The wine crater

Fig. 131.—Bronze Chimæra at Florence.

(Fig. 132) is exceptionally beautiful in its delicate lines of arabesque tracery.

There are some valuable examples in silver of the period of the late Roman Empire in the British Museum, which are the treasures of another "find." They consist of a bridal casket 22 by 17 inches, and 11 inches in height; another round bridal casket; dishes on a low stand (*Scutellæ*); oblong-shaped dishes or trays (*lances*); horse trappings and ornaments (*Phaleræ*); seated figures representing Rome, Constantinople, Alexandria, and Antioch;

various vases and vessels for holding perfumes and
unguents. This treasure was discovered in the vaults of a
house in Rome in 1793, where it was supposed to have

Fig. 132.—Wine Crater in Silver; from the Hildesheim Treasures. Antique
Roman.

been hidden from the barbarians who invaded and captured
Rome in the sixth century.

The bridal caskets have the portraits of the bride and

bridegroom in hammered or repoussé work, and mythological marine subjects. The style and execution is in the
usual coarse manner that characterized the work of the
period of early Christian Art, with some of the antique
traditions still asserting their influence in the style of the
design.

Tripods, candelabra, vases, bowls, caskets, spoons,
besides articles of personal adornment made in the precious
metals, have been found in the buried cities of Herculaneum and Pompeii, and in other places in Italy, France,
and Germany, of antique Roman design. (See Fig. 417 in
the previous volume of this work.)

The names of a few Greek and Roman goldsmiths occur
in the writings of Pausanias, Pliny, and Martial, one of
the earliest of which is named Mentor, who probably lived
in a subsequent near period to Phidias. Acragras and
Mys were the names of two others of a little later time.
Stratonicus and Tauriscus are two others who lived in the
third century B.C. Antipater is mentioned as the name of
a goldsmith by Pliny.

Pytheas was a famous worker in gold and silver, who
engraved figure compositions, and Posidanius of Ephesus
excelled in hunting and racing subjects. Praxiteles was a
silversmith who executed animal representations from the
life, and "Alexander the coppersmith" is mentioned in St.
Paul's Epistle to Timothy.

The metal work of the Byzantine period—from the
fourth to the eleventh century—is characterized by a
subservience of the design to the material employed; in
other words, what was lacking in good drawing and
modelling was replaced by splendour and magnificence in
the general effect.

The use of gold with enamels was a great feature in
Byzantine art and throughout the Middle Ages. When
the great Church of Santa Sophia was rebuilt by Justinian
in the sixth century, the best artists were employed to make
the great altar screen, and to decorate the sanctuary in

resplendent works in gold, silver, and enamels. The altar was made in marble plated with gold in which was set precious stones and crusted enamels. It was supported by pillars thickly plated with gold The canopy or ciborium of the altar rested on four silver-gilt columns, and this canopy was overlaid with plates of silver, on which were figures wrought in niello work. The canopy had an orb surmounted by a cross made of gold and inlaid with large precious stones. The screen in front of the altar had its dado or lower part of gilt bronze, and the pillars and architrave silver-plated. It had also statues and panels of silver, the latter being engraved with figures of saints in niello work. The ambo or pulpit had a canopy of plated gold set with precious stones. The sanctuary of Santa Sophia contained forty thousand pounds weight of silver, and the altar vessels were made of gold set with stones of the greatest value.

The above description is given by Mr. J. Hungerford Pollen, in his handbook of "Gold and Silver," to whom we are indebted for many of the illustrations and some interesting information on the subject of the precious metals.

It will be seen from this that Justinian had established a great school of goldsmiths and enamellers at Byzantium, and when Leo the Iconoclast in the eighth century, and Theophilus in 832, finally drove out the image-makers and many other goldsmiths from Constantinople—checking in a great degree the art of the metal-worker in the Eastern Empire—they were received with great welcome in Italy, Germany, and France, where they followed the practice of their art under more favourable auspices.

Under Basil the Macedonian, who died in 886, the images were restored, and a great encouragement given to all kinds of art; and during the reign of Constantine, his grandson (912-959), Constantinople was again a great art centre from which Italy and Germany procured their chief artists. The celebrated Pala d'Oro, or Altar of St. Mark's,

Venice, and the bronze gates of San Paolo, near Rome, were made in Constantinople.

The splendour and treasures of the imperial city remained intact until its capture by the French and Venetians in 1204, when a general sacking of nearly all of its treasures took place.

The Byzantine style of the scroll-work and acanthus was of the Greek type, and was admirably suited to show to advantage the rich quality of the precious metals, and a modified character of this leafage appears in the Romanesque metal work. The vine-leaf, grapes, and twisting tendrils were first used in a symbolic sense in the Byzantine style and subsequently in the Romanesque. The acanthus and the vine are treated very much alike in the conventional ornament of the latter style, which is really a connecting-link between the Early Gothic foliage and the Byzantine. This may be seen in the illustration (Fig. 133) of a portion of the base of the great candlestick at Milan, a work of the twelfth century.

A celebrated "find," known as the "treasure of Petrossa," was brought to light in 1837 by some peasants who were digging on the banks of Argish River, a tributary of the Danube. It consists of vessels of pure gold, vessels made of slices of garnet and other stones, a torque or collar of gold, a great dish, and some brooches of a large size. They have all been inlaid with precious stones, and have simple but well-designed ornaments. The workmanship is Byzantine, or it may have been done by Gothic artists after Byzantine models.

This treasure is now in the museum at Bucharest. The influence of the Byzantine school of metal workers spread, not only over the continent of Europe, but as far as England and Ireland; and many portable altars, shrines, and reliquaries were made to order in Constantinople, or given as presents to foreign churches.

During the seventh, eighth, and ninth centuries it was customary for kings and queens to present votive crowns to their churches: these crowns were treasured with other precious articles, and hung up in the sanctuaries.

Fig. 133.—Base of Candlestick, Milan Cathedral. (P.)

There is still preserved in the Cathedral at Monza the

Iron Crown of the Lombard kings. It was given to the cathedral by Theodolinda the Lombard Queen in 616. The Iron Crown is so called from its having a thin band of iron encrusted in the inside, said to have been made from a nail from the Cross. It is really a band or collar of gold, studded with tallow-cut precious stones.

St. Eloi, who rose from the rank of goldsmith to a bishop (588-659) made crowns and other articles for church uses for the Church of St. Denis at Paris.

The bronze-gilt chair of St. Dagobert (Fig. 134) is

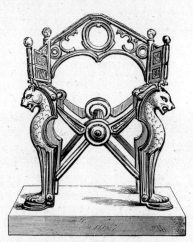

ascribed to him. He founded the Abbey of Solignac, near Limoges, where he established a school of working goldsmiths, which supplied many important works for various churches in France.

In the year 1858 at Guarrazar, near Toledo, in Spain, another valuable "find" was discovered, consisting of no less than eleven votive crowns or diadems, with other valuables, all buried close to the surface of the ground. The crowns are of pure gold,

Fig. 134.—Chair of Dagobert ; Seventh Century.

and are set with precious stones, such as sapphires and pearls. The rest of the treasure consists of three crosses, a large emerald stone, and several fragments of gold plates with chains attached.

The stones in these crowns, like those in the Charlemagne and Lombard crowns, and other jewellery of the Middle Ages, were "tallow-cut," that is, they were polished in the round or oval shapes, without facets, and were also known under the name of "*Cabochons.*" On one of the crowns of the above treasure—which is now in the Cluny Museum—is the name of "Beccesvinthus Rex" (A.D. 649-672), and another has the letters forming the name of King Suinthila (A.D. 621-631) (Fig. 135). Others of a smaller size were probably those of Spanish queens. The design and work of the articles forming this treasure are in a kind of Romanesque-Gothic. The crown of Charlemagne has already been described under the head of enamels (see Fig. 96). The art of the goldsmith was fostered to a great degree under the rule of Charlemagne. This monarch's great friend and adviser, the prelate Alcuin (735-804), was the chief spirit of his times in founding monasteries, which were, apart from their religious character, also great schools of art, especially in metal working, where all such articles as were required for church uses, as well as shields, swords, and jewellery for the king and nobles, were also made.

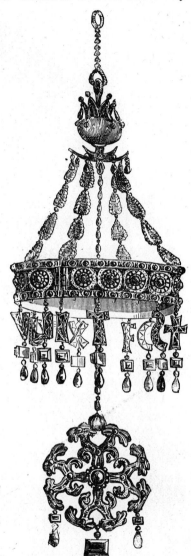

Fig. 135.—Votive Crown of King Suinthila; Seventh Century.

Charlemagne was buried with

most of his treasures about him, but his enamelled sword

Fig. 136.—Shrine of St. Patrick's Bell.   (S.)

and crown are the only objects which belonged to him
that now remain, both of which are at Vienna.   Gold,

silver, and bronze were worked in by Franks on the
Continent and by the Saxons in England as early as the
fifth and sixth centuries, many examples of which, consisting chiefly of articles of personal adornment, are now in

Fig. 137.—The Tara Brooch. (S.)

our museums. That the goldsmith's art was practised in
England in the days of Alfred (871-900) we have evidence
in the famous ring belonging to this king which is
described on page 121.

Another gold ring belonging to Ethelwulf, of the early ninth or eighth century, the enamelled vase or situla

Fig. 138.—Tara Brooch (reverse). (S.)

found in Essex, the golden altar of St. Ambrose at Milan, and the beautiful Irish chalice found at Ardagh have been described in the chapter on enamels, all of which show

evidence of the great skill of the European goldsmiths
from the seventh to the tenth centuries.

The tenth century was a barren one for Art in Europe,
except in some of the monasteries of France, Italy, and in
Ireland. In the latter country a great deal of good work
was produced—in metals especially—in the ninth and
tenth centuries. The amount of personal ornaments, such
as torques or collars of gold, bracelets, brooches, belt-
clasps, and croziers, shrines for sacred bells, and covers
for the Gospels, that were wrought in gold, silver, or alloys
must have been prodigious. The astonishing delicacy and
intricacy of the Celtic ornamentation bear eloquent testimony to the great skill of the early Irish artists.

The shrine of St. Patrick's bell, or the bell of Armagh,
is a splendid specimen of Irish art
(Fig. 136). It forms the cover of
the ancient square-mouthed iron
bell that formerly belonged to the
patron saint of Ireland, and is plated
with silver-gilt ornamentation and
gold filigree work in both high and
low relief. The ornamentation is
composed of twisted and interlacing
scrolls and knot-work, with some
elongated animal forms in the com-

Fig. 139.—Irish " Trumpet
Pattern."

position. It has crystals and coloured gems set in the
angles and other places. The large central stone is set in
imbricated work.

There are five of these bells in Ireland and two in Scotland, but none of them are so fine as the St. Patrick bell.
Another beautiful example of Irish metal work is the Tara
brooch (Figs. 137 and 138). It is made of white metal, a
hard bronze composed of tin and copper.

The gold and silver ornamentation on this brooch and
on the Ardagh chalice are of the same style of design and
workmanship, which would point out that these two fine
examples of Irish art were made about the same date,

perhaps anterior to the tenth century. The "trumpet pattern," which is not found on Irish work after 1050, occurs on the reverse side of the Tara brooch (Fig. 138).

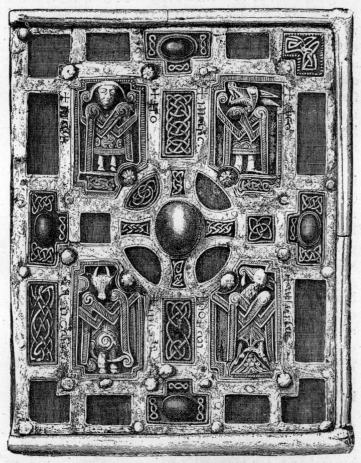

Fig. 140.—Cundach or Case of Molaise's Gospels. (S.)

The ornamentation is of an extraordinary beauty, both in variety of style and pattern and in the execution. It is riveted or fastened with pins and held by means of slender bars to the foundation.

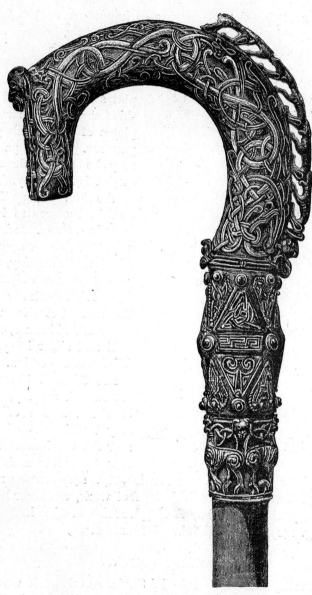

Fig. 141. —The Crozier of Clonmacnois.   (S.)

The *Cumdachs* or book-cases used as covers for the books of the Gospels were also important works of the Irish goldsmith's art. The illustration of the book-case or shrine for the cover of Molaise's Gospels is a unique

example (Fig. 140). This cumdach is made of plates of bronze, and on this foundation is riveted plates of silver with gilt patterns. In the panels may be seen rude and quaint figures or symbols of the four Evangelists, and in the centre is a cross in a circle. It dates from the first quarter of the eleventh century, and is one of the oldest of these Irish book shrines. Crosses and croziers were also made of bronze, with gold and silver inlays or relief ornamentation.

Fig. 142.—Irish Crozier of Bronze, Edinburgh Museum. (S.)

The Cross of Cong, of the twelfth century, now in the museum of the Royal Irish Academy, and the croziers of Lismore (end of eleventh century) and that of Clonmacnois (Fig. 141) are the most important examples of this kind of work, the latter being a very rich example. A simpler Irish crozier in bronze (Fig. 142) is in the Edinburgh Museum.

SPANISH METAL WORK.

During the Arab rule in Spain metal work was an important branch of the Moorish arts. The Arab rulers

had in their train many accomplished Eastern artists in
metal work, and such objects as caskets, jewellery, bracelets, rings, sword and dagger handles, and scabbards.

Fig. 143.—Sword of Boabdil, Madrid.   (R.)

The Moorish caskets are often made of wood, covered
with silver or gold plates, the ornamentation being similar

to that of the ivory carvings.   The Arab or Saracenic metal work of Spain is executed in repoussé, or is chiselled niello work, filigree, or enamelled, and the ornament is usually mixed with the Arab laudatory inscriptions.

Fig. 144.—Spanish Monstrance, 1537.   (S.K.M.)

The treasure found at Guarrazar, already noticed, shows something of the early metal work of the Spanish Visigoths.

Moorish arms, such as sword sheaths and hilts, are very artistic, as may be seen in the illustration of the sword of Boabdil (Fig. 143), the last of the Moorish kings. The hilt of this sword is made of solid gold, and is enamelled in blue, white, and red. The axle is made of ivory, and is elaborately carved.

Triptychs, altars, processional crosses, and other church furniture were made in Spain in the thirteenth and fourteenth centuries, of Gothic design.

In the fifteenth century there was an astonishing quantity

of silversmiths' work produced. This was owing to the

Fig. 145.—Spanish Chalice. (R.)

discovery of America and the consequent power and wealth
of Spain at this time. The silver throne of the King Don

Martin de Aragon belongs to this period, which still exists

ig. 146.—Spanish Pax.   (R.)

in the Cathedral of Barcelona. It is covered with a chased
ornamentation in the metal work, and has rich embroidered

work of gold and precious stones. Many silversmiths came from Italy, Germany, Holland, and France at this period and settled in Spain owing to the great demand for their services. Riaño gives the names of Enrique de Arphe, Jacome Trezzo, Mateo Aleman, Hans Belta, and others who were employed at this time, besides many Spanish goldsmiths.

A special feature of church furniture of this period in Spain was the *Monstrance*, or *Custodia*, an object of architectural design made in gold, silver, or bronze-gilt metals, which has a central part—the *lumule* or *viril*—generally made of rock-crystal, in which the sacrament was exposed; sometimes a sun with rays is represented on the monstrance, and usually it is surmounted by a cross in gold and set with jewels (Fig. 144). The designs are in the Renaissance and sometimes in the Gothic style, and they are often eight feet in height. Some of them are carried in procession on Corpus Christi

Fig. 147.—Spanish Jewel; Seventeenth Century. (R.)

Days. Many works in gold and silver are in Spain that have been made in Mexico, but of Spanish design, in which forms of American flora and fauna are worked into the designs.

A Spanish chalice of Gothic outlines with some Renaissance details is shown at Fig. 145. A beautiful pax of Renaissance design in the Kensington Museum is shown at Fig. 146.

The pendant jewel of the seventeenth century shows the beginnings of the decadence in design (Fig. 147), and the silver dish (Fig. 148), though very rich in effect, is a pronounced step in the direction of unrestrained space-covering that characterizes the design of the late seventeenth century in Spain as well as in other European countries.

Bronze-casting was practised in Spain by the Moors as well as the Spanish themselves. The Moorish hanging

Fig. 148.—Spanish Silver Dish ; Seventeenth Century.   (R.)

lamp (Fig. 149) is a beautiful specimen of bronze-working in pierced open-work. It bears the date of the Hegira, 705 (A.D. 1305). Important works in bronze of the Renaissance period, such as candelabra, monstrances, &c., are still preserved in many of the churches.

From the earliest historic times Spain has been celebrated for the excellent quality of its iron and steel arms and armour. The Romans patronised the Spanish armourers extensively for their swords and other arms after the Carthaginian War. The best swords were made at Bilbilis or Calatayud in Aragon, and were short and wide, with double edges —about 15 to 19 inches in length. A sickle-shaped sword was also made 22 inches in length.

Toledo blades were proverbial for their excellent tempering, and were famous as early as the days of the Romans. Seville was also noted for the excellence of its steel blades, and the Arabs, as we have seen, were highly skilled in metal working, and especially in the making of all kinds of arms and armour, including its ornamentation.

The celebrated sword of Boabdil had a Toledo blade, and including the hilt was 39 inches in length.

The Spanish warriors of the eleventh century had dresses, arms, and armour not unlike the

Fig. 149.—Moorish Lamp, Bronze; Fourteenth Century. (R.)

Normans, as represented on the Bayeux Tapestry, which
were in imitation of or borrowed from the military habits
of the Saracens.

The sword manufactory at Toledo was in its most

Fig. 150.—Spanish Rapiers.   (S. K. M.)

flourishing state during the fifteenth and sixteenth centuries; it was re-established in the last century, and is in
existence at the present day.

Two rapiers of the sixteenth and seventeenth centuries are represented at Fig. 150.

Muskets, crossbows, saddles, coats of mail, knives, scissors, and many other objects in steel have been made in Spain from the earliest periods, and many Spanish goods in manufactured steel even at the present day still preserve the Moorish forms.

Metal Work in Italy, Germany, France, and England.

In Italy during the eleventh century an endeavour was made to revive the art of the goldsmith, and many objects of Byzantine workmanship were brought from Constantinople, and also many articles for church uses were made within the walls of the great Benedictine monasteries throughout Italy. An important Romanesque example of metal work of the time of the Emperor Henry II. (1003-24) is now in the Cluny Museum. It is a golden altar front (Fig. 151) that was given by this Emperor to the cathedral of Bâsle, and is nearly 6 feet in width. Figures of the Saviour, three archangels, and a figure of St. Benedict, are in relief of beaten gold and stand each under Romanesque arches.

In England we read of reliquaries being made in the eleventh century having images of gold, the work of Richard, an abbot of St. Albans. Brithnodus, an abbot of Ely, Leo, and Elsinus are names of others who made reliquaries and objects in metal.

Hildesheim in Hanover was a centre of great activity in metal work in the eleventh century, and in the Cathedral of Hildesheim there are candlesticks, crucifixes, and chalices of this period.

At this time in Germany were made great coronas or crowns of light that sometimes spanned the nave of the churches, like that made by Bishop Bernaward (992-1022),

and his successor Hezilo for the Cathedral of Hildesheim,
a cast of which is now in the Kensington Museum.

The twelfth century was very fertile in important works
in gold, silver, bronze, and copper. Metal work was
carried to a high degree of elaborate finish and intricacy of
design.

Some wonderful achievements in casting, plating, and
gilding of metals have been performed during this prolific

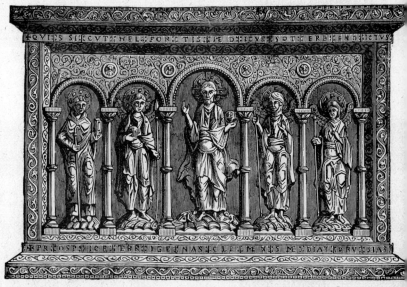

Fig. 151.—Golden Altar Front; from Bâsle. Cluny Museum. Eleventh Century.

period. The celebrated Gloucester candlestick, now in the
Kensington Museum, is a good example of the elaborate
style of the twelfth-century metal work (Fig. 152). This is
one of the most elaborate and intricate examples of ornamentation that could well be seen in the metal work of any
period. Nothing could exceed the fanciful ingenuity of its
design : it would, perhaps, have been better if some parts of
the design had been left plainer, as a foil for the others.

The material of its composition is a kind of white bronze, with a good proportion of silver in the alloy.

The churches of this century were, as a rule, furnished with large standing candlesticks or coronas for holding lights, many of which were of good design, were made of silver, and sometimes enamelled. The large seven-branched candlestick of the Cathedral of Milan — before mentioned—is an important work of this period, a copy of which is in the Kensington Museum. The material is gilt bronze, and the candlestick is over 14 feet in height; the design is extremely rich (Fig. 153), the base being composed of four winged dragons with voluted tails; the spaces between the dragons are filled with elaborate scroll-work, and symbolic subjects fill the volutes (Fig. 154). The lower boss is richly ornamented, but the other five are plain. Three pairs of graceful branches spring from the central stem to hold the lights.

The whole design is a reminiscence of the Jewish seven-branched candlestick. One

Fig. 152.—Gloucester Candlestick; Twelfth Century.

smaller in size is in the Brunswick Cathedral, and another one is at Essen.

Censers, reliquaries, and shrines were made at this period in the shape of little churches (Fig. 155). The reliquaries contained the bones of saints or other precious relics.

Sometimes they were made in the form of a human head, with a band or ribbon around it set with gems. This kind

Fig. 153.—Seven-Branched Candlestick in Milan Cathedral.

of reliquary was called a "chef"; one of this description is in the Cathedral at Bâsle.

The bronze censer (Fig. 156) of the twelfth century is a good specimen of the architectural design in the Roman-

esque metal work of this time. The reliquaries are usually
of copper-gilt and enamelled, or are occasionally in gold.
These objects have been noticed in the chapter on enamels.
The larger coffer-shaped ones with sloping roofs are
called *châsses*, some of which are six and seven feet in
length. Most of them are of copper-gilt and enamelled,
and are German work, made for the most part at Cologne

Fig. 154.—Lower Boss of the Milan Candlestick; Twelfth Century.

and in the Rhenish Provinces, and were generally of
Romanesque or Gothic design even up to the sixteenth
century.

The shrine of St. Sebaldus by Peter Vischer already
mentioned is a curious mixture of Gothic and Italian forms.
The celebrated shrine or silver reliquary of the Church of
Orvieto is made to represent the church itself; it is said to
weigh 600 pounds, and is enriched with panels of translucent enamel and small statuettes. It is the finest work

of the Italian goldsmith's art of the fourteenth century, and was made by Ugolino (1338), an artist of Siena. Heads of the croziers and bishops' pastoral staffs were often designed in elaborate architectural compositions, and generally speaking Gothic ornamentation is enthralled by architectural forms even to the smallest details when the plan of the object to be decorated is architectural, which happens in most cases; when, however, the plan is not so, the freedom and fancy of the designer revelled in the beauty of the

Fig. 155.—Shrine or Reliquary, Copper Gilt; Twelfth Century.

curving, twisting, foliage, and grotesque work, as may be seen in the metal work of the eleventh and twelfth centuries. The Gloucester and Milan candlesticks will afford examples of this.

In the twelfth century Limoges was very active in the making of articles for secular purposes as well as for religious uses. Common jewellery of enamelled bronze was exported to all parts, such as brooches or morses, buckles, armour decoration, and monumental plates with effigies, one of the latter being that of Aylmer de Valence in Westminster Abbey, made at Limoges and brought to England.

The monastic establishments were the schools and work-shops of all the art produced in the Middle Ages, and not only splendid examples of metal work, but manuscript illuminations, wood and stone carving, and many other kinds of works were produced within their walls. After the beginning of the thirteenth century the arts were passing into the hands of the laymen, and artists were at the same time beginning to receive greater encouragement from the patronage of wealthy persons.

Fig. 156.—Censer ; Twelfth Century.

Almost every kind of article was now made in gold, silver, and bronze, such as cups, jugs, bowls, standing

Fig. 157.—Mazer Bowl ; 1450 ; Ironmongers' Hall.

cups, mazer and wassail bowls, articles for the table, such as salt-cellars, ewers, basins, and nefs, etc.

The *Nef* was a kind of table ornament or sweetmeat dish in the form of a fully-rigged ship, and was sometimes mounted on wheels : the modern épergne corresponds to the nef. A *mazer* bowl was so called because it was made usually of maple wood—*masere* being the old word for maple.

These bowls have usually a silver or gold rim, and were often lined with silver, but the name is wrongly applied to bowls made entirely of metal, as it sometimes is. Fig. 157 is an illustration of a mazer bowl of the fifteenth century belonging to the Iron-mongers' Company of London. Salt-cellars were also important table decorations. The salt was put on the table in such a position as to mark the dividing line between the guests of different rank. There is a salt in the form of a giant, a work of the fifteenth century, at All Souls' College, Oxford, and some other salts of this period and earlier were often made in form of hour-glasses (Fig. 158).

Fig. 158.—Hour-glass Salt, given 1493, at New College, Oxford.

Very few specimens of household plate have come down to us from the thirteenth or fourteenth centuries, although we have many records of the great quantities of jewels and plate that belonged to the kings and feudal lords.

Spoons and knives were made and used at a very early period of the world's history, but forks do not seem to have come into general use until some time in the four-

teenth century. Sacramental cups and chalices, and all
kinds of drinking cups, were made at this time. The
beautiful cup of Gothic design with translucent enamels,
now in the Kensington Museum, is probably a work of
the fourteenth century, and of Burgundian origin. (See
Fig. 103.)

Three sacramental chalices are illustrated at Fig. 159,
and belonging to the fourteenth century, and two at Figs.
160 and 161, of the fifteenth century, all of which are
Gothic in design ; two also are given of the sixteenth century (Figs. 162 and 163), the latter being of Spanish origin
designed in the style of the Renaissance, which is inter-

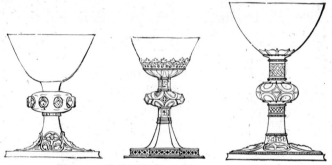

Fig. 159.—Gothic Chalices; Fourteenth Century.

esting as showing the development of the standing cup
from the chalice, this example being in the transitional
stage.

The difference between the Gothic and Renaissance cups
is very marked, the foot of the former being either trefoil,
or more often hexagonal in plan (Fig. 164), with the distinctive central knot or boss on the plain upright stem for
grasping purposes, while the Renaissance cups are usually
round in the plan of the foot, or sometimes octagonal, and
have a horizontal character which is obtained by the use
of mouldings cutting the cup into parts. (See Spanish
chalice, Fig. 163.)

This upright character of the Gothic cup is well empha-
sized in the beautiful enamelled cup belonging to the

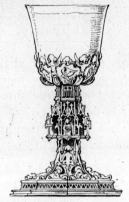

Fig. 160.—Chalice ; Fifteenth
Century.

Fig. 161.—Chalice ; Fifteenth
Century.

corporation of King's Lynn (Fig. 166), and the horizontal
features in the foot, stem, and bowl may be seen in the

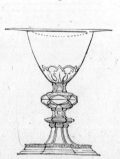

Fig. 162.—German Chalice, with
Paten ; 1520.

Fig. 163.—Spanish Chalice ; 1549.

standing cup of Renaissance design in the Corpus Christi
College, Cambridge (Fig. 165).

The base of the Gothic cup splays outwards from the
knot downwards, while the Renaissance base mouldings
may be enclosed by a line of the opposite curvature, forming a dome of a semicircular section ; and lastly the calyx
of the bowl of the latter cups is always a richly ornamented
feature, in opposition to the plain or almost plain bowl
and calyx of the Gothic varieties.   Many Gothic cups and

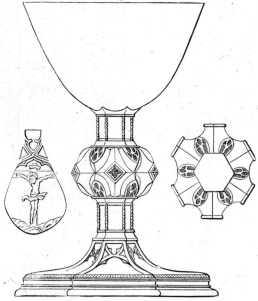

Fig. 164.—English Chalice, Corpus Christi College, Oxford ; 1507.   (C.)

hanaps show decided architectural constructions, as may
be noticed in some of the illustrations, and some have
quite a landscape treatment, as in the curious gilt metal
hanap (Fig. 167), which is probably of Nuremberg manufacture.

Clocks were also objects which received a pronounced
architectural treatment.   A favourite design was a church
tower, or a fortified tower, embattled, and having a spreading base, in which were open archways.

The goldsmiths of Italy in the sixteenth century were

Fig. 165.—Standing Cup, Corpus   Fig. 166.—Enamelled Cup at King's
    Christi College, Cambridge ;   Lynn; 1350. (C.)
    1599. (C.)

painters and architects as well, and a decided architectural construction is clearly seen in most of the gold and silver-smithery of this period. The monstrance (Fig. 168) is a good illustration of this, and another is the pax (Fig. 169). The church altar furniture and silver plate of the period also partook of the prevailing architectural features.

Benvenuto Cellini (1500-71) is the greatest name among the many great ones of the sixteenth century in the art of the goldsmith. Some of his work has already been noticed in the chapter on enamels. Cellini represents the art of the Italian goldsmith and enameller at its best period. He was famous for his designs in jewellery, in which he set precious stones in cartouche work combined with griffins, masks, and well-modelled little figures (Fig. 170). Many cups made in lapis-lazuli, sardonyx, and rock-crystal are attributed to him. He was also a successful worker in bronze, the best of his works in this metal being the statue group of Perseus and Medusa, and the colossal bas-relief of the Nymph of Fontainebleau, copies of which may be seen in Kensington Museum. A graphic and very interesting account of the casting of the Perseus group is given in his autobiography. A fine shield in damascene work by Cellini is in Windsor Castle. His smaller works in gold and jewellery probably exist in greater numbers than can be verified owing to the absence of his signature or other identifying marks. According to his own account, when besieged with the Pope, Clement VII., in the Castle of Angelo, by the Spanish, he unset the precious stones and jewellery, and melted down at the command of the Pope about two hundredweight of gold and silver crowns,

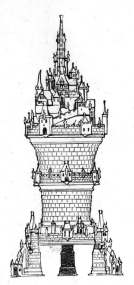

Fig. 167.—Hanap; German. (S. K. M.)

tiaras, cups, and reliquaries of ancient workmanship in order to convert them into money and medals as required by the Pope. This gives us a good idea of how the fine treasures of the Middle Ages must have been destroyed under similar circumstances, and excites our wonder how any valuable piece of goldsmith's work has escaped the melting-pot, which was generally the sequel to the pillaging of conquering troops or the exigencies of war.

Fig. 168.—Monstrance; Italian; Fifteenth Century. (S. K. M.)

Cellini's visit to France and his work in that country gave a great impulse to the style of the Renaissance, and his countryman, Primaticcio the sculptor, spread the style still further in France.

Some names of Italian goldsmiths about or immediately after Cellini's time are—Luca Agnolo, Valerio Vicentino, Pilote, Piero di Mino, Vincenzo Dati, Girolamo del Prato. The latter was a native of Lombardy. Benedict Ramel, François Desjardins, Delahaie, and François Briot are names of French goldsmiths of the sixteenth century. Many models of vases, ewers, plates, cups, and tankards were made by

Fig. 169.—Pax; Italian; Sixteenth Century. (S. K. M.)

Briot in pewter that are still in existence. These pewter models were usually made by goldsmiths, no doubt, as

models for their gold and silver work, or in some cases
were casts taken from the finished works, and kept as
mementos or as replicas in design of their more costly

Fig. 170.—Pendant, attributed to Cellini, in the Library at Paris.

works, and were also sold to those whose means would not
permit them to indulge in the more costly gold and silver
plate. Briot's pewter models are among the best examples

of design and workmanship in metal of the sixteenth century.

In Germany the art of the metal worker flourished in the sixteenth century in its greatest perfection at Nuremberg and Augsburg.

The German goldsmiths' work, especially at the end of the century, was almost identical with that of the Italian school. The similarity is seen in the details of the ornamentation, the masks and figures; the difference may be noted in the extraordinary development of the cartouche and strap-work of the German work, more especially in that of the Netherlands.

Many German artists of this time, who were chiefly engravers, designed for the goldsmiths and produced engravings from which goldsmiths' work and enamel paintings on metal were executed.

Virgil Solis, of Nuremberg, Theodor de Bry, of Liége, the Collaerts—father and son—of Antwerp, are some of the principal engravers who designed very largely for jewellery and other goldsmiths' work.

These German engravers and designers of ornament went under the designation of the " Little Masters," but in point of fact some of their work would compare favourably with the compositions of many of the so-called "Great Masters." Generally speaking, they were pupils or followers of Albert Dürer.

As a designer and engraver of figure work, Hans Sebald Beham must be placed first in the rank of the "Little Masters," and for ornament purely the name of Heinrich Aldegrever must head the list.

Albert Dürer, whose great name overshadows all German art, though he tried his gifted hand at ornament, as in the car of the " Triumph " and in the " Book of the Hours," designed for the Emperor Maximilian, was not altogether successful in the matter of ornament, for his work in this line is much too loose and florid, with much unrestrained and naturalistic flourishing.

Hans Burgkmair, of Nuremberg, his contemporary, was better at ornament than Dürer, and was the chief artist of that great work, the "Triumph of Maximilian," in which he strove to unite the Gothic and the style of the Renaissance. His work generally takes the form of elaborate heraldry.

Hans Holbein, as well as being a great painter, was also a famous designer for goldsmiths' work, and was a master in ornament, especially in the application of the figure to ornamental purposes. He was in some measure a pupil of Hans Burgkmair, and was thoroughly imbued with the spirit of the Renaissance. Holbein the elder—his father—was a well-known artist, who worked in the old German Gothic style.

The younger Holbein began his artistic career as a goldsmith, and his designs of sword and dagger handles, in which the figure forms so admirably follow the lines of the composition in a remarkable degree of ornamental fitness, reveal his fine sense and feeling for ornament.

In Italy the sculptor, Luca Signorelli, employed the figure and animal forms with an equal degree of skill, and with the same feeling for ornament. Both artists thoroughly understood the correct laws of ornamental composition, which was not by any means a universal gift with the artists of the Renaissance period.

Holbein designed many cups, one of which was a rich example of a standing cup and cover which was designed for Jane Seymour, one of the wives of Henry VIII. of England. The drawing for this cup is preserved in the British Museum.

During the sixteenth century the art of metal working in Germany, especially at Nuremberg, Swabian Augsburg, and Lübeck, reached a high state of perfection under the great patronage of wealthy families, such as the Fugger family, of Augsburg, and others. Holbein, and other German, Dutch, and Flemish artists, worked in England, and besides much German and Flemish Renaissance

work found its way into England, and influenced in a
great degree the style of the metal work of this country.

In addition to the gold and silver plate of the kings'
palaces and of private families, corporations and colleges
accumulated great quantities of plate, and before banks
were properly established, gold and silver plate and
jewellery were the chief store of wealth that could, when
necessary, be easily converted into money.

King Henry VII. had a service of plate valued at twenty
thousand pounds. This monarch employed the Italian

Fig. 171.—Apostle Spoons; 1566; at Corpus Christi College, Cambridge. (C.)

sculptor and goldsmith, Torrigiano, and other foreign
artists.

Henry VIII. also employed many Italian and German
artists and goldsmiths, and it is believed that Cellini
executed some of his finest jewellery for this king.

Not only Henry VIII., but his great lords and ministers,
had extensive collections of plate. Cardinal Wolsey had
a large safe or cupboard, barred all round for protection,
in which was displayed a goodly show of gold cups and
other sumptuous vessels for use at his table.

"Apostle spoons" were made at this and subsequent
periods, and were so called from their having little figures
of the Apostles modelled on the tops of the handles (Fig.
171).

The silver, gold, and bronze work in Queen Elizabeth's time in England was made in the style of the Renaissance, like that of Germany. Italian and German work at this time was almost identical (Figs. 172 and 173); and even when the Rococo decadence was prevalent in architecture, both on the Continent and in England, goldsmiths' work was the last industry that fell under its influence, especially when we compare it with the contemporary

Fig. 172.—Silver-gilt German Cup; Sixteenth Century.

pottery, furniture, and other decorative art. Of course, at the latter end of the seventeenth and during the eighteenth century, the design in metal work in France, and also in England, was sacrificed to display and ostentation; but at the same time a comparative purity of style is seen in much of the plate made in the reigns of William and Mary, James II., and Queen Anne, of English manufacture. The silver and gold plate of the "Queen Anne" period (1702-14) is highly prized for its beauty of design and massive character, some examples of which will be noticed presently.

In the metal work, especially in gold and silver of the seventeenth century, towards the middle of the century a certain heaviness of design gradually crept in ; although a good deal of fine work was still produced by the artists who belonged to the older schools, and, as a matter of

Fig. 173.—Bronze Candlestick ; Italian ; Sixteenth Century.

course, the best work belonged to the earlier part of the century.

A fine freedom of line and handling is seen in the Flemish salver (Fig. 174) of Renaissance design. The French example of a silver-gilt cup and cover is unusually simple for French work of this century (Fig. 175), and an English silver casket of the same date (Fig. 176) shows a similarity of style: the serpent handles and covers are almost identical.

About the middle of the seventeenth century silversmiths' work in Germany began to assume a bulbous or
lobed character, and gradually became more florid in
design (Fig. 177). This bulbous or gadrooned work was
carried out to a greater degree in English work of this
period, of which the gold cup at Exeter College (Fig. 178)
is a good example. The decoration of metal work in
England at this time consisted of flowers and foliage

Fig. 174.—Flemish Salver; Seventeenth Century.   (S. K. M.)

chased on the repoussé surfaces, and often large rich acan-
thus-leaves were used, especially on the vases and silver
furniture of Charles II.'s time. The lobed panel work of
Germany was developed in England into lozenge and pine-
shaped raised surfaces, and the details of the French Louis
Quatorze were added as decoration.

Tankards were made in silver, or sometimes in pottery
richly mounted in silver or pewter. The tankard has a

wide base, the body narrowing towards the mouth, and has

Fig. 175.—Cup with Cover, Silver-gilt; French; Seventeenth Century. (J.)

usually a cover (Fig. 179), while the beaker or drinking

cup is the reverse in shape—narrow in the base, and

Fig. 176.—Silver Casket; Seventeenth
Century.

Fig. 177.—Nuremberg
Tankard.

widening towards the mouth, and is without a handle or
cover.

Fig. 178.—Cup of Gold, *circa* 1660-70, at Exeter College, Oxford. (C.)

The English silver tankards were straight-sided, with

naturalistic decoration. Modern tankards for beer-drinking uses are made in pewter or Britannia metal.

In the Rhine Provinces, in Germany, and in Switzerland stoneware tankards with metal covers and mountings are still in use. Tankards in the seventeenth century were made with pegs inserted in the sides at regulated distances, so that each drinker might quaff his measured portion when the vessel was handed round.

In the reign of James I. many sumptuous objects in services and toilet furniture were made in gold and silver. The baronial halls in England were extremely rich in large pieces of plate: huge salvers, vases, basins, jugs, cups, toilet services, and even tables, chairs, mirror-frames, and fire-dogs were made in silver.

Fig. 179.—English Tankard ; Seventeenth Century.

In France, during the reign of Louis XIV., similar gold and silver vessels and sumptuous furniture were made in the rich and massive style of the period. Balin and Delaunay are mentioned among others who were skilful goldsmiths to that monarch, and who worked under the directions of the chief painter and tapestry designer, Lebrun.

England not only made a good deal of this silver furniture, but also imported it largely from France ; most of it, however, was melted down to pay for the wars of Charles I.

A few remaining examples are still at Knole Park, in Kent, consisting of silver tables, mirror-frames, fire-dogs, &c. (Fig. 180). Similar objects of this period are now at Windsor Castle (Fig. 181), of which copies in electrotype are in the Kensington Museum.

Some of the gold plate preserved in the Tower of London with the regalia is of this period.

After the date of 1660 gold and silver-smithery becomes

fluted and less florid in decoration, but some of it still keeps the gadrooned and bulbous character.

Towards the end of the century, in the time of William

Fig. 180.—Silver Fire-Dog at Knole Park.

III., the flutings were less in number, and consequently became larger in scale, and in the early part of the eighteenth century the metal work in England became plainer, depending more on the lines of its contour for effect than on its decoration (Fig. 182). Mouldings were plainer, and broad spaces of convex and concave shapes producing a massive and, in many cases, an elegant appearance (Figs. 182, 183), which gave to the Queen Anne plate a mark of great distinction.

About 1750 the forms in silver work partook, in many instances, of the prevailing fashion in the chinaware of that date, though without the extravagance in the decoration. From 1770, and for about ten years later, the designs became more attenuated, and were peculiar in having the

Fig. 181.—Silver Table at Windsor Castle.

dividing lines of the design composed of fillets of beads (Figs. 185 and 187). The beaded style of silversmiths' work and in all metal work, pottery, and furniture of this period was due to the development of classic design that took place in France and in England consequent on the discovery of the buried city of Pompeii in 1770.

The brothers Adam in England designed a good deal of silversmiths' work, of which the three illustrations given are examples of their style. Light wreaths, medallions, fillets of beads, festoons, masks, feet and legs of animals composed the decoration of the Adams' style.

The brothers John and Robert Adam had travelled in

Italy, and had brought with them pronounced classic ideas which not only influenced their own and other contemporary work in architecture and furniture designs, but in silversmiths' work also their influence was widely felt (Fig. 188).

In France the classic ideas were also very prevalent

Fig. 182.—Wine Fountain; 1710.   (C.)

about this period in silversmiths' work. The "Louis-Seize" candlestick (Fig. 189) is one of a pair from the Jones Collection in the South Kensington Museum, and is an admirable example of the style; though it is said to have been made at Turin in Italy in 1783, it is certainly

of French design. It has the square base so peculiar
to French work of this period, with the wreaths and

Fig. 183.—Candelabrum, Haberdashers' Hall, London. (C.)

medallions so characteristic of the style in question, that of
Louis XVI.

Another candlestick (Fig. 190) from the Jones Collection

Fig. 184.—Eighteenth-Century Bowl. (S. K. M.)

is probably Italian in style and manufacture, and belongs
to the early part of the eighteenth century.

At the time of the Revolution, and immediately after,

Fig. 185.—Tureen at Windsor Castle 1773.

Fig. 187.—Silver Vase;
1770.

Fig. 188.—Vase by
Adam.

Fig. 186.—Chocolate Pot; 1777. (C.)

the style of the silver work deteriorated in France. Vast
quantities of plate were seized and sent off to the Mint by

Fig. 189.—Candlestick, Silver-gilt; Louis Seize. (S. K. M.)

the Revolutionary army, and naturally an art like the goldsmith's, that ministered to the needs of luxury, was in
those times at a low ebb.

In England in the early part of the nineteenth century some good work was executed from the designs of Flax-

Fig. 190.—Candlestick, Silver-gilt; Italian; Eighteenth Century. (S. K.M.)

man and Stothard, chiefly in the classic style; the Wellington Shield may be mentioned as an example; but about

the middle of this century gold and silver work was characterized by even a greater degree of naturalism in design
than that of the French debased style from which it was
copied. Nothing could exceed the vulgarity and bad taste
in the design of silversmiths' work made about fifty or forty
years ago. All architectural principles that should guide
the design of relief modelling and construction were
thrown to the winds, and naturalism unnaturally applied
and mixed in any heterogeneous way was quite fashionable.
For instance, we have huge épergnes where stags and
other animals from the Highlands of Scotland or the
Welsh mountains are decorating silver rock-work from
which the tropical palms of Africa are seen to grow out of
their clefts, affording grateful shade to the natives of the
British moorland. The art of the silversmith in England
about this period had suffered more than any other artistic
industry, and in the matter of design it seemed to have
reached the twilight state of semi-insanity, and was utterly
devoid of any artistic merit.

A great improvement is, however, to be seen in the
work of respectable firms and in that of many private
craftsmen of to-day, but many shop windows are still filled
with costly work in the precious metals that are worthless
from an artistic point of view.

NIELLO-WORK AND DAMASCENING.

Niello-work has been mentioned on a previous page. It
was an important branch of the goldsmith's art, as well as
that of damascening. From the earliest times the nations
of antiquity have engraved on metals and filled up the
lines or grooves of the engraving with a black species of
enamel composition—*niello*—or with other metals such as
silver, gold, and electrum ; the latter process has been
called *damascening*, from Damascus, where gold and silver
inlaid in iron or steel was practised in the tenth and
eleventh centuries.

It was a favourite method of decorating metals during the Middle Ages throughout the countries of Persia, Syria, and in most European countries, especially on such objects as arms, armour, and different kinds of vessels.

The celebrated Italian metal-worker, Maso Finiguerra, worked extensively in niello, and to him is ascribed the discovery of the art of engraving on copper and printing from the copper plate. He was a goldsmith and a native of Florence, and was the pupil of Ghiberti and Masaccio. In the year 1452 he made a pax, on the flat panel of which he engraved a design to be filled in afterwards with the black composition of niello, but before he had completely

Fig. 191.—Italian Damascene Work; Sixteenth Century.

finished his work he took a "squeeze" in clay of the engraving in order to judge of the progress he had made, and from this squeeze he made a mould in sulphur, and filled it with a black pigment, and on pressing this sulphur block on a sheet of damp paper the pattern appeared similar to the niello effect. This led him to fill the lines of the actual silver plate with a more durable ink, and to print off impressions on paper. It was by thus experimenting that Finiguerra discovered the art of engraving and printing from the metal plate. The original pax with its impressions are preserved at Florence.

Damascening is executed in three ways. First, where the steel or copper is engraved with an undercut line and a thread of gold or silver is forced in by hammering or pressed by a burnisher into the grooved lines. Second, the plated method, where the plate of metal to be encrusted is enclosed between slightly raised walls in the foundation metal. Third, where the foundation metal is

Fig. 192.—Shield Damascened in Gold; Indian. (B.)

roughened by a sharp tool in all directions and the gold or silver is laid on thinly and pressed or hammered in. The last method is the latest and least durable. Sometimes the lines of the engraving are punched with holes at regulated distances, which serve as keys to hold the inlaid metal when hammered in.

The famous bowl called the " Baptistery of St. Louis,"
now in the Louvre, is made of copper inlaid with figures
of horsemen and hunting scenes. It is an example of
"Mosil work," or Mesopotamian damascening, of the
thirteenth century, in which silver only is used as the inlaid
metal.

A delicate design in Italian damascene work is shown
at Fig. 191, and an Indian example at Fig. 192. The
Italian example shows the Arabian influence in some of
the details of the ornament. The Japanese are perfect
masters in the art of damascening. Sword-blades of the
thirteenth and later centuries have beautiful designs inlaid
as intaglios or in damascene work; sword-guards of the
seventeenth and eighteenth centuries are remarkable for
this kind of decoration, and for the exquisite chasing of
the iron, which in some cases is cut out like fret-work, and
in others are carved as delicate as decorative ivory work.

INDIAN JEWELLERY.

The jewellery of India is one of the most important art industries of that country, and the trade of the gold and silver
smith is an established institution in every village and district. The variation in style and method of fabrication has
very marked features, according to the fashion that finds
favour in each locality. The extreme love for trinkets of
a brilliant and dazzling nature amongst all grades of the
people has in a great measure directed the fabrication of
Indian jewellery, which tends to make the most of the
precious metals by using them in thin plates or in a filigrain work, and in order to get the flashing effect and rich
colouring, scales or flakes of diamonds are more often used
than the more valuable and solid gems, and inferior gems,
or even coloured glass, are set to the best advantage, and
used indiscriminately : anything, in fact, is used in order to
get the gorgeous variety of brilliant colouring and dazzling

effect. Much of the Indian jewellery is of a flimsy character as regards its lightness and thin nature of the
material; but the latter is generally of the best quality, and
the artistic workmanship lavished on most of the jewellery
more than makes up for its want of inherent solidity.

Jewellery ought to be light in character and of good
design and workmanship if it is intended to fulfil its use in

Fig. 193.—Primitive Silver Bracelet; Dinajpur, Bengal. (B.)

decorating the person, as nothing is uglier than heavy
jewellery, which can only be valuable in the light of representing the wealth of the owner.

Some of the Indian jewellery is, however, fairly solid and
heavy, as in the chopped gold form of cubical, octahedron,
and oblong shapes of the metal which are strung on silk
cord as necklaces, and the nail-head variety of earrings
made at Ahmedabad and Surat in Western India.

Girdles, torques or neck collars, bracelets, and anklets

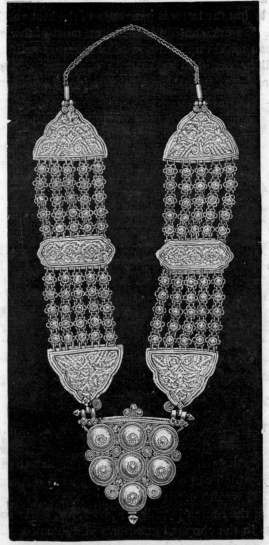

Fig. 194.—Silver Neck Ornament, from Sindh.　(B)

are made of twisted gold wire, which are common throughout India, and in the western provinces are made in the twisted form of the Matheran knotted and woven grass collars.

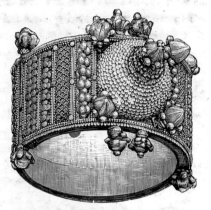

Fig. 195.—Native Silver Jewellery of Cuttack. (B.)

Some of the native jewellery in many parts of India still

Fig. 196.—Filigrain Jewellery of Cuttack. (B.)

keeps its primitive character and bears a great likeness

to the very early Celtic jewellery found in Ireland and in

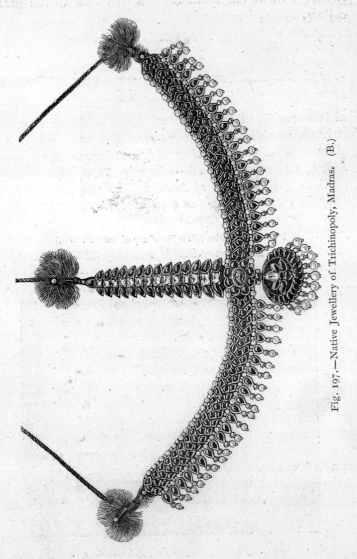

Fig. 197.—Native Jewellery of Trichinopoly, Madras. (B.)

other countries of Europe, which would probably suggest the same Celtic origin for all (Fig. 193).

The silver filigrain work of India, especially the designs of the Sindh jewellery and that made at Cuttack, Trichinopoly, and Travancore, recalls the methods of fabrication and design of the ancient Etruscan jewellery. (See Figs. 194, 195, 197.)

A certain analogy may also be noticed in the native jewellery from the above places to the Phœnician, primitive Grecian, and even Scandinavian, which goes a long way to prove the intercourse between, and the migrations of, the

Fig. 198.—Native Gold Jewellery of Bombay. (B.)

people of India, Thibet, Turkestan to Asia Minor and the continent of Europe.

Some Indian jewellery, though possessing shapes common to other countries, has very distinctive national characteristics in the decoration, which may be seen in the illustration (Fig. 198) of the gold plate from Bombay. In these cases the design is usually symbolical.

The Indian jewellers of the Mogul period have produced some exquisite work in the setting of gems on jade carvings and on small vases of jade.

The deftness and cunning of the Indian jeweller may
have been equalled by the Etruscans and ancient Greeks,
but he has not been surpassed in his delicate workmanship by any nation of modern times.

Iron Work in France, Germany, Belgium, Italy and England.

Ornamental iron work was executed in France and in
England before the Roman occupation of these countries,
but any early remains of this work that have been found in
either country are supposed to be of the Roman period.
The Romans were not skilled in the working of iron,
although well conversant with the manufacture of bronze
objects.

Remains of iron hasps, escutcheons, window grilles,
candlesticks, folding chairs, &c., have been found in France
and in England, of the Romano-Gaulish and British
periods, that have a great similarity of style, and, indeed,
up to the fifteenth century the style and design of iron
work in both countries were pretty much alike.

The most interesting examples of the blacksmith's art
of the Middle Ages—in England especially—are the hinges
to the church doors. The first hinges were simple single
straps of iron that passed from back to front of the door,
the socket being formed out of the solid piece at the angle
on one side. The front side of this strap by degrees was
clawed out, or otherwise elaborated, to cover as much of
the door as possible, so as to form an armour of defence
against predatory robbers, such as the barbarous Norse
pirates who were continually invading the British shores.

A favourite form of the hinge was the crescent shape ;
sometimes the hinge branched out in a simple crescent
with curved and bifurcated endings that may have sym-
bolized the snake or birds' heads, and often two or three of
these crescents branched out from a central bar. Between
the hinges additional bars or straps were sometimes run

Fig. 199.—Hinges, &c., to Haddiscoe Church.

across the door to strengthen it, and elaborate foliated
crosses often occupied the central part, as in Fig. 199.

On some of the old Norman doors, in addition to the hinges, as at Stillingfleet Church, there are designs in iron work which consist of mystical signs of Danish origin, such as a viking ship or sun ship, the swastika or fylfot, moon signs, and rude images of the human figure.

The crescent hinge may have had a symbolical meaning, perhaps Scandinavian, or it may have originated in the Saracenic crescent, and may have been brought from Sicily, the birthplace of Norman architecture.

The art of the blacksmith in the Middle Ages was more developed in France than in any other country of Europe, and the art of stamping the leaves, stems, and rosettes with steel or chilled iron dies and punches was practised there earlier than the thirteenth century, and at a period a little later in England. The ornament was in style very little more than the Romanesque type of the conventional vine, or other leaf of a like nature—the cinquefoil, trefoil, rosettes, and scrolls, but these few elements were used in the most effective manner (Fig. 200).

The magnificent hinges on the Porte Ste. Anne of Notre-Dame at Paris show to perfection the French stamping on the leaves and other parts. These unrivalled hinges (Fig. 201) are of the Early French style of the thirteenth century. Nothing, however, is known of their origin, nor even the name of the smith who forged them. Each hinge is composed of six large scrolls springing from the central bar or stem, all of which are richly clothed with spirals, foliage, birds, and dragons; the whole design is supposed to represent the terrestrial Paradise.

Exceedingly rich, but not so elaborated as the hinges of the Church of Notre-Dame, is the herse, or grille, of English work of the same period, which surmounts the tomb of Queen Eleanor in Westminster Abbey (Fig. 202). This fine example of English smithery was made by Thomas de Leghtone in the year 1294. It is a clever adaptation of hinge-work to the design of a grille. Mr. Gardner supposes Leghtone to be connected with Leighton Buzzard,

as the same kind of iron work as the Eleanor grille occurs
in the hinges of the parish church door of that place, and
also from the fact that similar work is found on many
other church doors of the same period in Bedfordshire—
at Eaton Bray and Turvey, for instance; also at Norwich,

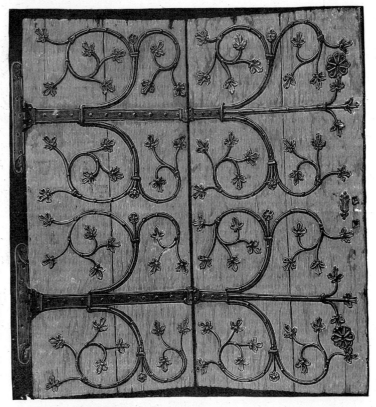

Fig. 200.—Press Door in the Church of St. Jacques, at Liége.   (G.)

Tunstall, Windsor, Lichfield, and Merton College, Oxford,
are examples of the same kind of work, which no doubt
was executed by Thomas de Leghtone and his assistants.

After the end of the thirteenth century examples are
scarce of genuine wrought-iron work, for the fashion

changed at that time in the manner of working the metal.
Sheets and bars of iron were cut in the cold state into
various patterns by the use of chisels and files, the pieces
being fastened together by rivets and small collars or ties

Fig. 201.—One of the Hinges to the Porte Ste. Anne of Notre-Dame, Paris. (G.)

of metal. Much of this work was done in Italy, in imitation of marble and wood panelling, and a very common
method consisted in making the grilles in Italy of riveted
quatrefoils. A fine grille of this character is in the

Fig. 202.—Grille or Herse on Queen Eleanor's Tomb, Westminster Abbey; 1294. (G.)

Church of Santa Croce of the date of 1371. In the churches and palaces of Venice, Florence, Verona, &c., there are many good examples of grilles that resemble in a great degree joinery work in iron.

In Germany the love for iron work was not developed so early as it was in France and England, and it was not until Gothic architecture took a firm hold in that country in the end of the thirteenth century that the first serious attempts were made in the use of decorative iron work, and, like their architectural forms, the German wrought-iron work was inspired by French examples.

German work in iron of the thirteenth century is very scarce: one of the best-known examples occurs in the iron work on the doors of the Church of St. Elizabeth at Marburg, near Cassel, which consists of branching scroll-work clothed with vine-leaf endings.

In the fourteenth century the Germans developed the French vine-work into lozenge-shaped leaves, and for a change interspersed them with fleurs-de-lis, and occasionally some tracery patterns, all of which were borrowed from the French. The stamped work of the English and French blacksmith was not developed in Germany.

In the fifteenth century German iron work was greatly influenced by the fine work which was being produced at this period in the Low Countries. Brussels had been noted for its extensive works in iron and steel from the fourteenth century. The brawny Flemish smiths were celebrated throughout Europe for their great achievements in moulded and hammered iron, such as in the spires of the cathedrals of Antwerp, Ghent, and Bruges, well-covers, railings, fonts, cranes, and grilles. The historical well-cover in front of the Cathedral of Antwerp has usually been ascribed to Quentin Matsys the painter, but as he was only twelve years old when this work was completed, it could hardly have been made by his hands. The explanation is that he has been confounded with another Quentin, a blacksmith and the son of Josse Matsys, the architect, smith, and clockmaker of Antwerp. The well-cover is more likely to have been the work of Josse Matsys. The design is Gothic in feeling and is very picturesque with its interlacing stems and vine-leaves, flowers, and figures. A rich font crane in iron work in the Cathedral of Louvain is said to be the authentic work of Josse, and a twelve-branched corona in the same church is ascribed to his son, Quentin Matsys. To the hand of the latter is also ascribed the rich Flemish gates of Bishop West's Chapel in Ely Cathedral.

Brabant was celebrated for its iron work, particularly in pierced and filed work in such things as locks, hinges, candelabra, tabernacles, and *guichets* (little windows or wicket gates), most of these objects taking pronounced Gothic architectural forms, for the most part being composed of flamboyant tracery and little buttresses (Fig. 203). Much of the Brabaçon iron work found its way into England and Germany. This work is characterised by its flamboyant tracery, which is found on locks of doors and Flemish coffers, and in the design of the guichets, a fine specimen of the latter now being in the Kensington Museum. The locks of the doors in St. George's Chapel, Windsor and in some other places are of Brabaçon workmanship. This Flemish style of lock work was imitated very much in England, but the workmanship was less refined although of a stronger character than the Flemish.

The Germans, especially of Augsburg, Nuremberg, and in the Rhine Provinces, more particularly at Cologne, developed the chiselled iron work to an astonishing degree of elaboration.

While the shapes of the lock-plates were of a decided Saracenic character, the design of the pattern ornamentation was either of an elaborate architectural composition, as in the large lock in the Klagenfurt Museum (Fig. 204), or of designs mainly developed from the thistle-plant.

The thistle was distinctly characteristic of German iron work, and also the trellis-work pattern as seen on the doors of the fifteenth and sixteenth centuries (Fig. 205).   Armo-

Fig. 203.—Tabernacle Grille from Ottoberg, Tyrol; Fifteenth Century.
(S. K. M.) (G.)

rial bearings fill the panels between the trellis-bands, with
richly forged rivets or nail-heads on the lozenge intersec-

tions. Sometimes the decoration was gilt or silvered, and
the ground underneath painted red or black. In the sixteenth and seventeenth centuries the iron work in Europe
and England partook of the character of the Renaissance,

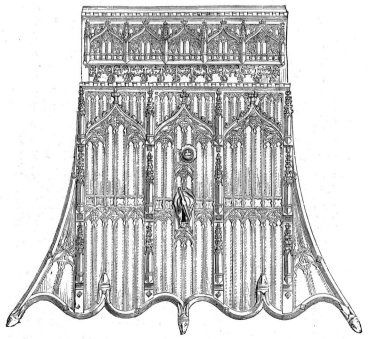

Fig. 204.—Lock, 18 inches high, in the Klagenfurt Museum; German; Fifteenth
Century. (G.)

and towards the end of the former century had all the
foliated character of that style.

The illustration (Fig. 206) shows a typical example of
French work of the end of the sixteenth century.

In Flanders, Holland, and in England, especially during
the eighteenth century, decorative iron work was again in
great demand, and some beautiful work in gates, grilles,
and railings were executed. Among the finest works of
this period are the celebrated gates or screens designed in

the style of the Renaissance and made by Huntingdon
Shaw for King William III. for his palace at Hampton
Court. These gates, which are fine examples of hammered
work, are now in the Kensington Museum. The iron gates

Fig. 205.—Iron-bound Door in the Monastery of Krems ; Late Fifteenth
Century. (G.)

and railings made in the reign of Queen Anne and later
were often of beautiful design, in which the capabilities of
the material were excellently expressed. Some fine examples still exist in the gates and railings of the old houses
in Cheyne Walk, Chelsea, and some good ironwork of this

Fig. 206.—Mirror, Wrought Iron ; French Work ; Sixteenth Century.

type may be seen in the screens in St. Paul's Cathedral. This beautiful style died out during this century, when a more extended use of cast iron crept in, and if we except the work of the late Alfred Stevens and of a few other designers and architects, there has been nothing of an artistic value that one can point out in England in the domain of cast-iron productions. In fact, it is a curious but common expression to say of a bad design for almost anything that it " looks like cast iron." Designers for cast-iron work might take some good hints from the old Roman or Pompeian bronzes.

CHAPTER V.

FURNITURE.

ANTIQUE: EGYPT, ASSYRIA, GREECE, AND ROME.

THE furniture of the antique nations has been noticed in some instances in the former volume of this work, especially in the cases of Egyptian and Assyrian examples, where fortunately we can point out the many representations of it that occur on the bas-reliefs. It is from these that we chiefly form an opinion as to how the palaces and interiors must have been furnished, for, owing to the great lapse of time, nearly every vestige of furniture of these old nations has passed away.

The British Museum and the Louvre contain a few Egyptian chairs or seats that have been made in ebony and ivory, which owe their preservation to the lasting nature of the material.

Two Egyptian chairs or thrones are illustrated at Figs. 146 and 147, in the first part of this work, and a wooden coffer at Fig. 149. At Fig. 148 carpenters are represented as occupied in chair making, the feet and legs of the chairs being designed from animals' limbs, and the stools on which the workmen are sitting are blocks of wood hollowed out at the top. The Egyptian couch was of a straight-lined design in the body with a curved head like an ordinary sofa, the legs, feet, and other salient points being carved with heads, feet, and tails of animals. Some boxes and coffers with gable tops dovetailed together, small toilet boxes having carved or painted decoration, and mummy

cases of cedar-wood having elaborate hieroglyphic decorations, may be seen in the British Museum and in the
Louvre. Chariot and horse furniture are well represented
in the reliefs and wall paintings. Egypt was famed for
chariot building, and exported them in trade to the surrounding nations. We read that King Solomon imported
his war-chariots from Egypt.

If examples of Egyptian furniture are scarce, the furniture of Assyria is practically non-existent, as the climate
of the latter country was not so dry or preservative

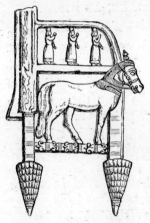
Fig. 207.—Assyrian Throne.

Fig. 208.—Assyrian Seat.

as that of Egypt, so that all examples that have not
been wilfully destroyed have long ago perished. Many
ornaments of bronze and of ivory decorations have been
discovered that have been used as mountings to feet, ends
or legs of seats, chairs, or thrones. The bas-reliefs of the
latter enable us to form a fairly accurate judgment of the
nature and style of Assyrian furniture, the decoration of
which was of a heavier and coarser character than that
of the more elegant Egyptian (Figs. 207 and 208). Forms
and parts of animals were used by the Assyrians and
nearly all Oriental nations as furniture decorations. The

human figure was used also, but generally in the representation of slaves or conquered peoples, who were degraded to the position of bearing the weight of the seat or throne of the monarch (see Persian throne, Fig. 256, first vol., from Persepolis, which was an adaptation from an Assyrian throne). The Egyptian chairs had also carved human figures as captives tied under the seat (Figs. 146, 147, first vol.).

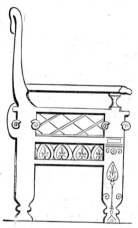

The furniture of the Hebrews was doubtless of the same kind as the Assyrian. From the description of King Solomon's throne it was apparently similar to those of the Assyrian kings. It had lions for the arm supports, and had six lions in gold and ivory on the six steps on either side of the throne.

Fig. 209.—Greek Chair.

In the manufacture of the furniture of the nations of antiquity the principal materials were—in woods, ebony, rosewood, walnut, pine, teak, and, above all, cedar-wood; ivory, gold, silver, bronze, and electrum were also much used for inlays and for solid mountings.

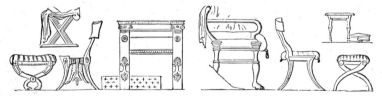

Fig. 210.—Greek Folding Stools and Chairs, &c.

The furniture and the chariots of the Greeks in their early period were simply copied from Egyptian and Asiatic sources, with less of the animal forms and more of plant forms as decorative details (Figs. 209, 210). Folding stools and chairs were made in wood and in metal, and the backs of the chairs were upright, or nearly so

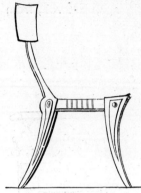

Fig. 211.—Greek Chair.

(Fig. 211); couches resembling modern sofas, elaborate footstools, and arm-chairs with sphinxes for the arms were made by the Greeks (Figs. 210, 212).

In the British Museum are some small models of Greek chairs made in lead, and wooden boxes showing the dovetail construction.

In the later Greek periods the furniture was inlaid with ivory, ebony, gold, and silver. Tripods were made of bronze, and had ornamented legs in the shapes of the limbs of lions, leopards, and sphinxes. The Roman bronze tripods were

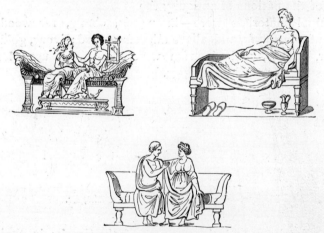

Fig. 212.—Greek Couches and Sofa.

very similar to the Grecian ones in design, and were not only used for sacred purposes in the temples, but also to support braziers for heating purposes, or for burning perfumes in the houses of private people (Fig. 213).

Hand-mirrors and *cistæ* were made in great quantities in bronze or in other metal alloys, in silver, and sometimes in gold. The mirrors were polished on the face, and had often rich designs of figure subjects. The Greek cistæ were cylindrical metal boxes that rested on feet designed from those of various animals, having a lid or cover, with

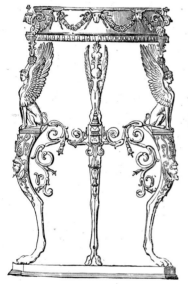

Fig. 213.—Bronze Tripod, Greco-Roman.

Fig. 214.—Folding Tripod, Roman.

a handle or knot usually of figure design, the whole surface of the body being covered with engraved figure compositions and ornamental borders. They were probably used to contain jewellery and trinkets. Some very fine specimens of these hand-mirrors and cistæ may be seen in the British Museum.

The furnishing of the houses of the Romans was very much of the same character as that of the Greeks and

Etruscans, from whom the Romans inherited all their
arts.

The interior plan and aspects of the Roman houses were

Fig. 215.—Roman Bronze Candelabra.

such as those of Pompeii and Herculaneum, described in
the first vol. Tables and tripods of bronze or braziers were
supported on three legs, some of which were made with

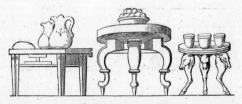

Fig. 216.—Roman Tables.

hinges for folding purposes (Fig. 214), and others were ot
sphinx and animal forms of a rich design (Fig. 213).
Lamp-stand designs were quaint and elegant and were
made in bronze (Fig. 215). Candelabra of architectural

design were carved in marble and were from six to ten feet in height (Fig. 217).

The Romans highly prized and paid good sums for tables that were made from the pollard cross grain of different hard woods in which the knots and grain showed to advantage, the beauty of the wood being brought out by hand-polishing and by staining it with various coloured dyes. Bird's-eye maple and the wood of the *cedrus atlantica* were much prized. The smaller tables, *abaci*, rested usually on one foot— *monopodium*—and larger tables had three or four legs, which had ivory claws or heads of animals as carved decoration (Fig. 216). Boxwood, beech, and palm, inlaid with ivory, ebony, and precious metals, were used in the materials of chairs and couches. The latter were also made in bronze (Fig. 218), and chairs of state were carved in marble, one of this kind being in the Louvre, a cast of which is now in the Kensington Museum (Fig. 219). The form of the Roman *curule* chair was like the letter X, and was so called because it could be folded and carried easily in the *curules* or chariots. It was used from the earliest times of the Romans down to modern days in

Fig. 217.—Marble Candela-brum, Roman.

Italy, and was often constructed of elephants' tusks, wood, or metal, with ivory feet. The curule chairs were carried about for outdoor use and for the theatre. The *sella* or *bisellium*, to seat two persons, was often a very

ornate kind of seat with turned legs similar to the couches
(Fig. 220).

In the houses of the Romans a separate room or ward-

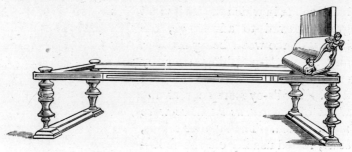

Fig. 218.—Couch in Bronze, Roman.

robe was fitted up to keep the dresses and clothes of the
family; this room had cupboards with doors and shelves,
drawers, and lockers.

Portable coffers and chests were used, in which they

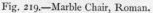

Fig. 219.—Marble Chair, Roman.

Fig. 220.—Roman Sella or Bisellium.

packed their clothes and valuables when carrying them to
and from their town and country houses. The Roman
furniture and wooden construction of their houses were

decorated with paintings and carvings of animals' heads, limbs, and feet, and with figures of heroes and masks, as well as with the usual architectural acanthus foliage. Veneering of woods was an art in which the Romans were skilled; both small and large designs or pictures in tarsia work were the chief decorations of the best furniture.

BYZANTINE, ROMANESQUE, SARACENIC, AND THE FURNITURE OF THE MIDDLE AGES.

The furniture, such as tables, chairs, beds, and the chariots, of the Byzantine period, was like the architecture in having something of the classic Roman mixture with some Asiatic Greek forms in its design. Scarcely any remains of such are now in existence, although we have evidence of the extreme richness of the sumptuary furniture and vessels of the great houses and palaces of Constantinople, for owing to the decadence and destruction of the Roman empire in the provinces, the capital of the East became enriched by treasures of the old Roman families, who naturally fled to Constantinople for protection for themselves and their valuable effects.

The old ivories known as consular diptychs have different varieties of seats, chairs, and footstools, on which the consuls are seated, represented in the carving. Many originals of these and casts from others may be seen in the Kensington Museum.

The chair of St. Maximian, preserved at Ravenna, is covered with ivory carvings, and is one of the finest examples of Byzantine work. It is described at page 138 and is figured in Labarte's "Art of the Middle Ages."

Much of the furniture of the early centuries of Christian art is represented in the Byzantine illuminated manuscripts. Beds and couches kept the old Roman forms with the turned legs. Chariots must have been used very much, as the old game of chariot racing was kept up by the Byzantines. The Iconoclasts of the Eastern Empire

under Leo the Isaurian (A.D. 726)—whose injurious rule
lasted about one hundred and twenty years—were respon-
sible for much destruction of sumptuary furniture, as well
as for other productions of an artistic nature, but at the
same time they were the indirect means of causing a new
development in art in the western parts of Europe, and
more particularly in the Rhenish Provinces, by driving the
Byzantine artists and craftsmen to these places, where
they were welcomed by Charlemagne, and by his powerful
nobles and Churchmen. In the course of time they succeeded in founding the school of art known as Rhenish-
Byzantine. The finest illustrations of this art are seen in
the magnificent enamelled reliquaries or shrines. The
gilt-bronze chair of Dagobert is of Romanesque design,
and is one of the earliest pieces of furniture of the Middle
Ages (see Fig. 134). Another mediæval chair or throne is
high seated, and exceedingly rich in design (Fig. 221).
It is of Scandinavian origin, and is a good example of the
Romanesque style of Northern Europe. Many forms of
the Romanesque are seen in the furniture and carving of
the Gothic style that immediately succeeded the former.

During the Anglo-Saxon period in England the ordinary
houses usually consisted of one room. Sometimes a shed-
like structure was erected against the wall of the room to
contain the bed of the mistress of the house, and as a rule
the inmates slept on a large table placed in the centre
of the room, or on benches on which bags of straw were
placed. Seats without backs, or stools, long settles or
benches with backs and carved ends or arms, were the
chief articles in furniture.

After the Norman Conquest domestic improvements
were multiplied, more rooms were added to the houses,
such as the solar or upper room, and the parloir or talking-
room, and some of the rooms had fireplaces, but not
chimneys. The principal room was the hall or assembly-
room, which had a fireplace in the centre, the smoke
escaping through the lantern light in the roof.

In the Norman times the principal additions to the
furniture of English manor-houses and castles were the
cupboard, presses or armoires, and chests. These pieces
of furniture were introduced from France. Sometimes the
portable presses and the chests were painted with tempera

Fig. 221.—Scandinavian Seat or Throne of the Middle Ages.

decorations, and were bound with wrought-iron clasps
and hinges, which were just beginning to come into use.

The bed-clothes and personal clothing of the nobles and
rich landowners began to assume a rich character, and
were often embroidered.

Tapestry and painted cloth hangings were imported ;

also pottery of an ornamental description was not only imported, but made in England at this time. All this applies to the homes of the rich only, for the poorer classes remained for a long period in a very primitive condition as regards their style of houses and their furniture.

Fig. 222.—Flemish ; Sixteenth Century. (P.)

Fig. 223.—German ; Fifteenth Century. (P.)

The construction of furniture and the panelling of chests began to exhibit some workmanlike appearances of good carpentry. Panels were placed in framework that was mortised and fastened with wooden pegs, which became the universal method of panelling throughout the Gothic period. Room panelling came into use in England in the early part of the thirteenth century, when pine timber was used at first for this work, but was displaced later by the more substantial oak. This oak panelling during the Gothic periods was often carved with elaborate tracery of an architectural character (Figs. 222, 223), and a common design was a carved imitation of a carefully folded textile, known as the "linen panel" (Fig. 224).

Fig. 224.—English ; Fifteenth Century. (P.)

Chests were used as tables, and the tops had inlaid checkers to be used as chessboards. They were also used as sideboards on which to place dishes of food, the dining-

table being a board which was placed on trestles, that
could be removed and packed away when not required
(Figs. 225, 226). A cross-legged chair and a three-legged

Fig. 225.—Dining Room; Fifteenth Century. (P.)

stool is shown at Fig. 228, which were common shapes in
the fourteenth century. The illustration, Fig. 227, is that
of a bedroom of the same period, and is taken from an

Fig. 226.—Dining Table on Trestles; Fourteenth Century. (P.)

English manuscript of the date of 1400. For these illustrations, and many others on the subject of furniture, we
are indebted to the work of Mr. J. H. Pollen on "Furni-

ture and Woodwork." The bed in the latter illustration
has a flat canopy, or tester, with embroidered hangings.
The walls of the room are panelled, and the floor is in
checkered parquetry. There is a curious seat that is

Fig. 227.—Bedroom Interior; 1400. (P.)

partly an open press, with pottery, and metal vases placed
as decoration on the top.

Chests, trunks, or *bahuts*, were at this period, and in the
time of the Normans, the most important articles in furniture : they were often made with inlaid wood decorations,
and had strap-work of iron and ornate hinges. They were
the usual repositories of the household valuables, money,
and other treasures, and were carried on horses or mules

when the family moved about from place to place. By degrees the chest, with the addition of a back and arms,

Fig. 228.—Seats; Fourteenth Century. (P.)

became the settles or principal seats in the living-room, and the back developed with an added hood or projecting covering into the daïs, or throne-like seat, that was placed at the end of the chief room—the place of honour.

Another and later development of the chest was to raise it on legs, and to add a back arrangement to it, with shelves for the display of household plate, to which was given the name of *dressoir*, or dresser, the latter in time developing into the modern sideboard.

Chests were also important articles of church furniture, in which the sacred vessels, treasures, books, and priests' garments could be locked up, and a particular form of chest

Fig. 229.—The Coronation Chair, Westminster Abbey. (P.)

kept in church vestries was the cope chest, which took

the semicircular shape of the copes when laid out flat in
these chests. Examples of these chests are still to be seen
in some of the large cathedrals.

Fig. 230.—Travelling Carriage; English Fourteenth Century. (P.)

The coronation chair (Fig. 229) gives a good idea of a
state chair of the early Gothic period in England.

Carriages of the fourteenth century were used for the
conveyance of women and children, but were not very

Fig. 231.—Travelling Carriage; English; Fourteenth Century. (P.)

common. They were long-shaped covered vehicles on
four wheels, with or without panelled sides, and were
painted and decorated (Figs. 230, 231). Carts for carrying
and for agricultural purposes were used in the Anglo-
Saxon and Norman periods in England, and in France

Fig. 232.—Table (Kursy); Saracenic. (L. P.)

at the same dates : these were two-wheeled vehicles, each
wheel being usually of one solid piece of wood.

The Saracens were very ingenious in the using of wood,
VOL. II.   S

as in carpentry, carving, and turning in the lathe. Their ingenuity and skill in carpentry and turning is seen in the Meshrebīya work and lattice, and in the carvings of the pulpit and door panels. This work has been noticed under the heading of Saracenic Architecture and Ornament in the former volume.

Regarding the furniture of the domestic dwellings of the Saracens, whether of Egypt, Arabia, or elsewhere, there was very little of a movable nature except the small tables and reading-desks. The tables of Saracenic design are usually small and of a greater height than width (Fig. 232). These tables or *kursys* are sometimes panelled with turned, latticed, or carved decoration, having stalactites under the top, as in the illustration, or in the kursys of a lighter construction are generally inlaid with ivory, ebony, and mother-of-pearl. Some of the richest variety are hexagonal in shape, are inlaid with brass and silver filigree ornamentation, and are of splendid workmanship. The next important article in movable furniture is the Saracen reading-desk, which is made in the form of a camp-stool, with cross legs. It is usually inlaid and decorated like the tables.

The divans are platforms raised slightly from the ground, and covered with cushions on the seats and backs. The carved cupboards or shelves on brackets placed behind and above the divans, on which vases and trays are kept for ornament or when not in use, complete the usual furniture of the Saracenic living-room. Seats or chairs of lattice-work (*dikkas*), on which the doorkeeper sits, are usually found in entrance-halls, and if we add the elaborate metal and coloured-glass lamps, the vases, the large metal salvers or trays, and the rugs and carpets, the furniture of a Saracenic house is complete.

ITALIAN AND OTHER FURNITURE OF THE RENAISSANCE.

In the early part of the fifteenth century and during the whole of the century the furniture of Europe generally was designed more or less on Gothic lines, but gradually the new forms that were now rapidly developing in the architecture of the Renaissance, but in a slower measure, began to assert themselves in furniture designs. Consequently, we find in many articles, such as armoires or presses, and cabinets, a mixture of style in the design—as, for instance, the upper panels would be in the Mediæval, and the lower ones in the Renaissance style, or the general construction would be Gothic, and the details and decoration would be Italian.

This was more often the case in the furniture and other art in Germany, where the Renaissance was tardily welcomed.

Styles of design in furniture overlap each other so much, especially in the Renaissance period, that it becomes very difficult to assign a correct date to many pieces of important work. Gothic designs continued to be used during the sixteenth century, although the Renaissance had been developing for a hundred years earlier. The most authentic means of fixing the date is when certain work can be proved to have come from the hand of a particular artist, or when there is a record of its having been made for a king or some great person, for the style is not always a sure proof of the correct date.

In the " Quattrocento " period (1400-1500), or fifteenth century, Italian furniture made for churches, palaces, or private houses, was usually decorated with paintings, sometimes on a gilt ground, which was prepared in a gesso material before the gold was applied, some parts of which had relief ornamentation.

Reliquaries, altar-fronts, panels of cabinets, chests, and marriage coffers were decorated in this way.

The work known as " tarsia," or certosina work, was made in great perfection about this time in Italy. It is inlaid work of a geometric character in design, or is composed of floral ornament, and sometimes consists of representations of landscapes and buildings. This kind

Fig. 233.—Marriage Coffer of Carved Wood; Italian; Sixteenth Century. (J.)

of inlay was derived from Persian sources, was developed chiefly by the Venetians, and was used mostly by them in the decoration of choir stalls, tables, chairs, cabinets, &c. Ebony, ivory, and metals were also employed in the Italian inlays of this period.

The Italian *Cassoni*, or marriage-coffers, were the most ornate and most imposing articles of furniture of the fifteenth and sixteenth centuries. They were placed in the long halls and corridors of the palaces and great houses, and were usually given as presents to newly married couples. They were generally used as the receptacle for the bride's trousseau and other treasures. In the latter century they were carved in walnut with sculptural mythological subjects, and had endings or corners of half-figures and half-foliage, as caryatids, with feet designed from the claws of animals to raise them from the ground (Fig. 233). The carving was relieved by gilding in parts, and sometimes the whole of it was gilt.

Other examples of an earlier date were covered with a finely modelled decoration of gesso work, and gilded, and in other cases the large panels in the front were painted with figure subjects in brilliant colours and heightened with gold.

A less costly kind of marriage coffer was made in cypress-wood, and fitted up in the inside with drawers, having the decoration on the surface engraved or etched in brown lines, with the ground slightly recessed and punched or stamped with a fine ornamentation.

In the Kensington Museum there is an extensive collection of Italian cassoni embracing all the above varieties. Chairs carved and gilt of the same style and period as the coffers were usually placed between the rows of the latter in the halls of the Italian palaces (Fig. 235). These chairs had their backs and legs richly carved, each part being made out of a single slab of wood.

The pair of bellows (Fig. 234) is a further illustration of the design and excellence of workmanship as shown in the

Fig. 234.—Italian Work; Sixteenth
Century. (P.)

work of the wood carvers of Italy in the sixteenth century, or "Cinquecento" period.

Another fine specimen of wood carving is the Italian stool (Fig. 236) of the same date, which is remarkable for its delicacy of treatment.

Another form of chair of a rectangular character, with or without arms, having an embossed leather or velvet covering on the back and seat, with turned and carved legs and rails, was made in Italy about this time (Fig. 237); it was much used subsequently in Spain, France, and in England, and has continued to be in favour down to the present day.

Cabinets were made in Italy and in France in which slabs of beautifully coloured and veined marbles and rare stones were inserted as panels in various shapes, to which the name of "pietra-dura" work has been given.

In the seventeenth and eighteenth centuries painted plaques of porcelain took the place of these marbles.

In England, France, Spain, and Germany, the great houses, both private and religious, and the king's palaces were elaborately furnished, and kept in a state of great splendour.

Churches were also furnished with elaborate stalls, pulpits, and rich utensils, but in the latter the style of the designs was still Mediæval.

In the reigns of Henry VII. and Henry VIII. in England the style gradually altered to the Italian forms of the Renaissance, and many Italian architects and carvers found work in this country in making furniture for the royal palaces, and besides, great quantities of Italian, Flemish, and French furniture were largely imported. Jean de Mabuse and Torrigiano were employed as architects and sculptors by Henry VII., and Holbein and some Italian artists designed furniture and goldsmith's work for Henry VIII.

Fig. 235.—Chair; Italian; Sixteenth Century. (P.)

In France, during the reigns of François I., Catherine de' Medici, and Henri II., a great activity took place in architecture and in all the industrial arts, in which that country not only imitated, but sought to excel, the work of the Italian schools.

As already mentioned, the French kings and Medicean princesses in the sixteenth century had invited from Italy Cellini, Primaticcio, Il Rosso, Serlio, and others, who succeeded in founding the style of the Renaissance in France,

and about the same time many French artists journeyed to
Italy to acquire the newer style which had been evolved
from the study of the old classic remains of that country.
Among the names of the principal French artists, sculptors,
and carvers of this period are those of Jean Goujon,

Fig. 236.—Stool of Carved Wood; Italian; Sixteenth Century.   (J.)

Nicholas Bachelier of Toulouse, Jean Cousin, Germain
Pilon, Philibert de l'Orme, Du Cerceau, who published
designs for all kinds of decorations and carvings, and
Hugues Sambin of Dijon.   Most of these men were architects and also designers of the heavy and rich furniture
that was characteristic of the French Renaissance.   Some

Fig. 237.—Chair Decorated with Gauffered Leather; Early Sixteenth Century;
Italian Style. (J.)

Fig. 238.—French Cabinet; Sixteenth-Century Work. (P.)

of these artists and their works have been noticed in the chapters on Renaissance architecture and metal work. The cabinet (Fig. 238) is a good example of the architectonic style of French furniture of the sixteenth century.

French wood carving is distinguished from the Italian of this period by the great use of the cartouche and strap-work (Fig. 239), which was so characteristic of the Henri-Deux style.

Fig. 239.—Carved Wood Panel; French; Sixteenth Century. (P.)

When the Renaissance had taken a firm root in Germany, the designers and carvers of altarpieces and of furniture generally proved themselves thorough masters of the style, and were especially skilful in the carving of wood, both on a gigantic and on a minute scale. Whole fronts of houses were elaborately carved in designs consisting of figure work, animals, ornament, and grotesques of a quaint and humorous description, while exceedingly minute works of figure subjects and animals were carved in box and other woods with a delicacy and quaintness often excelling the ivory carvings of the Japanese. Escritoires, buffets, cabinets, and other furniture, were made and exported from Germany into Spain and other countries.

Flemish and English furniture and carving were pretty much alike in the reigns of Elizabeth—the Tudor period of English art—and of James I., the Stuart or Jacobean. The pieces of carved furniture, both Flemish and English, were very solid and heavy both in the design and thickness of the material, which was generally of oak or chestnut. So much Flemish furniture was imported into England at this time, and the English-made work, being so close in resem-

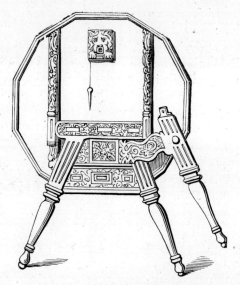

Fig. 240.—Elizabethan Table.   (P.)

blance to the former, that a great difficulty is experienced in classifying examples of this period. The table, Fig. 240, and the so-called "Great Bed of Ware," are examples of the furniture of the Elizabethan period (Fig. 241.)

In Spain the Italian style in furniture was introduced in the first instance by the great importations from Italy and Germany, but under such excellent native carvers and designers as Felipe de Borgoña (sixteenth century), and Berruguete (1480-1561), the style of the Renaissance soon

spread from Toledo to Seville and Valladolid, where great
quantities of carved and inlaid work and elaborate altar-
pieces were executed during the prosperous Spanish period
of the sixteenth century.

During the same century Venice and Florence were
famed for their marquetry—inlaid work of ivory and metal
—in cypress, walnut, and other woods, which art had been
imported from Persia and India by the Venetians, and
which spread rapidly through Europe until the furniture
made with marquetry de-
coration by degrees sup-
planted the heavier clas-
sical architectural designs.

This was brought about
chiefly in the West of
Europe by the Dutch and
French marquetry work,
developed during the seventeenth century.

Before leaving the Italian
sixteenth-century work we
must notice the mirrors,
with their elaborately
carved frames of Venetian

Fig. 241.—The Great Bed of Ware;
Elizabethan. (P.)

design and manufacture. In this century Venice was
renowned for the making of glass, for which it is still
famous, and certain privileges were granted by the State
exclusively to Venetian manufacturers of looking-glasses.
Two Murano glass makers named Andrea and Dominico,
who were the inventors, were granted in the year 1507
the sole privilege of making "mirrors of crystal glass"
for a term of twenty years. Previous to this time the
mirrors were made of various polished metals. The
frames of the Venetian mirrors were often elaborately
carved (Fig. 242), some of them being made in designs
that were strictly architectural in character, representing a
door, or window frame, with pilasters, frieze, and cornice,

and sill or plinth. These carved frames were often partly or wholly gilt, and were exported in considerable quantities. Pictures were framed in a similar way to the mirrors,

Fig. 242.—Venetian Mirror Frame ; Sixteenth Century.   (P.)

and carved and gilt frames were soon used all over Europe as picture frames. Later on gilt furniture of all kinds was made in Venice and was in great favour in the other countries of the Continent.

The manufacture of marquetry furniture by the Dutch in the seventeenth century has been mentioned as having helped in a great measure to change the style of furniture design from its former architectural character to a greater simplicity of construction. Large panel surfaces were used for the purpose of showing to greater advantage the rich and bright colours of different kinds of hard woods used in the marquetry. Both natural and stained varieties of various wood were arranged in the designs in juxtaposition, and a free and picturesque kind of ornamental foliage was employed mixed with large tulips, roses, and birds in the Dutch marquetry decoration. Other materials, such as ivory, ebony, and mother-of-pearl, were also used as inlays. In France a similar kind of marquetry was developed, but the design consisted more of figure subjects and imitations of ruins in landscapes. A complete change in the design of the furniture in the latter country was also effected by the same desire to get large surfaces on which the inlaid work could be seen to great advantage, and the spaces were not divided by architectural mouldings, or pilasters, as they had been in the preceding earlier work.

Towards the end of the sixteenth century, and during the earlier half of the seventeenth, the sumptuous furniture, the beds, and general furnishing of the better class of houses and palaces in France and other European countries, were characterized by the use of costly silk brocades, tissues, and embroidered coverings and hangings.

By thus seeking to give the furniture an appearance of the richest possible kind, such articles as chairs, couches, and beds lost in a corresponding degree their elegance and former constructive beauty. Under their gorgeous Italian and Oriental velvet coverings, their framed construction ceased to be visible. The above pieces of furniture still retained their sumptuous upholstery during the reign of Louis XIV., but the tables, armoires, cabinets, book-cases, pedestals, clock-stands and cases, came under the influence of the architecture of the period, when the

king's chief minister, Colbert, selected the best architects
and cabinet-makers of the day to design the furniture for
the palaces of the Tuileries, the Louvre, and Fontainebleau.
The greatest name connected with the design and manufacture of the magnificent furniture of the Louis-Quatorze
period is that of André-Charles Boulle, whose work is
known under his name as " Boulle." This celebrated furni-
tute is an elaborate kind of marquetry of which the materials
are rare woods, ebony, tortoiseshell, brass, mother-of-pearl,
and white metal or tin. The mountings, mouldings, and
other salient points are made in brass beautifully chased
and finished, some of the mountings being in the forms of
masks, foliage, cartouches, and animals' heads and feet as
termination.

André-Charles Boulle was born in Paris in the year
1642. His father, Pierre Boulle, was also a distinguished
ébéniste, or cabinet-maker, but his more eminent son possessed the artistic gift in a much higher degree. In addition to making his special marquetry from his own designs
Boulle also executed a good deal of his best works from
the designs of Jean Berain (1636-1711), his chief collabora-
teur. Berain's designs were more Italian in style, more
symmetrical in the composition of the ornament, and more
correct from an architectural point of view, than those
attributed to Boulle himself, whose designs had much of
the looseness and freedom of the prevalent Louis Quatorze.

At the death of Jean Macé, the king's ébéniste, in 1672,
who had formerly lived in the royal galleries of the
Louvre, the *logement* and office of ébéniste to the king
had become vacant, and Boulle on the recommendation of
Colbert, minister to Louis XIV., was appointed as the
successor of Macé, and was installed in his rooms in the
Louvre in the year 1673. He had previously executed
some important work for the king, and was known as the
ablest ébéniste at that time in Paris.

The origin of the Boulle marquetry can be traced to the
Indian, Persian, and Damascus encrusted inlays in ivory,

ebony, nacre, and metal, that found their way to Venice, Portugal, Spain, and France in the Middle Ages. These works consisted chiefly of caskets, coffers, and small pieces of furniture. In the inventories of Charles V. of France (1380) mention is made of lecterns and coffers of inlaid ivory or bone, in ebony, and similar works are mentioned in the inventories of Charles VI. (1418), and of Anne of Brittany (1498). These are the earliest notices of marquetry furniture that was made in France, and was probably an imitation of Oriental work.

In the Renaissance period François I. bought some magnificent furniture of Indian workmanship, inlaid with mother-of-pearl, from Portuguese merchants, and mention is made of chairs, tables, coffers, cabinets, and mirror-frames that belonged to Queen Marie de' Médicis (1600), the Cardinal d'Amboise (1550), and other great persons of the French Court, all of which works were made in marquetry.

In France before the sixteenth century, tortoiseshell, brass, tin, and exotic woods were used as inlays, in addition to the ivory, ebony, and nacre of the East. From this it will be seen that Boulle did not invent the celebrated marquetry that bears his name. He, however, brought this sumptuous form of cabinet work to great perfection, and under the patronage of Louis XIV. he had every opportunity to develop his artistic abilities to the utmost.

The method of procedure in the making of the Boulle marquetry was, first, to prepare the veneers of wood, shell, tin, and brass of the same thickness, each having perfectly plain surfaces ; these veneers were then glued together in pairs of opposite materials, according to the nature of the effect required in the finished work, and were held together firmly in a vice. The design was then traced on the surface of the upper leaf, and the veneers were then cut through the lines of the pattern with a burin, a sharp strong knife, or a fine saw ; thus four pieces of marquetry were made at one cutting. When the plaque forming the design was composed of tin or brass, which was afterwards engraved or chased, it was technically called "boulle"; and when the design was formed by the shell or ebony it was called "counter"; the two effects are together known as "boulle and counter," or *première et contre-partie.*

A later kind of Boulle work, known as the Second Style, has the shell veneers laid on a clouded vermilion or on a gilt ground.

Boulle was an artist of great excellence as a sculptor and chaser of metals; his mountings of foliage and masks which decorated his works are spirited in design and are skilfully chased and finished (Fig. 243). He executed a great number of costly pieces of his famous marquetry for Louis XIV. and the Dauphin of France, many of which found their way to England a century later. Examples of Boulle work fetch great prices when, as on rare occasions, they make their appearance in a sale. For instance, two armoires, or large cabinets, were sold at the sale of the Duke of Hamilton's Collection in 1882 for the sum of £12,075. The armoire (Fig. 244) now in the Jones Collection at South Kensington, is perhaps the finest piece of Boulle furniture in England. It is much finer and better designed than the Hamilton cabinets, and would probably, if now sold, fetch the above sum, or more, that was paid for these cabinets. It appears likely, from the style of the ornament, that it was designed by Berain.

After the death of Boulle his four sons carried on the making of this celebrated marquetry, but in a coarser and feebler style of design and of inferior workmanship. Other ébénistes tried to imitate Boulle work, but their efforts were not very successful, and were only inferior imitations.

In Germany in the seventeenth century, the most prominent names as designers and makers of furniture are Philip Heinhofer, Baumgartner, and Hans Schwanhard. The former was the maker of the celebrated Pomeranian Cabinet (1611-1617) which is now in the Royal Museum at Berlin.

In this century, in Italy, Andrea Brustolone (1670-1732)

was noted as a carver, gilder, and cabinet-maker who worked
in the extravagant style of the Louis Quinze (Louis XV.), and

Fig. 243.—Boulle Cabinet, ,S. K. M.)

in the first half of the eighteenth century (1700-77) Pifetti,
a Piedmontese cabinet-maker, was honoured by the Italian
Court, for which he executed many works in ivory carving

Fig. 244.—Boulle Cabinet or Armoire. (S. K. M.)

and marquetry work in the style of Boulle. Many other cabinet-makers and carvers were employed to make furniture and to decorate the queen's palace at Turin, among whom may be mentioned the names of Galleti, the successor of Pifetti, and Maggiolino of Milan, who chiefly made a kind of marquetry in light woods. We are indebted to Mr. J. H. Pollen's handbook on furniture for some of these names, and a list of many others will be found at the end of his useful book.

The French architect, Le Pantre (1617-82), designed furniture and decoration in the heavy classical style of the Roman antique, mixed with shell-work, grotesques, and little Cupids or "putti," and also engraved and published a book of studies of Roman ornament from sketches that his master, Adam Phillipon, had made in Italy. He worked with Le Brun, the painter and director of the decoration at Versailles. Le Brun's own work was heavy and dull, although he aimed at grandeur and gorgeousness of effect. He was director of the Gobelins tapestry manufactory, and his style of work was in harmony with the pompous ideas of Louis the "Grand Monarch." Madame de Maintenon says in one of her letters to a friend, that Louis was so fond of symmetry and stateliness in his architecture, as in other things, that he would have you "perish in his symmetry," for he caused his doors and windows to be constructed in pairs opposite to one another, which gave to everybody who lived in his palaces their death of cold by draughts of air.

Much of the more artistic kind of furniture was imported from the Continent into England during the seventeenth century, and a feature of this period was the highly decorative silver furniture already noticed in the chapter on metal work.

In this century and early in the following one, the art of wood carving was greatly developed in England, chiefly owing to the genius of Grinling Gibbons and to the influence of Sir Christopher Wren, the style developed being a

more or less realistic or baroque form of the Renaissance
(Figs. 245, 246). Gibbons carried out some of his carvings
to an astonishing degree of realism : bouquets of flowers,
festoons of fruit and flowers, birds, figures, and drapery
were executed by him in the highest possible relief, which
looked detached from the ground, and yet they usually
formed a part of the solid wood with the background. Ornament was carved with a singular crispness, and apparently

Fig. 245.—Carved Bracket ; English ; Eighteenth Century.   (P.)

without any hesitation on the part of the carver. Though we
may condemn the florid looseness of the style of Gibbons,
we must admire the dexterity of workmanship and general
technical excellence imparted to everything he touched.
Some of his best work may still be seen at Chatsworth,
Petworth House in Sussex, Lyme Hall in Cheshire, St.
Paul's Cathedral, and Trinity College Chapel at Oxford.
Many of the old English halls and manor houses also contain examples of carving done either by Gibbons or his

pupils and immediate successors, namely, Watson, Drevot, and Laurens.

Under the Regency of Philippe d'Orléans in France (1715-1723) decoration and ornament assumed a light and fanciful character, very naturalistic, but still having some classic details; of this style Claude Gillot is the chief

Fig. 246.—Mirror Frame; Seventeenth Century. (P.)

exponent. Watteau, his pupil, made a great name as a painter of pastoral scenes, *fêtes galantes*, and all kinds of light and daintily-treated subjects of a theatrical and artificial kind of composition. His colour was silvery and harmonious, and sometimes he decorated furniture with pastoral scenes.

The Rococo style had begun under the Regency, if not earlier, and such men as Oppenort, the De Cottes, father and son, François de Cuvilliés, the Italians Bernini and Borromini, and lastly the great apostle of the Rococo, Meissonier, were all designers of furniture or architects who belonged to the period of Louis XV., and who executed

Fig. 247.—Holy Water Vessel; English; Seventeenth Century.   (P.)

works that reflected the loose and unrestrained character of the times (1723-1774). Chinese and naturalistic elements were grafted on, or mixed with, the former Louis Quatorze, with an addition of still life that did duty for architectural form in objects of pottery and metal work, and a combination of shell work; all these elements made

up the style known under the different names of *rococo,
rocaille, baroque,* or Louis Quinze.

Furniture was made with curved and swelling panels to
show to more advantage the marquetry, or paintings on
gold grounds: these kinds of panels and friezes were
known as " bombé."

It is said that the Italian architects, Bernini and Borromini, were the first to introduce the rococo style into
France, but no designer went so far in the wildness of its
vagaries as the French Meissonier. His ornament fur-
nishes a perfect example of the want of balance and
symmetry. He designed for furniture, woodwork, silver-
smithery, and modelled decoration, all of which work
illustrated the broken shell-shaped panels with frilled and
scalloped edgings and curved mouldings.

Rooms were lined with looking-glasses having these
rocaille mouldings, which were well adapted to show to the
best advantage the glitter of the gold leaf that was used
inordinately on the furniture and decoration of the Louis-
Quinze period.

Pierre Germain, Jean Restout, and Jean Pillement are
well-known names of other designers of the rocaille
style.

Painted panels of pastoral scenes and flower groups were
the usual colour decorations of ceilings, furniture, carriages,
and a host of minor articles such as fans, étuis, snuff-boxes,
&c. The latter smaller articles, as well as the state carriages, were decorated with paintings in what was known
as the *Vernis-Martin* style. Martin was a decorator of carriages and an heraldic painter, who invented the particular
hard varnish or lacquer which bears his name. It was
quite likely that this was as near as possible a successful
imitation of the Japanese gold lacquer that decorated the
articles which were at this period imported from Japan by
the Dutch and Portuguese traders into Europe. Carriages,
tables, cabinets, and especially smaller articles like snuff-
boxes and needle-cases, were painted and decorated in

"Vernis-Martin." Some of the smaller objects were
beautifully mounted in chased gold.

It was quite a common practice to cover or to panel

Fig. 248.—Commode, with Lac Panels, and Mounts by Caffieri.   Louis-Quinze Style.

furniture with plaques of Japanese lacquer, and to mount
them in chased metal or ormoulu decorations. A unique
commode is illustrated at Fig. 248, made from panels of

very old Japanese lacquer and highly decorated with ormoulu mounts by Caffieri, a skilled chaser of the Louis-Quinze period.

In the latter half of the eighteenth century an improvement in the design of furniture and of ornament generally crept in, owing to the study of the ornamentation and design of the classic objects that had been found in the buried cities of Herculaneum and Pompeii. These cities had been discovered in 1713, and about forty or fifty years later books were published illustrating the buried remains, which helped to change the public taste, and by degrees a demand arose for designs of a more severe and classic kind.

The prevailing taste was then apparently gratified by the mixture or grafting of a certain quantity of classic forms with the former frivolous style of the Louis Quinze.

The style in furniture and in ornament now developed into what is known as the "Louis Seize" (Louis XVI.), and consisted in its ornament of a composition of thin scrolls, garlands, bows and quivers of arrows, ribbons and knots, medallions with classic cameo-cut subjects. Mouldings were fine and delicately ornamented, and of straight-lined variety; in fact, the straight line now re-asserted itself in architecture and furniture design (see Figs. 249, 250), in refreshing and healthy contrast to the tottering and riotous curves of Louis XV. and the Du Barry period.

Some of the most beautiful furniture expressive of the utmost elegance was made by Riesner and David, and was decorated with ormoulu mounts by Gouthière for the Queen Marie Antoinette. Riesner and Gouthière were the ablest men of their time, who generally worked together in the making and decorating of the finest furniture of this period. We are fortunate in possessing in the Jones Collection at South Kensington some of the very finest examples of this furniture, much of which was made for Marie Antoinette (Figs. 251, 252).

Riesner usually worked in light and richly-coloured

woods, such as tulip-wood, holly, maple, laburnum, purple-wood, and rosewood, for his marquetry work, and used oak for the linings and foundations.

The best pieces of David and Riesner were usually

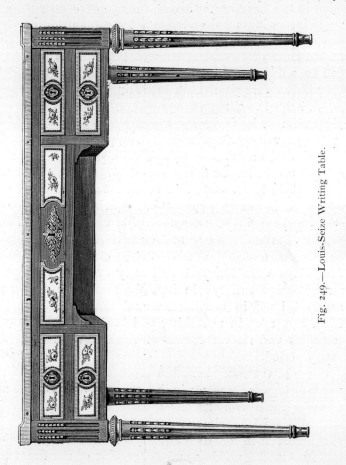

Fig. 249.—Louis-Seize Writing Table.

mounted in ormolu or bronze-gilt metal by Gouthière, who has never been equalled as a founder and chaser of this class of work. Prieur was also a good chaser of the Louis Seize period. Delafosse was an architect and designer of furniture and decoration of the period, whose designs were

of a more heavy and classical kind. Cauvet was a German
who worked in Paris, and designed graceful arabesques

Fig. 250.—Mahogany Cabinet with Sèvres Plaques.   Louis Seize.

and figure work, and who published a book of designs.
Lalonde designed work that might be classed in the same
category as that of Cauvet, and Salembier was a prolific

designer of a light and free kind of arabesque. Many of
his designs for silk may be seen in the fabric at the Silk
Museum in the Bourse at Lyons. Le Nôtre designed for
furniture, carving, and was also famed with La Quintinie
as a designer of the state and public gardens.

Fig. 251.—Escritoire of Marie Antoinette. (Jones Collection.)

In Italy the prevailing ornament in furniture and
decoration was more classical than in France. Piranesi,
Albertolli, Pergolese, and Bartolozzi are names of the
principal designers of this country in the eighteenth
century, most of whom published extensive works on

ornament. The latter two were brought to England by
the brothers John and Robert Adam (1728-1792), who had
travelled in Italy, bringing also with them classical ideas,

Fig. 252.—Table of Marie Antoinette, inlaid with Sèvres Plaques. (Jones
Collection.)

which they developed in England, and which influenced to
a great extent the style of architecture and furniture design
in this country. The Adelphi building and the houses in
Portland Place were built from designs by the Adams,

All kinds of furniture, sedan chairs, carriages, plate, &c., were made from their designs. Fine mouldings, medallions, rosettes, light garlands, capitals in classic form,

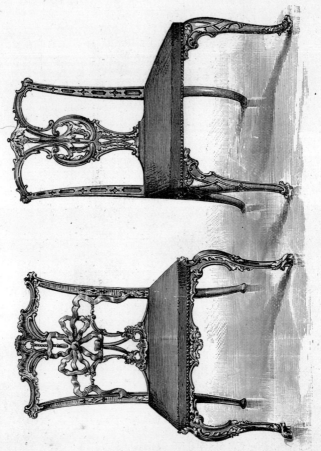

Fig. 253.—Parlour Chairs, by Chippendale. (L.)

fluted pilasters and columns, were all designed by them with the utmost restraint in style—even to coldness.

Thomas Chippendale was a famous cabinet-maker of the eighteenth century. His furniture, or even any good imitation of it, fetches a good price at the present time.

He published a book on furniture design and interior decoration in the year 1764. His sons are supposed to have made nearly all the best of the mahogany furniture known as " Chippendale."

The parlour chairs (Fig. 253) are good examples of Chippendale furniture, and the chairs made in the so-called

Fig. 254.—Chair in the Chinese Style, by Thomas Chippendale. (L.)

" Chinese style " (Fig. 254) are attributed to the elder Chippendale.

Sherraton and Heppelwhite are names of two other well-known cabinet-makers, who made excellent mahogany furniture in the last century, both of whom published works on the subject at the latter end of the century.

The names of Gillow, Lichfield, Lock, and Copeland are those of eminent English cabinet-makers and decorators of this period, the two former firms being still in existence in London.

In France, after the Revolution (1792), a more decided

Fig. 255.—Stool and Chair, Carved and Gilt Mountings ; Empire Style. (L.)

phase of the dry and heavy classicisms was apparent in the furniture design and decoration of the period (1801). This return to classic heaviness has been attributed to the influence of the academic painter David, but is more likely to have been a pandering to the national worship of Napoleon and the French Empire. It seemed to have been the universal desire to make everything echo or

Fig. 256.—Cabinet of Red Chased Lacquer (Japanese) and Porcelain Dish. (J.)

reflect in some measure the glory of the Emperor Napoleon I. The meanest thing had some symbol or allusion by the way of decoration that should remind everybody of the greatness of the new monarch and of the French

Empire, and consequently the heavy and ponderous style
of that period was known as the "Empire Style." The
furniture of the Empire was usually made in mahogany,

Fig. 257.—Lacquered Boxes; Sindh.   (B.)

decorated with mountings in brass or bronze, of sphinxes,
griffins, Roman emblems, and antique scrollery (Fig. 255).
   Percier and Fontaine are names of French cabinet-

makers and designers who worked in the Empire style, and who published a book of their designs.

In England the style was copied, and we find that endless imitations of the French fashion in tables, sofas, chairs, cabinets, and clocks were designed after the same antique ideals.

In this country, during the earlier half of the present century, the mediæval Gothic style was partly revived in architecture and in furniture, mainly owing to the efforts of Augustus W. Pugin, the architect. He designed many pieces of furniture, and published a work consisting of Gothic designs in the year 1835. Notwithstanding the efforts of Pugin and some other eminent architects and " purists," no particular lasting impression was made in this direction.

If we except a few of the best cabinet-makers' shops, where in the present day some furniture of good design is made, the majority of such work is now made by machinery, or is often too much the work of the upholsterer, and is consequently less artistic and more mechanical both in design and construction.

Fig. 258.—Lacquered Leg of Bedpost; Sindh. (B.)

Some of the most beautiful furniture of Japanese and Chinese manufacture is made in carved wood and lacquered in black or red. Cabinets with drawers and quaintly contrived cupboards and recesses (Fig. 256) are made by the Japanese, finished in lacquers, and inlaid with ivory and mother-of-pearl. The Chinese are especially skilled in carving red lac-work. Some vases of great dimensions and of exquisite workmanship in this material may be seen in the Kensington Museum.

Lac-work is also executed with great skilfulness by the natives of India. Bracelets, armlets, or *golias*, are made of lac in various colours, the golden decorations of which are made from tinfoil and varnished with a yellow varnish made of myrrh, copal, and sweet oil boiled together. Boxes, bed-posts, and other furniture, made in wood or *papier-mâché*, are lacquered and decorated with flat renderings of flowers and conventional shapes of animals and birds (Figs. 257, 258). All kinds of toys, weights and measures, cooking utensils, circular playing-cards, turnery, &c., are objects in small wares made in the choicest lac-work of India.

CHAPTER VI.

TEXTILE FABRICS.

WEAVING is an art that has been practised from pre-historic times. Grasses, shreds of bark, rushes, bast, &c., were at first woven, and used as articles of dress and coverings such as we see in use to-day among the uncivilised tribes of the world. The loom is also a very ancient invention, and must have been used much earlier than we have any record of it.

One of the oldest varieties of fabrics made in the loom is that of linen, the threads of which are prepared from the fibrous parts of the flax plant stalk. We have not only Biblical evidence of the weaving of linen by the ancient Egyptians, but the actual material itself, which has been proved by the strictest scientific analysis to be the product of the flax plant.

The oldest kind of Egyptian linen was that used for the swathing bands of the mummies, and was formerly known under the erroneous name of *byssus*, the latter being a material woven from the filaments or beard of the *pinna marina*, or sea-caterpillar.

The various methods and processes used in the manufacture of linen are well illustrated in the Egyptian paintings and bas-reliefs, such as the beating of the flax, combing, spinning, and weaving in the loom. Some of the Egyptian linen was exceedingly fine in texture and perfect in workmanship: a piece of linen found at Memphis had 540 threads to the inch in the warp.

Linen yarn and the raw flax were exported from Egypt

by the Phœnicians and Carthaginians to Greece, Italy, Germany, Spain, and probably to the British Isles. The Greek women wove linen for their garments, as the women of most European countries have done in the ancient and Middle Ages. Germany, Holland, and Belgium have from early times been the chief countries for linen manufacture in Europe. Perhaps at the present day the city of Belfast in Ireland is the most important seat of linen industry in the world, and Dundee in Scotland might claim the second place. For the last two hundred years the linen trade of Ulster has been in a flourishing condition. The English Parliament from the days of William III. to the present time have encouraged and promoted the trade, but the initial success of this industry was owing in a great measure to the skill and energy of Louis Crommelin and the Huguenot colony, who came to the North of Ireland from France after the Revocation of the Edict of Nantes (1685), and in the year 1699 finally settled at Lisburn, near Belfast. A similar colony of French Protestants, who were weavers by trade, settled in Scotland in 1727 under their leader, Nicholas d'Assaville.

A great epoch in the history of weaving dates from the time of the invention of the Jacquard machine, which caused a revolution in nearly all branches of weaving. Jean-Marie Jacquard (1752-1834), the inventor of this machine, was a native of Lyons and a silk weaver by trade. The Jacquard machine is attached to any ordinary loom, and its work consists in mechanically selecting and raising the warp threads, when the shuttle passes across the loom, the action being regulated by means of cards with pierced holes through which the lifting cords or needles pass, the holes in the cards being arranged or cut in accordance with the preconceived pattern that ultimately figures in the woven cloth.

The first Jacquard machine used in England was set up in Coventry in the year 1820.

Silk and its manufacture by the Chinese was known and

understood from a period anterior to the date of 2700 years before the Christian Era.

Perhaps the first knowledge of silk products in Europe was due to the conquest of Persia and portion of India by Alexander the Great, who came in contact with the Chinese, or some people who lived beyond India, and who had probably worn silken garments. To these people the Greeks gave the general name of the *Seres*. This name was not only given to the people beyond India by the Romans, but to the silkworm itself. Aristotle, Virgil, Dionysius the Geographer, and later Pausanias, mention the *seer* or spinning-worm, from which the rich and valuable Oriental garments were made. Pliny says that the Assyrians made silk from the *bombyx* and taught the art to the inhabitants of the island of Cos. Pamphile, the daughter of Plates, made the finest woven silk in the island of Cos. It is supposed that in the first instance the raw material found its way from China, through India, Persia, and Arabia, to the Grecian Isles, and eventually to Italy and Western Europe. In European countries silk at first was mixed with wool or linen, and garments of this material were worn by the Romans.

The thin gauze-like silken garments of Cos were of a pure quality and were imported to Rome in the second century and were reckoned worth their weight in gold. About this time great quantities of the raw silk were brought from the East by the overland route and by sea, and in the end of the fourth century silk had become so cheap as to be within the reach of the common people (Marcellinus, A.D. 380). Tyre and Berytus were the chief seats of silk manufacture from which the Roman markets were supplied.

In the year 552 an event is recorded that revolutionised the manufacture of silk in Europe. The story is related that two monks, either Greeks or Persians, were sent as ambassadors to China, and there learnt the arts and methods of silk production from the natives. They suc-

ceeded in secretly conveying in their hollow cane walking-
sticks a quantity of silkworms' eggs which they brought
to Constantinople, where they were hatched in warm
manure, and the grubs were fed on the leaves of the mul-
berry-tree.   Very soon after this a royal factory was set
up in the palace at Constantinople. Women weavers were
pressed into the Emperor's service, and a state monopoly
was set up for the manufacture of silk fabrics.

The introduction of the silkworm did not cheapen the
price of silk; on the contrary, the production of the royal
looms were sold at excessive prices, and far beyond those
paid for the material before the silkworm rearing period
in Europe.

The court of the Eastern Empire did not hold the silk-
weaving monopoly long, for very soon after the secret of
the rearing of the worms spread to the Peloponnesus
and the isles of Greece, where, from the sixth to the middle
of the twelfth centuries, Europe was supplied with nearly
all the silk it required.

In the year 1130 Roger I., the Norman King of Sicily,
brought a colony of silk weavers from Athens and induced
them to settle in Palermo, where an extensive silk industry
was already developed under the former Saracenic rulers,
who were vassals of the independent Fātimy Khalifs of
Egypt, during the ninth and tenth centuries.

After the introduction of the Greek weavers into the
Palermo workshops we find the Siculo-Arabian designs
altering from the older circular panels of Saracenic ornament, which consisted of the designs of birds and animals
placed back to back, or *vis-à-vis*, of Mesopotamian origin,
to bands of birds, animals, and fishes, grotesque and otherwise, mixed with foliage and scrolls containing mock
Arabic inscriptions.

To trace the analysis of patterns in silk fabrics is to trace
the historical development of the fabrics themselves, for
pattern and manufacture, historically considered, have
developed side by side.

When we consider the varieties indicated by the names of Byzantine, Saracenic, or Arabian in its various forms, Italian and French, we shall find that in the order mentioned the chronological development of material and pattern run concurrently.

Silk, in its raw state, during the first few centuries of our era arrived in the principal towns of Asia Minor, in Alexandria in Egypt, and in Byzantium (Constantinople), from China, by the way of the Indian Ocean and the Red Sea, and overland by caravans.

The Persians and the Byzantine Greeks, from the first to the eighth centuries, monopolised the Western silk manufacture, as they already possessed the looms on which they had made linen, woollen cloth, and carpet tapestry. It required very little adaptation to convert them into silk looms, and towards the early part of the seventh century the new material had firmly established itself in Persia, Syria, and Constantinople.

The patterns for the most part were symbolic and large in character, and nearly all of them had their origin in the " Homa," or sacred " Tree of Life " (Figs. 259, 260), with the worshippers on either side consisting of kings or other personages in the act of adoration, such as we find as a common theme engraved on the Assyrian cylinders, wall decorations, and bronze platters, which had its origin in the older Egyptian forms. Where the Sacred Tree, with animals instead of human forms, was made a feature of in the silk fabrics, the stuff had a Persian development derived from Babylonian sources, but the Greeks or Byzantines used this pattern for the sake of expediency, and not in a symbolic sense.

There is a piece of very old Byzantine silk in the Kensington Collection, and also a piece of the same material in the Silk Museum at Lyons, which consists of a design of winged personages wrestling with lions; the pattern is woven in strips, and the colour is a red ground with white, gold-coloured, blue and green figuring. The style of the

design and peculiarity of the weaving prove it to be of a
date anterior to the eighth century. This particular Byzantine tissue has the red weft of the ground executed in
five different shades of the red colour thrown crosswise
(*lancé croisé*), each shade alternating in three threads by
three ; the warp is thick, and the shuttle passes right across
the width, all the material being pure silk—these are the
marks by which Byzantine fabrics are known.

It is only in genuine examples of Byzantine Greek fabrics

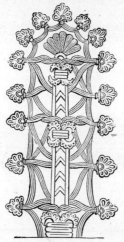

Fig. 259.—Assyrian Homa
or Sacred Tree.

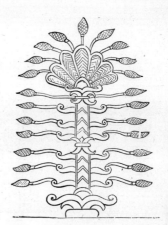

Fig. 260.—Tree of Life, Assyrian.

where we find the human figure is used in the design, or
animals of a free and natural type, as the Byzantine silk
designs were invariably taken from Greek mythological
sources and scriptural subjects. Genuine examples of
Byzantine fabrics are very scarce, and the one described is
a genuine example of great value.

When the Arabs under Mohammed had conquered the
countries of Persia, Syria, and the countries south of the
Persian Sea, they found already in these places the manufacture of silk in a flourishing state. From this time—the

ninth century—until the fourteenth, we find that from the borders of China and India in the east to Africa and Spain in the south and west—which embraces the countries conquered by the Saracens—the silk industry was carefully fostered under the Mohammedan rule. Next to precious stones in importance and value the chiefest treasures of the Khalifs of Bagdad, Cairo, Fez, and Cordova were silken goods. The bazaars of the chief towns were filled with the precious material, and silk fairs or markets were held periodically, chiefly at Antioch, Rey, Erzeroum, Ispahan, Jerusalem, and Mecca. The Mussulman laws forbade the faithful to negotiate with the (Christian) infidels, but there was a saving clause that helped them out of this difficulty, which allowed them to bargain with the Jews, and these middlemen did not scruple to do business with either the Christian infidel or Mussulman.

The Jews were then, as they are now, the bankers, merchants, and dealers in silk and precious stones, and even before this date they were the purveyors of all kinds of articles of luxury to the wealthy Romans of the south, the Gallo-Romans of the west, and the Goths of Northern Europe.

Notwithstanding the laws of excommunication then in force, Italian Christian merchants, as well as Jews, traded with the Mohammedan world, and both Jews and Italians travelled over Asia Minor, North Africa, throughout Italy, Sicily, Spain, France, and England, distributing the products of Saracenic looms, and establishing silk manufactories in Christian countries, notably in Sicily and Italy. Shawls, dress goods, and hangings were then the principal articles of silk manufacture.

Persia was the original place from whence came the best patterns and materials; it was really the fountain-head of textile designs, and from thence they spread over Arabia into North Africa, Sicily, and Italy, the patterns being modified according to the popular taste of the different countries and by the introduction of various symbolic features.

TEXTILES OF INDIA.

The textiles of India form an important section of the industrial arts of that country. The materials used in the woven and embroidered fabrics are silk, cotton, wool, hair, coloured grasses, jute, gold, silver, and various tinsels.

Among the chief artistic productions in textiles are the *kincobs,* or silken brocades, made at Ahmedabad and Benares, the embroidered muslin of Dacca, the pile carpets of Malabar, the rugs of Madras, and the shawls of Cashmere.

The native excellence, however, in the design, colour, and manufacture that has characterised these textiles for centuries past is now in danger of extinction—and great mischief has been done already—from the influence of European designs, the introduction of magenta and aniline dyes, and by the competition with European markets, resulting in the production of cheaper forms of Indian goods. It is only in the case of a few instances where the textiles are made to order, or under the patronage of some of the remaining Indian princes, that the traditional superiority of manufacture is still maintained. Another exception is the production of the silk brocades, or kincobs (Fig. 261); this is owing in a great measure to the demand for these goods by the Chinese and other Orientals, who have not yet adopted the Western ideas of imitating the European style of dress.

Some of these kincobs are highly ornamented with interwoven gold or silver-gilt patterns of floral form, others are ornamented as in the "happy hunting-ground" patterns of Benares manufacture, with flowers, birds, and animals. This particular form of fabric is no doubt a survival, through Persian channels, of the embroidered garments of the ancient Babylonian monarchs.

In the production of cotton goods the trade of the native caste of weavers has suffered very much by the great importation of Manchester cottons, and by the establish-

ment of monster cotton power-loom factories at Ahmedabad
and elsewhere. Many natives of the weaver caste have
been obliged to take to agricultural and other less lucrative

Fig. 261.—Kincob of Ahmedabad. (B.)

pursuits, owing to the partial ruin of their trade by English
competition.

Cotton-printing is still, however, an important native

industry, especially in the city of Lucknow, where the colouring and design are still superior to that of the English or French chintzes. Some of the best Indian, or rather Indo-Persian, ornament is found on the printed calico *palampores*, or bed-coverings, made at Masulipatam and other places. Calicoes woven in varying stripes of coloured threads, checks, and tartans of all hues, are among the specialities of Indian textiles, the material being used for trouserings, skirts, and petticoats.

The once-famous Dacca muslins, that on account of their gossamer-like appearance have been known under the names of "evening dew" and "running water," are now almost non-existent, a cheaper and coarser variety taking their place. Muslins from Dacca and other places embroidered with silk are still greatly used in India, and are largely exported to the surrounding Eastern countries, including Turkey and Egypt.

Cotton fabrics interwoven with golden thread were formerly made in great quantities to meet the wants of the once-powerful native rulers and the Court retinues, but now, since the English rule in India, this kind of fabric with many others of a sumptuous nature are much less in demand.

Printing patterns in gold and silver foil is a common method of decorating dark purple or deep green cottons; muslins are also stamped with patterns in gold.

Fine gold and silver-gilt wire is used very much in India for lace-making, weaving, and embroidery. The natives excel all Europeans in the art of wire-drawing and in the making of gold and silver foil, tinsels, and spangles. These industries are carried on chiefly in the cities of Delhi, Lucknow, Ahmedabad, and Lahore.

Silk manufacture is still a flourishing industry in many parts of India, but, on the other hand, in some places it has declined very much owing to European competition. The *tasar* or *tusser* silk is a native wild silk, from which a coarser variety of silk is now manufactured in increasing quantities, and is exported chiefly from Bengal. It is a useful material, but has not the brilliancy or sheen of the ordinary silk. Plain silk cloth is made in the Punjaub, and the damasked or figured variety is made chiefly at Bhawalpur.

Cashmere has been famed for centuries past for its beautiful woollen shawls made from *pushm*, the wool of the Cashmere goat, and from camel's hair wool; the woven material of the latter is known as " camlet."

The principal design on the Cashmere shawls is the cone pattern decorated with a mixture of small flowers, the fillings between the cones being also a diapering of small floral forms. The cone patterns are also found on metal work, enamels, and carvings from Cashmere and its neighbourhood. On the genuine shawls the ornamentation is embroidered in wide borders, centrepieces, and corner groups of flowers. The Cashmere shawls have been imitated in woven shawls by the French and in the Paisley shawls of Scotch manufacture. Some of the costliest Cashmere shawls are embroidered with a " terrestrial paradise" of singing birds, flowers, animals, and figures.

Indian ornament or decoration, from its mosaic-like or flattened-out character, is extremely well suited to the decoration of textile fabrics. The native ornament consists of a variety of flat renderings of the daisy (*sventi*), the lotus, the shoe flower (Figs. 91, 92, 261), knop and flower patterns, parrots, peacocks, lions, tigers, elephants, men on horseback, hunting or fighting, &c., and is always rendered in flat tints of alternating colours on flat grounds, in such works as enamels, tiles, pottery, wall paintings, lac-work, and textiles of all kinds. Though at times the vice of Indian ornament is illustrated in a riotous use of small detail, on the whole it is well suited for the decoration of flat surfaces. In the artistic products of the Moham- medan people of India, or descendants of Persian settlers, the ornament invariably consists of Persian or Saracenic types; the former is distinctly seen in the Masulipatam rugs, carpets, and *palampores*, and the latter in the various art work of the Mogul period, as, for instance, in the inlaid marbles and other work of Agra. (Fig. 293.)

The Sassanian Persian designs in silk, as we have seen, were derived from the more ancient Assyrian and Babylonian embroideries, the motives of which were invariably the Tree of Life, or "Grove of Ashareh," with divinities, priests, or royal worshippers on either side, the whole usually enclosed in circles.

In the Persian and in the later Mesopotamian Mōsil-work animals took the place of the human figures, and were often placed back to back, divided by a stem or piece of floriated ornament—a reminiscence of the sacred tree—and still enclosed in a circular band. The animals were generally lions, cheetahs, or were griffin forms, all treated as ornamental abstractions, and the intervening spaces between the circles were filled up with forms of parrots or other birds, conventionally treated.

The early Saracenic designs were copies of these (Fig. 262). Later Saracenic designs had less of the bird and animal forms, and more of the purely Arabian ornament, with the addition of horizontal bands of Kufic inscriptions such as texts from the Koran, laudatory compliments to and names or titles of Sultans and Khalifs for whom the fabrics were made (Fig. 263).

It is singular that the rich silken fabrics made for and by the Saracens had nearly always representations of animals in the designs, although this was contrary to the laws of their faith; but this may be accounted for by their practice of copying or adapting the forms of decoration already in use in the countries they had conquered, and their lack of originality in design during their earlier days was, perhaps, the strongest motive in causing them to adapt ready-made inventions to their own uses.

The wearing of pure silken garments was also forbidden by the Mohammedan religion, but the Saracens got over that difficulty by the mixture of a few cotton threads with the silken web. The Egyptian Mamlūks (1250-1390) were very prodigal in the use of silk for dresses, banners, tent hangings, carpets, and horse clothing, supplied from the looms of Cairo and Alexandria, and imported from the Eastern centres.

In the thirteenth century the silk industry of the Saracens was in its greatest vigour, with designs mostly in

Fig. 262.—Silk Damask; Eleventh Century; Early Saracenic (L. P.)

imitation of the Persian school, and in the fourteenth the same motives were used, but arranged in rows of horizontal bands—which is essentially a Greek method—and was due to the influence of the Greek and Christian Coptic designers. A good example of this style may be seen in the peacock design, Fig. 264.

On account of the seaboard of Asia Minor having a mixed population of Jews, Christians, and Saracens, silk fabrics from that country were decorated with imitations of Persian designs, having the "homa" or "tree of life," Christian elements, such as the cross, seen in the "tree of

Fig. 263.—Silk Fabric of Iconium; Arabian; Thirteenth Century. (Lyons Museum.)

life" (Fig. 265), and also imitations of Arabic writing. The Syrian examples of textiles are not so good in material or workmanship as the Byzantine or old Persian.

Fig. 264.— Arabian Silk Wall Hanging of the Fourteenth Century. (J.)

The most interesting development in the design of silk fabrics is that which took place in Sicily. The Sicilians were first taught the art of spinning and weaving of silk and the rearing of the silkworm by their rulers the Saracens of Egypt, and the early designs of the Siculo-Arabian style have, in addition to the Persian cheetahs, Indian parrots, and antelopes, such animals of African origin as the giraffe, elephant, gazelle, and other fauna of that continent. Gold, silver, and cotton threads were used with the silk in these fabrics.

Fig. 265.—Apostolic Tree of Life, with the Cross Emblem.

Mention has been made that in the twelfth century, when the Normans conquered Sicily, of their bringing silk weavers from Athens and from other parts of Greece to work at Palermo. Here and at this time (1130) a distinct alteration of the design took place by the introduction of the Greek classic and Christian elements of ornament in mixture with some of the older Saracenic forms.

Mock Arabic inscriptions were also used very much in these Sicilian fabrics; this may have been done by Christian designers ignorant of Arabic, in order to give to the fabrics an appearance of Saracenic work, which, perhaps, made them sell better when exported (Fig. 266).

Another peculiarity of the Palermitan silks is the multitude of elements found in the designs. All kinds of fabulous animals and birds are used as in heraldic blazoning : sunbursts, cloud-forms, Christian emblems and elements occurring as forms of angels with swinging censers, initials of sacred names, and emblematic plants. The use of these heraldic and Christian elements was in a great measure due to the influence of the Crusaders in the Middle Ages. The favourite colouring of the Sicilian silks was dark red grounds and green foliage; the birds, animals, and mythological

Fig. 266.—Silk Damask ; Sicilian ; with Imitated Arabic Characters.   (R.)

elements were usually woven in gold threads as in the example given (Fig. 267).

Towards the end of the fourteenth century and during the fifteenth the designs became more floriated, the vine and pomegranate, with vase forms, were used and were really

developments from, and did duty for, the sacred tree of the
early patterns, and instead of a circular framing the flamboyant or ogival diaper lines were introduced. This repeating framework was derived from the Saracenic Pointed

Fig. 267.—Silk Damask; Sicilian; Fifteenth Century. (L. P.)

architecture and adopted in the ogival Gothic at this date
(Figs. 268, 269).

During the sixteenth century the pineapple was used
very much under a variety of modifications as an ornamental form in fabrics (Fig. 269), and often in company
with the pomegranate. This came about after the discovery
of the West Indies, from where the pineapple had been

imported into Europe (Fig. 270). Large-pattern damask diapers, brocades, and velvets were now made in many places in Italy, with patterns based on waving lines or ogival forms enclosing bilateral schemes of ornament, all of which were reminiscences of the " tree of life " patterns, and

Fig. 268.—Silk Damask ; Florentine ; Fifteenth Century.

in all may be traced the strong influences of Saracenic design.

From the fourteenth to the sixteenth centuries, and even later, Lucca in Tuscany, Genoa, Florence, and Venice were celebrated for the manufacture of silken brocades and velvets, which have been used for the dresses of priests, kings, and noblemen, as well as for hangings.

The dress patterns of those days were all of a very large size of diaper, such as are now only used for hangings and furniture coverings. The Venetian and Spanish pictures

Fig. 269.—Diaper in Velvet Brocade ; Italian ; Sixteenth Century.

of the period contain many illustrations of these patterns
on the dresses of the figures and hangings of the chambers.

In France the silk weaving industry was first established

Fig. 270.—Velvet Brocade; Italian; Sixteenth Century.

at Lyons about the middle of the sixteenth century. The
designs of the first efforts of the French weavers were very

similar if not copies of the prevailing Italian school, but
soon after became more floral in character, and more and
more realistic renderings of flowers and foliage, until about
the eighteenth century, when they partook of the same
character as the pottery and furniture decoration, which
has been already described.   During the Mediæval and
Renaissance periods France, like England, imported silks
and velvets from Italy and the East, and their linen and
drapery from Flanders and Germany.

Bruges in Flanders was especially famous during the
sixteenth century for its silks and velvets, and Yprès was
even more so for its fine linens and damasks.

Very little silk was manufactured in England prior to
1629, when about this date a company of silkmen was
formed in London.   The Revocation of the Edict of
Nantes in 1685 had the effect of firmly establishing the
manufacture of silk in England by the colony of French
refugees who settled at Spitalfields, St. Giles's, and Soho
in London, and at Canterbury, Norwich, and Coventry.
The trade soon afterwards spread to Manchester, Maccles-
field, and Paisley in Scotland, and the first silk mill
for spinning and throwing was erected at Derby by
John Lombe in the year 1717, which was worked by water
power.

The designs for the patterns of English silks have always
been more or less imitations of the prevalent French styles,
and, in fact, England depended largely until late years on
the efforts of French designers for nearly all of its textile
patterns.   This is not the case, however, to-day, for very
few foreigners are now employed as designers by English
manufacturers.

The chief seat of the velvet manufacture in Germany at
the present day is Crefeld; Switzerland produces great
quantities of silk, which is made chiefly at Zurich and the
villages on the banks of the Lake of Zurich, at Bâsle, and
other places.

China, the birthplace of silk, and younger Japan are still

famed for their delicate fabrics in this material, from whence the raw products are imported extensively into Europe. In America the silk industry has made great headway of late years, the principal seat of the manufacture is the town of Paterson in New Jersey.

England has always held its own in the manufacture of woollen goods of good material, mostly of plain cloth, but sometimes inwrought or woven with designs of figures, animals, and foliage patterns. At Bath, Norwich, Worcester, and in the abbeys and great religious houses during the Middle Ages the monks employed a good deal of their time at the loom, and considerable quantities of their work were exported to the Continent during the fourteenth century. The town of Worsted in Norfolk has given the name —worsted—to a cloth made there from a new preparation of the woollen yarn, which consisted of a special twisting of the threads so as to make the yarn of a harder texture. This cloth has been used for church vestments, hangings, and bed coverings.

Cotton, the woolly product of the cotton-tree, and the cloth made from it, has been known in India and the East from the earliest times.

Pliny mentions cotton under the name of a fabric called *oxylina*, made from the cotton that grew about the branches of the *xylon* or *gossypium* tree, or shrub, which grew in India, Upper Egypt, and Arabia.

The Romans imported cotton fabrics from India, and the priests of ancient Egypt used it for their dresses.

The cotton plant was cultivated by the Moors in Spain about the beginning of the tenth century, and they were the first people in Europe to make cotton fabrics. They are also credited with the invention of fustian-making (Spanish, *fustes*), a cotton material woven and afterwards cut precisely like velvet; it is generally thought that as fustian preceded the manufacture of velvet, the making of the latter may have been suggested to the Italians by the Spanish fustian.

In the year 1585, after the sacking of Antwerp, some
Flemish weavers settled at Manchester—now the great
seat of cotton manufacture in England—and commenced
the new industry of cotton spinning and weaving.   Before
this date Manchester and its neighbourhood were noted
for the weaving of linen.   The linen yarn was imported
from Ireland, woven at Manchester, and the cloth sent
back for distribution and sale in Ireland and other parts
of the kingdom.

The power of production in cotton goods was enor-
mously increased by the inventions of Arkwright with his
water-frame spinning machine, Hargreaves, who in 1770
invented the spinning-jenny, and by Compton, who
improved on the latter by his invention of the mule-jenny
in 1779.

In 1785 Dr. Cartwright invented an automatic loom,
which others improved on, when finally Horrocks, of
Stockport, in 1803 brought to a successful issue his
invention of the power-loom now in general use.

Cotton printing and dyeing in colours have been successfully practised in India, Asia Minor, the Levant, and
in the East generally from the earliest times.   The patterns
found in the commoner prints and chintzes of to-day have
still reminiscences of Indian and Persian ornament.

Most of the English designs in cotton prints of the more
important classes have a strong tendency to floral patterns
of a naturalistic type, the outcome of the imitation of
French silk patterns that were common in the early part
of this century.

Calico block-printing was introduced into England
about the middle of the eighteenth century by Robert
Peel—the grandfather of the first baronet—who cut his
own blocks.   Printing by means of cylinders was invented
in 1785.   Previous to the invention of calico printing
"painted cloths" of linen and other fabrics were used as
hangings and in the general furnishing of English apart-
ments.

EMBROIDERY.

The earliest method of decorating textiles was that of embroidering. It has been called "painting with the needle," and is even an older art than pattern weaving. In some of the oldest monuments of art that are still in existence, as the bas-reliefs of Egypt and Assyria, there may be seen representations of the embroidery that formerly decorated the kings' garments (see Figs. 162A to 165, former volume), and we have seen that these were the models for some of the earliest woven patterns. At first embroidered patterns would be simple geometrical designs, and afterwards symbolic units mixed with simple floral forms, as many of the older Egyptian embroidered patterns usually were, until by degrees the higher forms of patterns with figures or personages and animal forms were developed by the Chaldeans and Assyrians.

The latter nations, with their inherent love of barbaric splendour and Asiatic predilections for georgeous colouring, surpassed the Egyptians in the art of embroidery.

The Persians and surrounding nations inherited from the older races this love of colour and early traditions of design, which are still seen in their tapestry, carpets, and embroidered work of all kinds.

The ancient Phrygian and Lydian people, who inhabited a portion of Asia Minor, were cultured races whom the Greeks and Romans always regarded as the inventors of embroidery—"*phrygio*" being the Roman word for embroiderer. The Phrygian embroidered patterns were mostly geometric, but in the later periods plant and animal forms were also used. Most of the decoration of the Ionian Greek pottery, consisting of bands of animals, birds, rosettes, and lozenges, are copies from the embroidered work of Asia Minor. To-day, even, the women of these parts embroider their bodices, aprons, head-coverings, and towels in an almost similar style of ornament.

The rock-cut façades of the Phrygian tombs, unlike the

imitated timber constructions of the Lydian tombs, have sculptured decorations that have been copied from geometrical forms of embroidery, and in many cases these façades resemble an embroidered curtain or carpet that would be hung up to serve the purposes of a door to the entrance of the earlier square domestic wooden buildings, of which the Phrygian and Lydian tombs were imitations in stone.

The Assyrian thresholds (Fig. 166, former volume) and many other sculptures and wall decorations in painted tiles of Chaldean and Persian origin were usually copies of embroidery, all of which clearly shows that embroidery and pattern weaving preceded stone, wood, and metal sculpture.

The Greeks were highly skilled in making embroidery. Homer repeatedly alludes to this art as an employment for women. Helen of Troy and Penelope wrought beautiful robes and hangings in their looms, embroidering them with rich needlework. On a Greek vase from Chiusi, Penelope is represented at work on a loom of the " high warp " (*haute-lisse*) or vertical pattern which is used so much to-day by the embroiderers and carpet weavers of the East. We have many allusions in the Bible to those who made all kinds of cunning needlework. Josephus says that the veil of the Temple at Jerusalem " was a Babylonian curtain embroidered with blue and fine linen, with scarlet and purple, and of a texture that was wonderful."

In England, during the Anglo-Saxon times, embroidered work had a great reputation, so much so that it was greatly prized and in request in France and other parts of Europe, where it was known as " Anglicum Opus." From an inventory of Charles V. of France (1364-80) we learn that he had a room furnished with English " hullings " or hangings embroidered in blue, with figures of lions, eagles, and leopards. Embroidery was the chief occupation of Anglo-Saxon and Anglo-Norman ladies. Bede and other old historians frequently extolled the excellence of design and workmanship of the English embroidered palls, copes, corporals, chasubles, and hangings. After the Conquest and during the Norman period all kinds of heraldic devices were introduced amongst the ornament and floriated patterns; sometimes stories and romances were illustrated with the needle, and belonging to this order the famous Bayeux Tapestry may be mentioned, which represented in the form of a long frieze the Conquest of England by the Normans. It is supposed to have been wrought by Queen Matilda and her maidens, but was probably made to the order of Odo, Bishop of Bayeux, and brother-in-law to the Queen. It is not only a celebrated piece of needlework, but is an invaluable record of the costume of the period (Fig. 271). A coloured photograph of it is now in the Kensington Museum.

Fig. 271.—Norman Archer from the Bayeux Tapestry.

About the date of the thirteenth century various technical names were given to the different kinds of embroidery, such as "*opus plumarium,*" or, as it is now called, "feather-stitch," a kind of needlework where the stitches are laid lengthwise, and not across, overlapping each other like the feathers in a bird's plumage; "*opus pulvinarium,*" or "cushion" style, where the work is done in cross and tent stitch; "*opus pectineum,*" where the embroidery is made to represent or imitate weaving, and had the design carried through from front to back of the foundation material. The Opus Anglicum, so highly prized, seems to have been a kind of chain-stitch embroidery, giving a granulated surface. The workwoman would start, for instance, in the case of executing the face of a human figure, at a point in the centre of the cheek or chin, and work around it in a circular method, and where the hollows and dimples would

Fig. 272.—Part of the Orphrey of the Syon Cope; in the South Kensington Museum.

occur, a heated metal rod with a small bulb at the end of it would be used to press down the cavities.

In the well-known Syon Cope, an English embroidery of this period (Fig. 272), both the old feather-stitch and the chain-stitch are used as above described.

The *Crewel* stitch is a combination of the long and short

Fig. 273.—Carpet from Persia, embroidered in Gold and Silver on Dark Blue Velvet; Early Eighteenth Century. (S. K. M.)

feather-stitches, and is adapted for shading effects. In the stitches known as chain, knotted, and button-hole stitch the thread is looped; but lies flat in satin-stitch, crewel, darning, tent, and cross stitches. Satin and darning stitches can be worked so that the design appears the same on both sides of the cloth, but chain and crewel stitch only produces the design on one side of the material.

Gold thread has been used very much in all ages in embroidery, and silver thread also, but unless the latter is

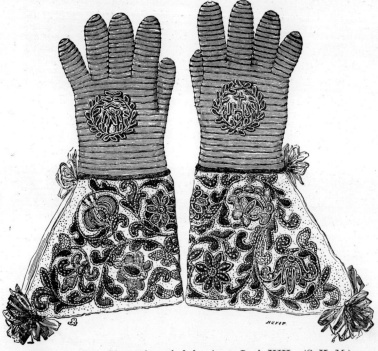

Fig. 274.—State Gloves, formerly belonging to Louis XIII. (S. K. M.)

varnished or lacquered it goes black by tarnishing. Gold " passing " is a silver-gilt thread wound around silk.

In old embroideries and woven tissues a gold thread was made of thin parchment gilded and twisted around silk: the Japanese used gilded paper in the same way, and sometimes the pure gold was used in thin, flat, beaten-out strips for both embroideries and woven fabrics.

In Persia and in the East generally an extensive use is

made of cloths of gold and silver embroidery (Fig. 273) as well as closely-covered needlework in silk and wool, and another modern kind is white silk embroidery on white cambric or calico.

Cut work or "appliqué" is another form of embroidery, where flowers, foliage, ornament, and figures are separately wrought with the needle, and the spaces cut out of the ground material into which these pieces were inserted. Many examples of Spanish, Rhenish, and Florentine needlework may be seen in the Kensington Museum, in which the architectural portions of the design are woven, and the figures of saints and other subjects worked on fine canvas and inserted in the panel spaces. Another and commoner kind of appliqué work is where the ornamental shapes are cut out of silk, velvet, linen, or woollen material, and sewed on to the cloth foundation, an edging material being used consisting of silk cord, gilt leather, or gimp. Appliqué work is more adapted for hangings and furniture coverings than for dress material, though it was formerly used for dresses. The illustration (Fig. 274) gives a very good idea of the style of ornament in Spanish or French embroidery of the Renaissance period.

TAPESTRY.

Tapestry weaving is an art that requires greater care and skill on the part of the workman than any other branch of textile manufacture, especially in that kind known as "storied tapestry," in which is woven a design or picture copied from a previously executed cartoon.

Tapestry is woven in the "high warp" (*haute-lisse*) or in the "low warp" loom: in the former case the loom is vertical, and in the latter horizontal. The largest sized and the more important kinds of tapestry, such as the "Gobelins," are made in the high warp looms.

On account of the skill required, the accuracy and difficulty connected with the weaving of storied tapestry, it takes a long time to educate and perfect the training of a tapestry weaver—who must be an artist himself, so much being left to him in the selection, harmonizing, and shading of the different colours, even after the design is made that he is required to copy.

In tapestry weaving the warp is covered by the woof on both its sides. The warp is divided into two leaves or parts by a thread, and by a glass rod or tube called the *báton de croisure*.

"To form the web, the workman takes a shuttle mounted with wool or silk, the end of which he fastens to the warp to the left of the space to be covered by the colour in his shuttle; then passing his left hand between the two leaves, separated by the *báton de croisure*, he draws towards him the thread which this shade is to cover; his right hand, passing between the threads, lays hold of the shuttle, which he brings to the right, and his left hand taking hold of the coats brings forward the back thread of the warp, while the right hand returns the shuttle to the place from which it was first moved. This passing and returning of the shuttle forms what is called two shoots or a course." (De Champeaux).

One of the great difficulties of the weaver is the shading off or gradation of the colours, which is rendered more difficult by the design being reproduced on the wrong side from the position of the weaver. Hatching and stippling are resorted to in order to prevent a harsh or mosaic-like appearance, and it is here that the great skill and artistic knowledge of the weaver are most required. An extraordinary number of tones and shades are used in an important piece of work, all of which require to be fast dyed in colour in order to secure durability of tone in the fabric. It is said that M. Chevreul, the late famous French chemist and director of the dyeing department of the Gobelins, had composed a chromatic prism of 14,420 different tones.

The best wool used in principal tapestry works on the

Continent has always been imported from Kent in England.

The art of tapestry weaving was originally acquired from the East, where carpets of a floral and ornamental design were woven in the imitation of the old hand-made embroideries. In Europe the names of Sarazins or Sarazinois tapestry were given to these products from the fact that they were made and exported by the Saracens. Perhaps the earliest woven tapestries of Europe were the Flemish, which were first made towards the end of the twelfth century. The towns of Arras, Oudenarde, Lille, Brussels, Valenciennes, Tournay, and Bruges were celebrated for the manufacture of tapestry, of which the town of Arras was the most important, hence the old name of "Arras" used in England for all kinds of storied tapestry.

Flanders was a rich and powerful country during the fourteenth and fifteenth centuries, and at that time the ports of Bruges and Antwerp were the greatest in the world. The various trades were protected by the great corporations or guilds against the encroachments of the nobles on their rights, and the most sturdy and turbulent of all the guilds was that of the Flemish weavers, by reason of their numbers and general prosperity of their trade. The product of the Flemish looms found its way to all parts of Europe and particularly to England, and as far as design and workmanship were concerned, and in the flat treatment of the former to the material, these old Flemish tapestries have never been excelled. The flat decorative treatment in the figure subjects of the earlier work, consisting of allegorical designs and romances by such artists as Roger van der Weyden, Stuerbout, Hugo van der Goes, and other artists of the Van Eyck school, were singularly appropriate to the material, and immensely superior to the more gorgeous effects of colour and misapplied shading of the later French tapestries. Examples of this earlier work are still in existence in the museums and palaces of Europe.

Louis XI., King of France, took the town of Arras in 1477, and this was practically the death blow to the manufacture of tapestry at that place, but immediately after this event Brussels under the Burgundian rule rose to great prosperity. Artists and tapestry weavers flocked to Brussels, which soon became a great centre of this industry. Designs were sent from Italy by the Popes and other princes to be woven in tapestry, and many of the best Italian and Flemish painters made designs for the Brussels ateliers. Pope Leo X. had the tapestries—now in the Vatican—from the celebrated cartoons by Raphael, made in Brussels. These cartoons are now in the Kensington Museum. They were bought by Charles I. from a tapestry manufactory of Brussels by the advice of Rubens.

Giulio Romano, the Italian painter, Lucas van Leyden, Bernard van Orley, Jean Mabuse, and other artists of the Renaissance period, furnished designs for Brussels tapestry.

Owing to the occupation of Flanders by the Spanish (1555-1648), the palace at Madrid contains the most extensive collection of Flemish tapestries in existence, which had been chiefly acquired during that period.

Tapestry making declined and was almost non-existent during the religious wars of the sixteenth century, but was re-established and became once more a flourishing industry in the seventeenth century, and a decree was passed in 1647 for its support by the State.

The subjects of the storied tapestry were now of a more naturalistic order: hunting scenes, landscapes, and rustic figures were woven from the designs of the Dutch and Flemish painters of the period, and many of the designs were copied from French tapestry.

The family of Pannemaker, celebrated at a former period in Brussels, set up an important atelier in Lille about 1647, which remained in full working order for about fifty years. Another well-known tapestry master named Guillaume Werniers (1701-1738) executed many compositions designed by Teniers.

Among the earliest tapestry manufactories in France was the one established at Fontainebleau in the year 1539 by Francis I. It was managed by Philibert Babou, the king's architect, and Serlio, the Italian architect and painter, designed some of the tapestries. The same manufactory existed under Henri II., with Delorme for its director and Ducerceau as the chief designer. Many tapestry weavers were attracted to France from Flanders and Italy at this period, and a colony of Flemish weavers who had settled in Paris were joined to the house of the Gobelins—a long-established family of scarlet wool dyers—in the Faubourg Saint Marcel in 1603. The house of the Gobelins had been under royal patronage for some time previous to the year 1667, when it was bought by Louis XIV. and henceforth became a royal monopoly.

Lebrun, the painter to the king, was appointed director. Some very heavy and inappropriate compositions of this painter were copied in the Gobelins tapestry, but besides these, many purely decorative and ornamental designs with rich borders were also produced. This was a period of great activity at the Gobelins factory, when nearly three hundred workmen and artists were employed. Mignard was the successor of Lebrun as director of the works (1690), then Mansard the architect. After him came the Duc d'Antin as director (1708-36), and then M. de Marigny, under whom many large paintings were reproduced in tapestry, and smaller designs of Boucher and others. This celebrated factory, like that of the Sèvres porcelain, still remains under State care and patronage.

Several other tapestry manufactories existed in Paris from the early days of the Gobelins, and a new kind of tapestry-carpet called the Savonnerie—a kind of velvet carpet made in imitation of the Oriental Turkey-stitch, was introduced into France under the patronage of Henri IV. (1580-1610), the looms being set up in the Louvre. This carpet manufactory was united to the Gobelins factory in 1826.

At Beauvais a celebrated manufactory of low warp tapestry has been in existence from early times, and though some of the Beauvais compositions are equal to the high warp productions of the Gobelins, the work as a rule consists of a smaller and more ornamental character of design.

Rheims, Aubusson, and Felletin have also been centres of the French tapestry industry. Aubusson carpets and tapestry have been noted for their soft and delicate textures, and have been used very much for furniture upholstery.

Italy has produced some good storied tapestry in the sixteenth century (Fig. 275), but has been more celebrated for its velvets, &c.

England has been content to import more tapestry than it has ever manufactured, although many important works have been executed at different times in this country. Probably the earliest piece of genuine English tapestry is that which still adorns the old St. Mary's Hall or Council-chamber in Coventry, and may have been made in the fourteenth, or early fifteenth, century.

In the laws of Edward IV. (1344) tapestry making is mentioned, and in the reign of Henry VIII., and the year 1509, Sheldon and Hicks set up a tapestry manufactory at Barcheston in Warwickshire.

The most important tapestry works were those set up at Mortlake, near London, in the reign of James I., by Francis Crane, and which were liberally supported by James and his son Charles I. During the reign of the latter monarch the Mortlake works furnished a great many important hangings for the royal palaces of Windsor, Hampton Court, Greenwich, and St. James's, among which were the reproductions of the celebrated cartoons of Raphael, which Charles I. had purchased from Brussels. Some of these tapestries are now preserved in the " Garde Meuble " at Paris. Mythological subjects, framed with rich borders, were designed by Francis Cheyne, a native of Saxony, who was the principal artist employed at the

Fig. 275.—Dismissal of Hagar and Ishmael by Abraham   Italian Tapestry;
Sixteenth Century.

Mortlake works. During the wars of the Commonwealth the factory was closed, but was re-opened at the Restoration of Charles II., who passed some Acts for the encouragement of English tapestry making, and put restrictions on the great importations of foreign tapestries. The latter king employed Verrio the painter to make designs for the Mortlake textiles. On the death of Francis Crane, the founder, in 1703, the works were finally closed.

Unimportant tapestry works were in existence at Soho and Fulham about the middle of the eighteenth century. Another attempt at tapestry weaving was made by a French Protestant refugee named Passavant, who established a factory at Exeter about the end of the seventeenth century, and of late years there has been an attempt made to carry on tapestry weaving at Windsor under the patronage of Her Majesty.

Some excellent work, equal if not superior to some of the best Flemish tapestry, has been successfully made by William Morris from the designs of Sir Edward Burne-Jones.

England has given great attention to the manufacture of low warp carpets, in which she is only excelled by some of the best products of Oriental looms. The manufacture of printed and woven carpets now forms one of the most important factors in the national prosperity of England. Brussels carpets are now made chiefly at Kidderminster; originally they were made at Wilton. Axminster and Kidderminster carpets are made in Glasgow, Wilton, and Kilmarnock, and Wilton carpets in Yorkshire.

Turkey carpets are imported chiefly from Smyrna. Persia, India, and Tunis are still great centres of the Eastern carpet industry. The carpets from these places are in great request in Europe for their beauty of colour and design and for their great wearing qualities.

Carpets were originally used as *portières*, table and couch coverings, but have gradually become coverings for floors, owing to their cheapened cost of production.

LACE.

Hand-made laces are divided into two great classes —the "needle-point" and the "pillow-made"; the former is made with a needle on parchment, and the latter by twisting or plaiting threads from bobbins on a pillow.

Needle-point lace is an offspring of embroidery, and pillow-made lace is the highest artistic development of twisted and plaited threads. The foundation lines or threads of the pattern, various kinds of grounds, and the edging in needle-point lace, are usually worked over with a button-hole stitch in the ordinary course of making, while this distinguishing feature of needle-point lace is absent in the pillow-made varieties.

The earliest forms of lace were known as "lacis," or darned netting, and a species of embroidery called "cut-work." One kind of cutwork consisted in cutting, vandyking, or scalloping the edges of collars, cuffs, or garments into various shapes, and overcasting the edges with the button-hole stitch; another kind was when an embroidered design was wrought on stretched network, and the pattern wrought in looped stitches with the needle. This was the transitional form between embroidery and lace work.

"Lacis," or darned netting, was worked in regulated stitches on a ground formed in squares, called "reseuil," and sometimes it was formed of pieces of linen cut out and applied to the net. Ornamental open-work of cut linen and other material embroidered with silks of various colours, gold and silver threads, and woollen yarns, were made before the sixteenth century. All these varieties, though akin to lace work, required some kind of a foundation, but lace consists of a combination of threads alone, and has no foundation.

Pattern-books were published in Venice of designs for "cutworks" and embroidery of all kinds as early as 1527,

and later, in 1531, a book was published by Tagliente,
giving the descriptions and methods employed for making
the various stitches used in embroidery for hangings,
costumes, and altar-cloths. Some of the geometric designs in this book have been used for point-lace patterns.
The term used by the Italians, *punto in aere* (*aria*), or
"point in air," is thought by Mr. Alan Cole to mean
needle-point lace. The geometric design (Fig. 276) of

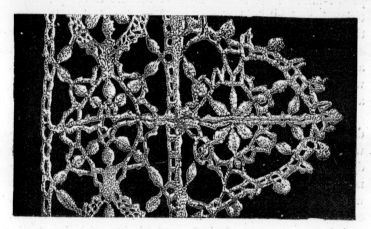

Fig. 276.—Genoese Point Lace.

Genoese point is something very much akin to the *punto
in aria* patterns.

At Antwerp and Cologne, and other cities in Germany
and Flanders, imitations of the Venetian pattern-books
were published, which served the lace makers of those
countries for their patterns.

The Flemish lace workers imitated to a great extent the
Venetian patterns, and in later years those of the French.

Lace is made in silk, cotton, flax, and sometimes in gold
and silver thread, aloe-fibre, and hair.

In the early kinds of lace the pattern was united by
single threads covered with button-hole stitch, and edged
with little loops, the flowers or pattern made of compact

" clothing," or woven threads (Fig. 277D), and the ground in its simplest variety by meshes made by plaiting (Fig. 277A), as in the Brussels and Honiton four-thread ground, or in other varieties, by simple twisting (Fig. 277B).

The ground or mesh (*réseau*) is usually hexagonal, and is worked together with the pattern in the Valenciennes, Mechlin, and Buckingham laces, but in the Brussels and Honiton the ground is worked in afterwards, or the pattern is sewn on. Other fancy grounds or "fillings" are called "modes" or "brides," which consist of little ties ornamented with "picots" or small loops (see Figs. 280, 284). A more elaborate form of fillings may be seen in the

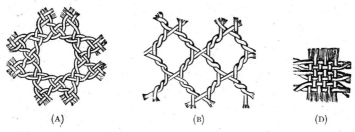

(A)   (B)   (D)

Fig. 277.—A, Brussels ground ; B, Two-thread Mesh ; D, Woven Ground.

Brussels and Alençon lappets (Figs. 278, 279); in the latter may be seen lozenges and flat hexagons of a solid character set in frames of hexagons and on the intersections of the squares. This groundwork has been termed *réseau-rosacé*.

The outline around the pattern in some laces is called the "cordonnet" ; it is an important feature of the Alençon point lace (Fig. 279), where it consists of a horsehair overcast with a button-hole stitch of thread ; it is also a distinctive mark of the pillow-made Mechlin lace (Fig. 283), but never occurs in the true or *vraie* Valenciennes.

The oldest of white hand-made laces is the Italian needle-point variety, which is a development of embroidery. It is difficult to give the exact date of the invention of needle-point lace, for in the earliest specimens of Italian work, in which the patterns are copied from the geometric designs of the Venetian pattern-books, they are usually a mixture of needle-point and of plaited and twisted work, but the latter may have been done with a hooked needle, and not pillow-made. On the other hand, before point lace was so universally made by the Vene-

Fig. 278.—Lappet   Brussels ; Eighteenth Century.

tians, the pattern-books were published about the middle of the sixteenth century for *merletti a piombini*, or " lace made with leaden bobbins "—probably a species of pillow-made lace—and some Italian work of this kind is still in existence that is quite as early in date as that of the oldest needle-point variety. This would prove that there was little or no difference in the age of either invention, although perhaps priority ought to be given to the needle-point variety.

Guipure is a name that has been given to lace in which the flowers are united with ties or "brides picotees" (Fig. 280), but the term guipure is more properly a kind of filigree work made with stiffened cords like gimp or wire,

Fig. 279.—Lappet ; Point d'Alençon ; Eighteenth Century.

the pattern being formed of gimp bent into a flattened design by the needle, and united where the forms touch each other (Fig. 281).

The patterns in the early laces were, as we have seen, purely geometric forms, such as squares with circles enclosed, divided by radiating lines and diagonals, rosettes, lozenges, and small trimming borders of rectangular panels, all worked on foundation lines that resembled in some degree the main lines of a spider's web.

By degrees these patterns developed into a more solid massing of the flower forms, and the ties, or brides, became more irregular, but at the same time more evenly distributed.

Sometimes, as in Venetian point lace, the brides had little flowers worked on them, and in many instances the larger forms were raised to a considerable height or thickness.   The groundwork in some of the scroll designs of

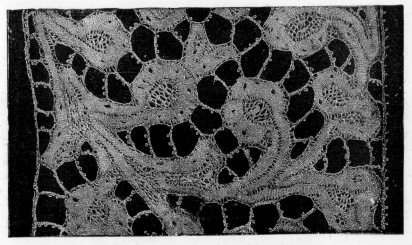

Fig. 280.—Guipure; Flemish; Seventeenth Century.

Venetian point laces is composed of regular hexagons, and this was the starting-point of the future hexagonal mesh grounds.

Raised scroll work is peculiar to the Venetian point laces of the best period—the end of the seventeenth century.

Flemish lace was mostly of the pillow-made variety, but some point work was also executed, principally at Brussels. Mechlin, Lille, and Valenciennes were all famous for their pillow-made laces.

Returning to the development of patterns in lace, we find that France led the way in design from the early years of the eighteenth century. Prior to this time, Colbert, the Minister of Louis XIV.—whose far-sightedness in the matters of art did so much for France—succeeded in establishing lace-making centres at Alençon, Argentan, Quesnoy, Arras, Rheims, &c., and the patterns of lace then in favour partook of the prevailing style of Louis-Quatorze ornament with a mixture of floral forms, more or less realistic in character (Fig. 279). The latter

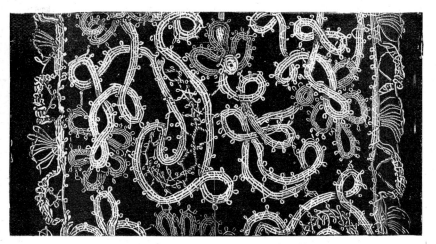

Fig. 281.—Guipure Lace; Italian; Seventeenth Century.

illustration is that of a lappet of "point d'Alençon" fabric, which is the most elaborate and most expensive of all French laces. Another French point lace is that known as " point d'Argentan," and if not a variety of Alençon lace, is very much like it. This lace is noted for its clear and strong-meshed ground.

Valenciennes lace, made in the French town of that name, is one of the oldest pillow-made laces, dating from the fifteenth century; the best Valenciennes, however, has been made at Yprès, and is a very soft and flat variety of fabric, with the meshes plaited, not twisted, has no cordonnet around the edges, and is very floral in design. "Fausse" Valenciennes is an irregular and slightly coarser variety than the "vraie" or true Valenciennes. Mechlin lace is similar in design to Valenciennes, but has the cordonnet outline, and has the meshes of the ground partly twisted and partly plaited (Fig. 283).

Lille and Arras laces have fine single grounds : four of the six sides of the mesh are formed by the twisting of two threads, and the other two sides by simply crossing

Fig. 282.—Finest Raised Venetian Point.

the threads. Lille was formerly famous for its black straight-edged laces. Chantilly laces were made in white and black silk, but now similar black silk laces are made at Bayeux in Normandy, and at Auvergne, an old-established centre. Laces are now made in all kinds of materials.

Brussels lace has always been a much-prized variety : it is made both in the "*point à l'aiguille*" or needle-point, and in "*point plat*" or pillow-made, and sometimes it is a mixture of both, where the flowers are made separate in

needle-point and are worked in afterwards to the various
"modes" and mesh or net grounds. The Brussels mesh
is peculiar in having two of its hexagonal sides longer
than the other four, the former two being plaited with four
threads, while the latter four are composed of a two-
thread twist, and the cordonnet is well raised around the
pattern and is plaited. The patterns in Brussels lace are
of all kinds, but are chiefly imitations of French designs;
it is a common thing to find Alençon and other French
patterns copied in this lace. In France, Brussels lace

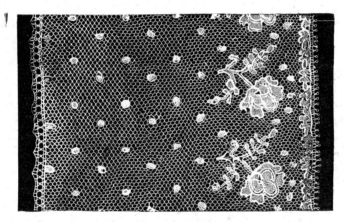

Fig. 283.—Border of Mechlin Lace.

was known by the name of "point d'Angleterre," from
the fact that great quantities of it were imported, and also
smuggled into England during its prohibited importation
in the lace-weaving period of Charles II.

Ancient Spanish point-lace was like the Venetian raised
work, but much of the so-called Spanish lace was really
Flemish, and was largely imported from the Spanish
Netherlands.

Honiton in Devonshire, and Buckinghamshire are the
chief centres of the lace making in England. Honiton
lace is pillow-made, and is similar to Brussels in fabrica-

tion, the designs of which were originally sprigs of flowers, but have developed to a kind of guipure work held together by "brides" (Fig. 284).

Buckinghamshire lace is also pillow-made, and resembles Flemish lace in design, but is a little more irregular and weaker in drawing.

Irish lace is known under the name of Carrickmacross — a kind of cut linen work; Limerick—a species of embroi-

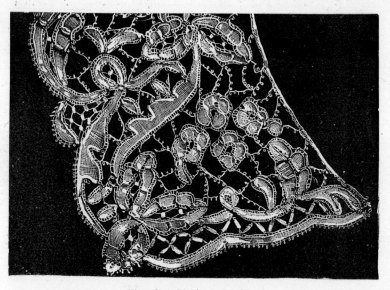

Fig. 284.—Honiton; Modern.

dery; and point lace, made in Ulster and elsewhere in Ireland (Fig. 285).

Many efforts have been made in recent years to revive the Irish lace-making industry, which have been attended with a good measure of success, particularly in the schools attached to the convents.

A great modern revival of lace making has taken place in the island of Burano, near Venice, which dates from the year 1872. This is due to the energy and ability of

Madame Bellario, assisted by the patronage of the Queen of Italy and other members of the royal family. The variety made is the needle-point, and the designs are mostly good copies of the old Venetian and seventeenth-century French patterns.

Machine-made lace has been brought to an advanced state of perfection, and Nottingham in England, where the first machines were set up, is now the great centre of this industry. The machine on which lace is made is a development of the stocking-knitting machine,

Fig. 285.—Irish Point; Modern.

and lace nets were first made on these machines about 1770. Heathcote, of Nottingham, invented the bobbin net machine, and Leaver invented the lace machine which is still in use with various improvements and modifications. Almost any kind of lace can now be imitated by the machine, but it is easily distinguished from the hand-made varieties by the greater regularity of texture, the absence in the machine-made point lace of any imitation of the button-hole stitch and of the elaborate plaiting that is found in the pillow hand-made laces.

CHAPTER VII.

MOSAICS.

THE word mosaic is applied generally to a decorative work executed with small cubes or tesseræ made from various coloured marbles or enamels, cut into convenient sizes according to the requirements or scale of the design.

These cubes of enamels or marbles are placed in a bed of cement which is first spread on the surface of the wall or panel. The composition of this cement has varied in the different periods and countries and according to the nature of the ground which receives it.

The Italian method is to spread on the wall a thick coating of mastic cement composed of marble dust or powdered stone, lime, and linseed oil; when this cement is partly set a coating of fine plaster is laid on the top and brought up to the level of the intended surface of the mosaic; the design is traced on this surface, and the plaster is then cut away with a fine small chisel, little by little, just sufficient at a time to receive a small quantity of the tesseræ or cubes, which are first dipped in moist cement and inserted in their proper places, matching the colour copied from the cartoon. When the work is finished the surface is brought to a uniform level by a polishing process.

Some of the earlier kinds of mosaic were composed of pieces of marble or other stones cut in geometric slabs or rectangular shapes; this kind was called by the Romans *lithostratum*, and was used chiefly in pavements; *opus sectile* is a kind of pavement mosaic made of different colours, the marbles being cut into small regular portions; *opus tesselatum* is a variety of the *opus sextile*, but has its component parts made of geometric forms in which straight and parallel lines predominate in the design; and *opus vermiculatum* has its tesseræ composed of small cubes or bits of enamel (glass mosaic), terra-cotta, or marble, which are cut into all kinds of shapes, so as to form a more pliant or softer contour to the proposed design. This latter variety is used in picture mosaics and in the goldsmiths' work and jewellery made at the present time in Rome and Venice.

Another kind of mosaic used in pavement is that known as *opus Alexandrinum*. Large slabs of different coloured marbles have been used as floor pavements and as wall linings, both on the exterior and in the interior of churches and other buildings in Italy and elsewhere. Most of this work is of a geometric pattern; the different pieces of stone, marble, terra-cotta, or enamel, being cut into exact shapes to fit a preconceived pattern, form a species of inlay, and do not therefore come under the head of a true mosaic. Coloured marbles and precious stones have been used in the decoration of furniture by the Italians and French, which is known by the name of "Florentine mosaic," or "pietra dura."

A species of mosaic work resembling enamels in appearance was executed by the Egyptians, a method in which stones and coloured pastes were cut to fit into metal shapes, as may be seen in the pectoral ornaments and diadems (see Figs. 142, 143, former volume).

In the Museum of Turin there is an Egyptian sarcophagus inlaid with precious stones, but it can hardly be called true mosaic work.

The Greeks were very skilful in mosaic, and were doubtless the inventors of the enamels used by themselves and by the Romans afterwards under the name of *musivum* —from whence the word mosaic is derived. The Italians called these enamels *smalto* or smalts.

Nearly all the remains of antique mosaic that have been preserved to our days have been executed in Italy or in countries that were under the Roman sway, but usually the work has been done by Greek artists or under Grecian influence.

Pliny mentions the name of Sosus, a Greek artist, who

Fig. 286.—Roman Mosaic, from Woodchester.

came to Italy to execute mosaics. To this artist is ascribed the celebrated mosaic of the doves perched on the rim of a basin—*Cantharos*—one of which is drinking from the water in the vessel. This mosaic is now in the Capitol at Rome, and came originally from the Villa of Hadrian. It is related by Pliny that Sosus made a floor in mosaic decorated with fragments of a repast, such as realistic representations of the remains of bones, vegetables, fish, a mouse gnawing at a nut, &c.

Great pavements, with all kinds of animated figures, both realistic and fanciful, representing combats of animals, fighting gladiators, circus and hunting scenes, with the figures sometimes of life size, in combination with allegorical subjects, tritons, nereids, and other marine deities, were common in the antique period in Italy.

These great pavements were usually found enclosed in frames or borders composed of ornament, or of smaller

Fig. 287.—Roman Mosaic, found at Avignon.

designs of birds, fishes, and marine animals. The borders, however, are often modern work, and are generally restorations or additions. Besides being found at Rome and other places in Italy, these large Roman mosaics have been found at almost every place that was formerly a Roman province.

Many good examples have been discovered in France, chiefly in the Basses-Pyrénées, and in England, at Woodchester, Withington in Gloucestershire, London, and other places (Figs. 286, 287).

The Roman mosaics executed in the provinces were,

however, of a ruder kind than those found at Rome and at other places in Italy (Fig. 288).

In the Græco-Roman collection at the British Museum may be seen representations of colossal figures in mosaic from Carthage, and a floor pavement 40 feet by 12 feet from Halicarnassos. One of the most important examples of Roman mosaic was found in the seventeenth century in the Temple of Fortune at Palestrina—the ancient Praeneste. It represents landscape scenes placed in superimposed sections, through which runs a river, supposed by some authorities to represent the mouth of the Nile ; islands are

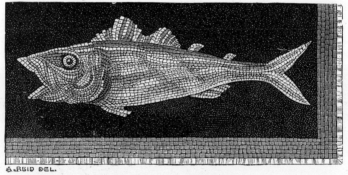

Fig. 288.—Ancient Roman Mosaic.

represented on which are monuments, temples, trees, farms, climbing plants, animals, and figures engaged in agricultural and hunting pursuits. The animals depicted are chiefly those which are native to Egypt ; besides these there are some fantastic creatures represented common to the mythology of that country, as well as to Greece and Rome ; the inscriptions and names of the animals are rendered in Greek characters, Greek being the official language used at that period in Egypt and at the Court in Rome, as well as being the native language of the artists who executed the work. All this goes to strengthen the opinion formed by the Abbé Barthélemy, in opposition to others, that this great mosaic picture represents the voyage of the Emperor Hadrian on the Upper Nile, through Egypt, to the Elephantine Island.

Mosaic pavements with subjects of combats of lions and bulls in a savage landscape, executed in the same manner as the Palestrina mosaic, have been found at Pompeii in the ruins of Hadrian's Villa, a building which he had constructed in imitation of the various styles of architecture of the different countries which he had visited.

A celebrated mosaic, of a much higher and earlier order of art, is the representation of the Battle of Arbela, or Issus, now preserved in the Naples Museum. This battle was fought between the Greek and Persian forces in the year 331 (B.C.), in which Alexander the Great was victorious over Darius the Persian. Alexander is represented on horseback in the act of throwing his lance at a Persian satrap; horsemen, chariots, and foot soldiers are all represented with great vigour and in correct drawing; the whole composition is excellent, and represents the Greek army in the decisive moment of victory.

This great work was found in the House of the Faun at Pompeii in the year 1830, and is immeasurably superior to anything of its kind hitherto found in that buried city. It has, no doubt, been a copy in mosaic of a picture or fresco painted by a Greek artist. Important portions of the work are missing, but enough remains to testify to the beauty and greatness of this monument of Grecian art. Fig. 289 represents the head of a Persian soldier in the mosaic.

A border was found with this work which represents a river with alligators, hippopotami, aquatic birds, and river plants, all disposed in a careless manner; this border is evidently a later Roman addition to the work.

Another antique mosaic picture in the Museum at Naples is the seated figure of the tragic poet found in a house at Pompeii.

Fountains, columns, dados, wall panels, as well as floor

decorations, were common objects of mosaic treatment with the Romans, and many houses of the better classes at Pompeii have been lavishly decorated with this imperishable material. A singular peculiarity was the almost exclusive representation of the human figure on

A.REID DEL.

Fig. 289.—Head in Mosaic, from the " Battle of Issus."

floors, while the wall spaces only received ornamental compositions.

It appears from this that the Romans never thoroughly understood the true value of mosaic as a means of architectural decoration, and it was not until about the fourth century of our era that the walls and vaults of churches at Rome were treated with pictorial mosaic. For a long time in Italy the character of the design was strongly influenced by the old classic traditions, which impregnated the germs of the early Christian art of the catacombs of S. Calixtus and S. Agnese (see Figs. 332, 333, former vol.). This influence hardly ever passed away from the works of Italian artists, for down to the sixteenth century there has been many examples of church decoration in which a mixture of Pagan and Christian elements are found.

The remaining mosaics of the central cupola in the church of S. Constance at Rome consist of a Pagan composition—the "Triumph of Bacchus"—worked out in the Roman style, and another vaulted compartment in the same church has a mosaic decoration consisting of a vine spreading over the whole surface, amongst the branches and leaves of which are children gathering the grapes. At two of the sides are grape-laden waggons drawn by oxen, and figures pressing out the grape juice in the vats. From the subjects of the mosaics in this building it was formerly thought to be a temple of Bacchus ; but as the vine is one of the commonest symbols of the Christian faith, and as a mixture of Christian and Pagan elements was a very common occurrence in the age of Constantine, there is no hesitation in describing these mosaics, and the church itself, as early Christian work.

A very important mosaic of the fourth century still exists in the apse of the Church of S. Pudentia at Rome. The design is not altered from the original, but much of the work has been restored at different times.

A colossal figure of Christ is enthroned in the centre of a composition which has an architectural background of temples and churches. St. Peter and St. Paul are represented on either side of the central figure, with other sacred personages, and above in the clouds float the sacred emblems of the Evangelists.

After Constantine removed the seat of his empire from Rome to Byzantium (330) mosaic decoration was used in many of the Eastern churches in Macedonia and other places in the Byzantine empire, but it was not until the sixth century that the decided Byzantine Greek style was developed in mosaic work—notably in the mosaics of the great church of Santa Sophia. During the fifth century at Rome, and more especially at Ravenna, the basilicas and Christian churches were decorated on the vaulted ceilings, walls, arches, and spandrels with mosaics, of which the general design and ornamental details were still strongly influenced with the spirit of the antique ; but although these works retained much of the dignity pertaining to the latter, they were gradually losing the correctness of drawing which had characterised the mosaics of the fourth century.

In the chapter on Early Christian Architecture, in the former volume of this work, pages 288-300, we have drawn attention to some of these mosaics.

The church of Santa Sophia was burned down in 533, and the rebuilding of it was finished and the church consecrated in 559. Much of the interior was shortly afterwards covered with mosaic decoration. Near the summit of the cupola was a colossal figure of Christ enthroned, with his arm raised upwards in the act of blessing ; below the sacred figure were ranged the Apostles, and in the lower pendentives were groups of people. In the chancel below is a figure of the Virgin enthroned, with the Infant Christ standing on her knees ; in the great niches are figures of martyrs and bishops, and in the spaces above the pillars figures of the prophets.

On the walls of the narthex, Christ is represented seated on a throne, the crowned figure of Justinian prostrate at his feet, and on the gold background are the heads of the Virgin and St. Michael. In colour the mosaics are sober and refined, the expressions and attitudes of the figures solemn, and often beautiful ; the costumes follow the style of the antique.

According to Salzenberg, who published his great work on Santa Sophia at Berlin in the year 1854, the colouring of the draperies of Christ and his Apostles is white, the Virgin has blue robes, and the other figures of prophets, angels, and martyrs are in varied colouring. The shades of the folds in the draperies are expressed by quiet blues and greens, the lights being heightened by silver markings. All the mosaics have a ground of gold, and bands of gold enrich the garments of Christ. Although many of the great mosaics of this church belong to the sixth century, some of them are, however, works of a later period. Among other arts, Justinian encouraged mosaic decoration in the highest degree, and is said to have ornamented the palace of his capital with mosaic pictures representing the victories of his armies.

Some famous mosaics were executed during the sixth century at Ravenna, notably in the basilicas of S. Apol-linare-Nuovo, S. Apollinare-in-Classe, and S. Vitale; in the former there is a fine mosaic, the subject being the Kiss of Judas, and a group of figures where Pontius Pilate is represented washing his hands after the trial of Christ, both of which works again show the antique influence.

In the beautiful basilica of S. Apollinare-in-Classe the figure of Christ is represented standing and blessing with uplifted hands, surrounded by the symbols of the Evange-lists and a flock of sheep; the angels Gabriel and Michael and the Transfiguration are also represented.

The Church of S. Vitale, which was built somewhat after the model of Santa Sophia, has the celebrated mosaics representing processions in state of the Emperor Justinian and the Empress Theodora, who presided at the dedication of the church. The dresses of the principal personages in these mosaics are richly decorated with Byzantine geo-metric patterns, figured embroidery, and jewellery. In the apse of the church is the celebrated youthful figure of Christ, who is represented without a beard ; it is remarkable for its benign expression and softness of its adolescent beauty. The mosaics of S. Vitale are distinctly Greek in character, unlike those of the two former churches, which were executed by Roman mosaicists brought from Italy to Ravenna by Theodoric the Ostrogoth in the early years of the sixth century.

The seventh century was almost barren in mosaic works, and the eighth century does not seem to have produced more than a few tentative efforts, mainly in countries outside Italy.

It is related that Adrian I., who was Pope between the years 772-795, gave permission to Charlemagne to remove several mosaics from churches at Ravenna, the materials of which were used in the decoration of the dome of his chapel at Aachen (Aix-la-Chapelle). These mosaics were destroyed by fires in the years 1656 and 1730. Some drawings of them were made before the second fire by Ciampini, and published by him at Rome in 1699. These works were not, however, of any great artistic value. The art of the mosaicist was fast becoming only a caricature of its former self, for the work of the ninth century was characterized by exceedingly bad drawing and savage colouring. Uninviting and even terrible representations of Christ, of the Virgin, angels, martyrs, and prophets were only too common. It may be said with good reason that in Rome and in the West during the ninth century, that the zenith of ugliness had been attained in the design of mosaics, and in place of the careful grouping and correct drawing of the works of the fourth to the sixth century we have instead figures of great dimensions and multiplication of attributes.

At the time we speak of there was not this decadence of art in the Eastern Empire, for many fine mosaics were executed to the order of Basil the Macedonian (867-886), under whose protection art generally was much encouraged. Some of the mosaics of Santa Sophia and of other churches and palaces at Constantinople were executed during this period.

However, from the tenth to the twelfth centuries the art of mosaic decoration, with a few notable exceptions, was in a slow state of decadence in the East, but the old Greek artistic spirit broke in other and in new directions, as we have witnessed in the wealth of Byzantine enamels, carved ivories, bas-reliefs, repoussé work, miniatures, and illuminated manuscripts.

In the eleventh century some fine mosaic floors were executed in France. Examples of this date were found in the old churches of Sordes in the Department of Landes, and of Lescar in the Basses-Pyrénées. Some of these pavements have ornamental compositions of geometrical interlacings and conventional foliage, and others have hunting scenes in which animals, figures, and birds are treated flatly, after the Persian or Oriental manner of inlaid work or like textile designs.

In the thirteenth century towards the latter end, in the dawn of the Renaissance, design in mosaic began to feel the reviving influence in common with all Italian art. In the mosaics of this century executed at Rome we see something of the poetry and dignity which belonged to the great works of the fifth century. This turning-point was in a great measure due to the influence of Cimabue, the founder of Italian painting (1240-1300), who was then a great personality in Italian art.

The most important mosaics of this period in Italy were those which decorate the tribune of the basilica of St. John Lateran at Rome, executed by Jacobus Toriti between the years 1287 and 1292, and those of the tribune of S. Maria Maggiore in Rome, executed also by Toriti during the last few years of the thirteenth century and finished about 1302.

The design of the former mosaics is simple in arrangement. On a gold ground, symmetrically arranged, are the figures of six saints and Apostles, with smaller figures of St. Francis and St. Anthony of Padua advancing towards a central cross, from underneath which flows the four rivers of Paradise into the Jordan beneath. Above is the celebrated head of Christ, the face having a benign expression.

This was formerly supposed to be of an older creation, but it is quite likely to have been designed by Toriti. The head is surrounded by a plain gold nimbus, and around and above it, on a blue ground with clouds, is a glory of angels in the form of an arc. Below this, on the wall of the tribune, between pointed window openings, Christ and the Apostles are represented on a smaller scale.

In the tribune of S. Maria Maggiore the design is grander and more decorative than the St. John Lateran mosaics, and indeed ranks as the finest work of art of its period. In a large central medallion of the apse Christ and the Virgin are enthroned, Christ being represented in the act of crowning the Virgin. A crowd of angels are on either side and at the lower parts of the medallion. The ground of the latter is blue, sown with golden stars ; beyond, on either side of the adoring angels, are the upright figures of Apostles and saints on a gold ground, and above them, filling the upper surrounding space, are conventional vines in whose scrolly branches birds of various kinds are found. Below this composition the River Jordan is represented, and the walls of the tribune are occupied with small compositions representing scenes in the life of Christ. In the loggia of the same church are a series of well-designed mosaics inscribed with the name of the artist who designed them—Philippus Rusuti—who is not known with certainty to have executed any other work. They had been formerly ascribed to the Florentine mosaicist Gaddo Gaddi, a friend of Cimabue ; he died in 1312.

Gaddi, according to Vasari, had been invited to Rome to complete the unfinished mosaics of Toriti at the Church of S. Maria Maggiore after the death of the latter artist, and he occupied himself with the storied mosaics representing the foundation of that church in a series of four compositions. It is still, however, a matter of doubt as to how much of these mosaics belong to the hand of Rusuti or Gaddi. The latter artist executed some subjects in the dome of the Baptistery at Florence, in the Cathedral of

Pisa, and the mosaics which decorate the inner lunette in the portal of the Cathedral at Florence.

Gaddi followed the style and aims of Cimabue; his work was poetic in conception, and in his execution he leaned to the Byzantine methods, but in drawing and composition he was greatly excelled by the Roman mosaicist Toriti.

The celebrated Roman family of the Cosmati were excellent mosaicists. Giovanni Cosmato, son of the elder artist of that name, executed some fine work on the tomb of Gonsalo Roderigo in the Church of S. Maria Maggiore, and on monuments in S. Maria sopra Minerva. A variety of mosaic was much used in Italy at different times, the earliest dating from the sixth century, which consisted in decorating pulpits, screens, and small altars with a geometric inlay of small squares and lozenges of gold and coloured tesseræ which were inserted into grooves of white marble (Fig. 290).

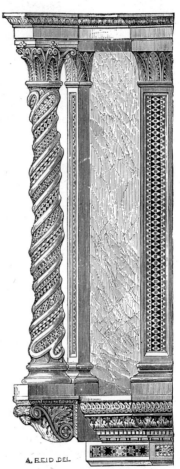

A. REID DEL

Fig. 290.—Geometric Mosaic, Church of Ara Cœli, Rome.

About the year 1351, Pietro Cavallini, a native of Rome and a supposed pupil of the painter Giotto, was commissioned to execute some mosaics in the Church of S. Maria Transtevere at Rome.

The design and style of these works were strongly influenced if not partly copied from the frescoes of Giotto in the Arena Chapel at Padua.

Cavallini also executed in mosaic the celebrated Navicella, from the design by Giotto, which decorates the vestibule of the old basilica church of St. Peter's at Rome. This work represents a ship in which the Apostles are seen, and Christ and Peter are figured walking on the sea.

With the exception of a few notable works in St. Peter's at Rome, in St. Mark's at Venice, some unfinished work of Domenico Ghirlandaio (1449-95), and the work of Pesselli in the Church of Or-San-Michele at Florence (1416), the fifteenth century was not a prosperous period for mosaic. This is accounted for by the rapid development of the Italian schools of painting, which advanced during this century with incredible swiftness, and as painting advanced, mosaic decoration retreated before its more popular rival. The mosaicist had to make room for the fresco painter, who soon became the successful competitor of the former in the work of church decoration.

Regarding the mosaics of St. Mark's at Venice, it may be stated that they date from the eleventh century to the nineteenth.

The interior of this church is richly decorated on the vaults and upper parts of the walls with mosaics on grounds of gold, the other parts are covered with various rich marbles, and the floor is mosaic designed in the Byzantine style. In the twelfth century the principal apse, the cupola of the choir, and some of the chapels were decorated in mosaic. The great central cupola has mosaics of the eleventh century representing the *Virtues*, and twelfth-century work with the subjects of the "Virgin with Angels and Apostles," the "Evangelists," &c. To the same century belong the mosaics in the cupola of the choir, consisting of the figures of Christ, the Virgin, David and Solomon, and symbols of the Evangelists; the figure of St. Clement in the vault of the terminal chapel of St. Clement is ascribed to the twelfth century, and the mosaics of this chapel representing the life of the saint are thirteenth-century work.

The most important mosaic of the latter century in St. Mark's is that which decorates the façade, the subject being "The Dedication of the Church."

From the remains of the original mosaics which have not been remodelled by the restorers of later times, it has been seen that the work of the above centuries at St. Mark's kept to the spirit and traditions of the Byzantine school. The work of restoration, however, has been so great in modern times that nearly all the mosaics belonging to a date prior to the sixteenth century have been executed afresh, so it can hardly be said there are any perfect or genuine Byzantine mosaics left.

Those of the sixteenth century in St. Mark's are more like paintings in their general effect than monumental works for the decoration of the fabric. Pictorial effect and an appeal to the emotional faculties were aimed at by the artists and governing body of the church, rather than simplicity or a feeling for the decorative fitness of the material. The painters Titian, Pordenone, Tintoret, Paul Veronese, and the sculptor and architect Sansovino made designs for the mosaics, and their cartoons were interpreted by mosaicists, the principal of whom were Vicenzo and Domenico Bianchini, the brothers Zuccati, Bozza, Rizzo, Gaëtano, &c.

In this century, at Rome, in the cupola of the Chigi Chapel in S. Maria del Popolo, a celebrated mosaic was executed by the Venetian mosaicist Luigi da Pace, from a design by the great painter Raphael. It bears the date 1516, and has for its subject the Creation of the World. The Almighty is represented surrounded by seraphim, and in eight compartments are mythological figures representing the planets. Angel figures of great beauty are seated on the signs of the Zodiac, which occupy the lower parts of the mosaic.

During the seventeenth and eighteenth centuries the

principal mosaics executed in Italy were those which decorate the Church of St. Peter's at Rome. In these periods the Pontifical fabrique or studio for the production of the smalto and for the execution of the mosaics was in a state of activity. The fabrique had various locations in the vicinity of the church from the time of its establishment in 1528, and was finally set up in the Vatican in 1825 by Leo XIII. The most important period in the history of the Pontifical ateliers was during the early half of the eighteenth century, when it was under the direction of Pierre-Paul Cristofari, who was assisted in the production of the variously coloured material by the chemist Mattioli.

The mosaics which cover the cupolas, the altars of the various chapels, the pendentines, tympani, and other spaces, have been executed by mosaicists who were not the designers of the subjects.

This was the general practice in the Renaissance periods. One noteworthy exception to this rule may be noticed in the work of the artist Muziano de Brescia, who executed the mosaics of the Gregorian Chapel at St. Peter's from his own designs, for which work he received the commission from Pope Gregory XIII. (1572-1585). Muziano was an imitator of Michelangelo, and is best known by his work in mosaic. As a rule the mosaics of St. Peter's, like all those of the Renaissance period, are not to be compared for dignity and repose with those of the early Christian era, nor did they fulfil the true aim of monumental wall decoration, but sought rather to imitate as closely as possible the finish of oil or fresco painting. The "Transfiguration" after Raphael is not a success as a mosaic. It is believed to have been executed by Cristofari from a drawing enlarged from the original by Stefano Pozzi (1708-1768).

In the great cupola the mosaic has for its subject "The Eternal Father," surrounded by cherubims. In other compartments are angels in adoration, cherubims, Jesus, Mary, John the Baptist, Paul, the twelve Apostles and their attributes. These mosaics are from designs by the Chevalier d'Arpin (1560-1640), and rank among the best works of their kind in St. Peter's.

In the present century there has been some noted revivals of mosaic decoration in France and in England.

During the first thirty years of this century a royal manufactory was set up in Paris under the superintendence of Belloni, an Italian artist who came from the Pontifical atelier of Rome. Mosaic work of all kinds was executed at this studio, such as miniatures, pictures, and *pietra-dura*, or Florentine mosaic, for the encrusted decoration of furniture, as well as important works for pavements, which were designed in the classical style of the period. The principal work of Belloni is the pavement of the " Salle Melpomène" in the Louvre. It is a composition divided into five compartments, each having figure subjects, and has an extremely rich border of frets, foliage, and rosettes.

Some fine mosaics of a more recent date are the decorations of the *foyer* and other parts of the Grand Opera House in Paris, executed from the designs of M. Charles Garnier, the architect of the building, M. de Curzon, and others, by the mosaicists Salviati and Facchina of Venice.

The new cathedrals at Marseilles and Lyons have been recently decorated with mosaics more or less in the style of the Ravenna work of the fifth century, but the principal part of these works consists of ornamental compositions, such as doves with olive-branches, monograms, stars, and borders of romanesque ornament. Some still more recent work is the decoration of the apse of the Pantheon in Paris, from the designs of M. E. Hébert and the late M. Galland, who furnished the ornamental designs.

In England, during the present half of this century, there has been several attempts to popularise mosaic decoration. Full-length figures of the chief ancient and modern sculptors, painters, and architects have been designed by Lord Leighton, Sir E. J. Poynter, E. Armitage, V. Prinsep, W. F. Yeames, F. W. Moody, and others; these have been executed in glass mosaic and in English ceramic mosaic, and form part of the decoration of the South Court in the Kensington Museum.

In the Houses of Parliament a mosaic has been executed from the design, "St. George," by Sir E. J. Poynter; and other examples are the mosaics on the monument to Prince Albert designed by Sir Gilbert Scott.

But the most important efforts during the last few years are the mosaic decorations in St. Paul's Cathedral.

From the year 1863 until 1892 the eight spandrels of the dome were filled with mosaics, the subjects being the four Evangelists, designed by Mr. Watts, R.A., and Mr. Brittan, and the four greater Apostles by the late Alfred Stevens. The work of these spandrels was carried out by Dr. Salviati of Venice.

In the spring of 1891 Mr. W. B. Richmond, R.A., undertook the great work of designing the cartoons, and of superintending the mosaic decoration of the eastern end of the cathedral, including the apse, the original sanctuary bay, and the choir.

The central panel in the roof of the apse is occupied with a representation of "Our Lord in Majesty," seated on a rainbow throne, and clothed in light-coloured robes. The background is composed of a great whirl of wings; the sun and moon are also represented. The panels on either side of this subject contain figures of the recording angels, which are Byzantine in style of design; as the whole of the mosaics are, but perhaps not so much in degree as the figures of these angels. Mr. Richmond had made a special study of the Ravenna mosaics, and was no doubt rightly influenced by the style of design and methods of execution of these early works.

The three saucer domes of the choir have subjects representing respectively the creation of birds, fishes, and animals of the land; and the pendentives of the saucer domes are each filled with figures of angels, their arms being extended, as if in the act of bringing down messages from heaven to the earth. Inscriptions in Latin, consisting of appropriate scriptural texts, explain the subjects of the pendentives.

The spaces at the sides of the clerestory windows are occupied with figures of the Sibyls, Prophets, builders of the Taber- nacle or House of God, scenes from the Old Testament, and some secular figures.

Fig. 291.—Mosaic from the Alhambra.

The general effect of the mosaics is very rich, and the colouring exceedingly harmonious.

The smalto tesseræ used was made from opaque glass of many colours and shades, and the fractured edge was

Fig. 292.—Saracenic Mosaic, from Monreale.

shown in every case as the surface of the mosaic; this was done in order to get greater brilliancy of colour, and to catch all the possible light that is reflected from the walls and floor of the church.

Portland stone composed the panels, and brick was the

background material of the saucer domes, and in order to get a bed for the cement and tesseræ, these surfaces had to be cut away to a certain depth so that the mosaics would come flush when finished with the original surface. The tesseræ were inserted into a bed of red mastic cement, made chiefly of a mixture of red lead and linseed oil, a cement which ultimately sets as hard as the stone itself. The execution of the work was entrusted to Messrs. Powell of London, who employed a large staff of skilled assistants in this successful achievement.

The Saracens employed mosaic—as in the Alhambra in

Fig. 293.—Indian Mosaic, from the Taj Mehal.

Spain—in the form of small tiles—*azulejos*—of glazed earthenware cut into geometric shapes, from which they made up their characteristic rectilinear patterns, and used this form of decoration to a great extent for walls, but rarely for floor pavements (Figs. 291, 292).

Some beautiful examples of mosaic work in the nature of inlaid marbles and precious stones occur in the Mohammedan buildings in India, the chief of which are the Taj Mehal at Agra (Fig. 293) and the great palace at Delhi. The latter has been noticed in the chapter on Indian Architecture in the former volume, and an illustration of the inlaid marble hall is given at Fig. 329 in the same volume.

CHAPTER VIII.

GLASS.

THE manufacture of glass is of great antiquity. The invention has been ascribed to the Phœnicians, but specimens of glass beads, amulets, plaques, vases, and small phials or bottles have been found in some of the oldest Egyptian tombs. In the British Museum there is a small piece of blue opaque glass in the form of a lion's head, which bears the prenomen of the Egyptian monarch Nuntef IV., belonging to the Fourth Dynasty (B.C. 2423-2380). There are also paintings on the walls of early tombs representing bottles with red wine, as well as figures engaged in glass-blowing.

Fig. 294.
Glass Vase or Bottle; height, 3½ ins. (B. M.)

A number of glass bowls, vases, and bottles from Nimroud may be seen in the British Museum, the earliest specimen of which is an Assyrian transparent glass vase with two handles, and is inscribed with the name of the monarch Sargon (B.C. 722-705). This is supposed to be the oldest known specimen of transparent glass (Fig. 294).

Many long-shaped little bottles — *alabastron* — of pale greenish, and others of brilliant colours, with slightly varied shapes, have been dug up from the ruins of Assyrian palaces, and have been found in most of the ancient tombs in Greece, Italy, and in the islands of Cyprus, Sardinia, and Rhodes. These little bottles have been made by the

Egyptians, Assyrians, Phœnicians, and Greeks, and their shape, being consecrated by use, remained unchanged for many centuries; they were portable objects of barter, as glass beads also were with the Phœnicians, who distributed them in trade to all parts of the countries bordering on the Mediterranean (Figs. 295, 296).

Common forms of the Phœnician glass bottles were small vessels in the shapes of heads, and of dates, grapes, and other fruits, which were blown in moulds. These vessels probably came from the great workshops of Tyre and Sidon; some of them bear the names of their makers—Eugenes, Ennion, and "Artas the Sidonian."

The shapes of many of these vessels are decidedly Greek, and if not Greek in manufacture, have been copied from the shapes of Greek pottery.

The colours used were yellow, turquoise, and white on blue, green, or brown, and a common arrangement of these was in zigzag or wavy alternating lines; in other examples the surface was

Fig. 295.
Phœnician Alabastron.

reeded, as may be seen in the alabastron, Fig. 295.

Ancient Roman glass is of great variety in colour, and many specimens show the highest technical skill combined with great artistic beauty. The lovely iridescent effect on Roman and other antique glass is due to the chemical changes of the surface decomposition, and in other instances to the minute flaking of the glass, which reflects the light at various angles, and thus producing the prismatic hues.

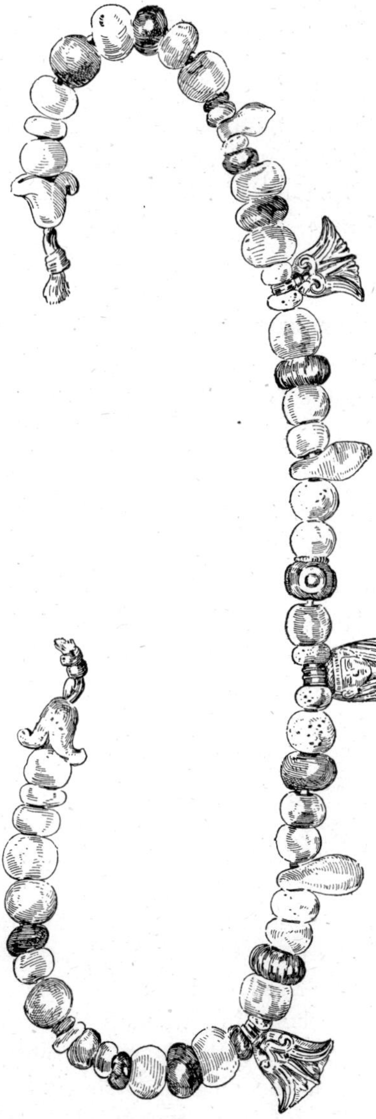

At the time of the Roman occupation of Egypt, during the period of rule under the Ptolemies, glass making was a great industry in the latter country. It is said that the Romans learnt the art from the Egyptians, and it is known that many of the latter were brought to Rome to practise their art as glass-blowers.

The making of the glass known as *mille-fiori* was taught to the Romans by the Egyptians, and was extensively e.nployed in vase and bottle

Fig. 296.—Necklace of Glass and Gold, Phœnician. (B. M.)

making by the former; the Venetians from the fourteenth century have imitated the Romans in their uses of mille-fiori glass for bead making and other purposes, with great success.

The method of making this variety of glass consists in arranging a number of thin rods or threads of glass of the required variety of colours, gold being sometimes used; these united rods were then fused together by heat, and drawn out or twisted, so that when transverse sections were cut the pattern would always be the same.

Another way of mixing the colour in glass, which was employed by the Egyptians, Romans, and later by the Venetians, was in the making of regular patterns of mosaic-like designs of the various colours, and another was in imitating the precious stones and marbles, such as onyx, agate, serpentine, porphyry, and murrhine; the latter is supposed to be a variety of agate, with red and purple shades. The murrhine glass examples of Roman manu-facture are very rare.

The Romans used these glass imitations of the precious stones and marbles to line their walls and floors, as in mosaic work.

Egyptian and Roman glass in their transparent varieties have such colours as yellow, purple, blue, green, and pink; opaque colours are generally found in shades of yellow, blue, green, and black. The most valuable kind of glass was that of the clearest white or crystal; this, it would appear, was the most difficult to make, as the commoner clear variety had usually a slight greenish or bluish hue.

The Romans made a special variety of glass ware which consisted of interlaced bands of opaque white or coloured glass, ingeniously made to form a pattern by twisting them with clear or coloured transparent glass, like that of the elegant lace-glass variety known as the " vitro di trina " of the Venetians (Fig. 302).

In the arts of glass cameo and intaglio engraving,

and in the imitation of gems, the Romans were exceedingly skilful.

The cameo engraved glass was produced by placing a layer of white opaque glass on a ground of transparent blue, the design being formed by cutting away the white surface to the blue ground, leaving the blue as the background; the remaining white which formed the design was then carefully finished by engraving. Light and shade

Fig. 297.—Ancient Roman Glass Bottle. (S. K. M.)

was produced according to the thicknesses of the cameo left by the engraver.

The celebrated Barberini or ˙Portland Vase, in the British Museum, is made in a blue and white cameo. This splendid work of art was discovered in a marble sarcophagus near Rome, which is supposed to have been the tomb of the Emperor Alexander Severus. The vase is ten inches in height, is two-handled, and has for the subject of one side a figure decoration representing Thetis consenting to be the bride of Peleus, attended by Poseidon and Eros; on the other side is Peleus and Thetis on Mount Pelion, and on the bottom is a bust of Paris. The ground is transparent blue glass, and the subjects are beautifully engraved in cameo out of the superimposed white layer.

A similar kind of vase, but smaller, was found at Pompeii, and is now in the Museum at Naples, and the remains of the Auldjo Vase in the British Museum is also in a similar style, the cameo decoration of it consisting of vine-leaves.

Fig. 298.—Roman Glass Tablet in relief.
(S. K. M.)

Intaglios and cameos, sometimes of a large size, were copied in glass from gems; these were usually cast in moulds, and many of them are of high value as works of art. (Fig. 298).

The Romans made window glass of small squares or oblongs, which was manufactured by rolling it on a plate.

In the early Christian period gold leaf was used as a means of decoration on glass: sometimes the gold was annealed to the surface, and sometimes it was placed, as the making of the gold smalto for mosaics, between two layers of thin glass, and afterwards fired. Patterns and figure subjects were executed in gold foil, and formed the decoration of glass dishes and bowls, the broken remains of which have been found in the Christian tombs of the Roman Catacombs.

Though extensive glass works are known to have existed at Constantinople and at Thessalonica between the ninth and thirteenth centuries, there are scarcely any remains of Byzantine glass in existence that can with certainty be ascribed to the Eastern empire, unless we except the five cups and two shallow basins of thick green glass that are decorated with Byzantine ornament, and which form part of the treasure of St. Mark's at Venice. Glass was used in the windows of Byzantine churches and, of course, in the making of the mosaic tesseræ.

It is highly probable that glass objects were made in Syria, and at Damascus especially, since the Roman period, yet examples of the earlier work from these parts are very rare. The celebrated gold cup of Chrosroes (A.D. 531-579) is a Persian work which has been set with glass lozenges and rosettes. Other examples are small glass weights, discs, or tokens, and a Saracenic glass basin in the Cluny Museum at Paris, which has been made either in Egypt or Syria, and is known to date between 1279 and 1294.

With the above exceptions there is no authentic work that can be pointed to which dates earlier than the fourteenth century. The finest examples of Saracenic glass, some of which may be seen in our museums, are the beautiful enamelled glass mosque lamps (Fig. 299). They mostly date from the fourteenth century, and are usually decorated richly with Arabic inscriptions—sometimes with the name of the artist—in gold and coloured enamels.

In the city of Damascus glass cups and other vessels of great beauty were made at this period, having enamelled Saracenic decorations.

The "cups of Damascus" were much prized, and according to the inventories of the kings of England, France, and Germany, we learn that they were set in gold stands or mounts, and were usually presents to Western monarchs, brought by their ambassadors from the East.

The cup kept by the Musgrave family, and known as the "Luck of Edenhall," is made in enamelled Saracenic glass, and has a leather covering of fifteenth-century workmanship.

Venetian blown glass has always been renowned for its

Fig. 299.—Enamelled Oriental Glass Bottle and Mosque Lamp.

beauty, both in its elegance of form—as in the wineglasses, goblets, and cups—and in the beautiful opalescent hues of its delicate colouring.

The making of glass in Venice began to assume great importance in the fourteenth century, but many small glass furnaces were in operation for more than a hundred years prior to this date.

The Venetians apparently, in the early period of the Renaissance, studied very closely the remains of the Roman glass, and eventually imitated and produced nearly all the kinds of glass that in former days were made in ancient Rome.

Another direct cause which led to the advancement of the glass makers' craft in Venice was the parricidal conquest of Constantinople by the Christians of Rome, aided by the fleets of Venice, in 1204, for after the sacking of the Byzantine capital, most of the portable works of art of every kind—including the bronze horses that had been brought from Rome to Constantinople by its founder, and which now adorn the front of St. Mark's—were carried off to Venice, and it is more than likely that after this the glass mosaic workers, among other Byzantine craftsmen, had come to Venice, where they found employment in the rising republic.

The work in the mosaic decoration of St. Mark's doubtless helped to develop the making of glass in Venice, and the lagunes were rich in marsh-loving plants that would yield alkali and furnish the fine sand requisite for its manufacture.

Mention is made in one of the documents in the archives of Venice, dated 1090, of one Petrus Flavianus, who was a "phiolarius," or glass maker, and the trade regulations of the glass makers' societies or corporations are preserved at Venice and Murano, which show that in the thirteenth century they had become important bodies.

Glass furnaces were becoming so numerous in Venice that the Great Council decreed, in 1291, they should be demolished, but permitted them to be set up outside the city, in the suburban districts. In the following year, however, the decrees were altered to the effect that the small glass workers might remain in the Rialto (the city proper), provided fifteen paces were left between each atelier. These decrees were made to guard against a possible spread of fire.

It is supposed that this had the effect of moving many of the principal glass works to Murano, a district of Venice which had become renowned for the production of Venetian glass, and where to-day the eminent firm of Salviati & Co. have their extensive works.

The glass house at Murano, which was known as the "Sign of the Angel" in the early half of the fifteenth century, was the most renowned of the ateliers of that century. Angelo Beroviero was one of its earliest directors, who was succeeded by his son Marino in that position. The latter was a head or master of the Company of "Phioleri" (Glass Makers' Corporation) in 1468, which was a very strong society at that time and enjoyed exceptional privileges from the city council.

The intercourse of Venice with the East furnished the Venetian glass makers with patterns of Damascus and Egyptian glass, and the enamelled and gilded Oriental varieties were imitated and improved on by the Murano artists. Some of the products of this period are preserved in the museums. The illustration (Fig. 300) is from a Venetian enamelled cup of green glass in the Kensington Museum.

In the sixteenth century the glass-making furnaces of Murano had increased to a great extent, and were placed under the special protection of the Council of Ten. Owing to the jealousy at this time of other European States, Venetian glass-blowers were bribed by offers of money and large salaries to set up furnaces abroad, and laws were then made forbidding workmen to leave the country to carry on glass making in other places under the penalty of death. This, however, did not prevent Venetian glass-blowers from taking service under the protection of foreign rulers in such countries as Flanders, Spain, and England.

The natural consequences followed, that the exports in glass from Venice to foreign countries became lessened, so much so that the workmen of Murano complained of being thrown idle for several months in the year.

Venetian glass has been made in many colours, such as blue, green, purple, amber, and ruby, and in variegated mixtures of clear or transparent and opaque glass. The

Fig. 300.—Venetian Enamelled Glass; Fifteenth Century. (S. K. M.)

clear variety is remarkable for elegance of shape and fantastic designs of handles or wings, consisting of twisted and knotted interlacings, which were generally executed in blue or red colours and attached to the sides of wine-glasses and other vessels (Fig. 301). One beautiful variety of glass is clouded with a milky-like opalescent tint, which

Fig. 301.—Venetian Glass of the Sixteenth Century. (J.)

is supposed to be produced from arsenic. The opaque white glass is made by the addition of oxide of tin to the usual ingredients.

Glass was made by the Venetians to imitate precious

stones, were streaked, splashed, or spotted with various colours, gold, and copper; the aventurine spotted glass was obtained from a silicate of copper.

The *latticinio* variety was formed of rods of transparent glass enclosing lines of opaque white glass forming patterns. The *vitro di trina* is the so-called lace-glass (Fig. 302); the latter and the mosaic-like or *mille-fiori* glass were made by the Venetians in imitation of the Roman varieties. Another variety was that known as *a reticelli*, in which ornament of opaque network sometimes enclosed air bubbles. That known under the German name of *Schmelz* is the variegated or marble opaque glass made in the Murano furnaces, which imitated chalcedony, lapis lazuli, tortoiseshell, and jasper. Crackled glass was made by the sudden cooling of the half-blown material; this was again heated and drawn out in order to increase the spaces between the crackled lines.

In the sixteenth century the forms of the Venetian

Fig. 302.—Venetian " Vitro di trina." (S. K. M.)

glass vessels were of the Renaissance type; the long shanks and the wide bowls gave them an appearance of elegance and grace. The light and thin character of the material had also a great deal to do with the fragile look of elegance in Venetian glass of this period; the glass of the former (fifteenth) century was of a much thicker kind.

The lightness and superior strength of Venetian glass was due to the absence of lead in its composition, which is so much used in the modern flint glass.

The materials of the composition of the clear Murano glass are supposed to be—one part of alkali, obtained from ferns, moss, lichen, or seaweed, and two parts of pebbles of white quartz or fine clean white sand, and a small quantity of manganese, all well mixed together and melted in the furnace.

The colouring matter is produced from the oxides of various metals, as in the vitreous coloured glazes used in the enamels for glazed pottery.

Vessels and objects in endless variety have been made by the Venetians, such as ewers, basins, drinking-glasses, bottles, standing cups, bowls, goblets, large and small candlesticks, beads, and mirrors, and were exported in great quantities to all parts by the Venetian galleys.

Bead making at Venice was a separate trade, and was one of great importance in the sixteenth and two following centuries. The makers of the small beads were called the "Margariteri," and those who made the large beads were known as the "Perlai." The beads were made from small sections broken or cut off from rods or tubes of glass and placed in an iron pot that was made to rotate, so that the motion prevented the beads from adhering to each other, and at the same time formulated their spherical shape.

Mirrors were made by the ancients of polished metal and from slabs of black obsidian—a kind of natural glass. In mediæval times they were made of clear glass behind which was placed a sheet of lead foil. Glass mirrors were made in Venice from the year 1507, when methods had been discovered of polishing the glass and of applying the "foglia," or layer of metal leaf, to the back. After this date the making of mirrors soon developed into great importance, and the "Specchiai," or mirror makers, had their own corporation. Like the other glass wares of

Venetian manufacture, the mirrors were exported to all parts of Europe.

Some good examples of sixteenth-century mirrors and mirror-frames in glass cut into ornamental shapes, with bevelled edges and engraved, are preserved in our museums and in old houses.

Glass painting for windows was known and practised in Venice as early as the fourteenth century. The very early Italian stained glass used in windows is said to have been executed for Leo III. in 795.

Besides the painted or stained glass used in church windows during the Middle Ages throughout Italy, there were glass manufactories in Rome, Verona, Milan, and Florence for the production of similar wares as those of Venice.

In France and Spain glass making was carried on at various places from the days of the Romans; antique fragments of glass have been dug up in Normandy and in Poitou. In the latter province glass making flourished from a very early date up to the fifteenth century. It was revived in 1572 by the Venetian Fabriano Salviati, who came to Poitou and set up a glass workshop. At Paris, Rouen, Normandy, and in Lorraine glass was made prior to the sixteenth century. The Normandy glass was of a coarse kind, made chiefly for windows and common utensils, but many of the Venetian varieties were made at the other places named.

Some Venetian glass makers came to Paris in 1665, when an establishment was formed for the making of mirrors, and about the same time another factory was set up at Four-la-Ville; these two factories were united by the French Minister Colbert, and were under the patronage of the king. We find that soon afterwards, and especially in the Louis-Quinze period, large panels and wall spaces were filled with glass mirrors as interior decorations.

Glass was made in Spain in the Ibero-Roman period, as the remains of glass vessels and necklaces have been found in tombs, and the ruins of Roman furnaces have been found in the valleys of the Pyrenees. It is supposed that the art was carried on under the Gothic kings of Spain, and also by the Moors in the thirteenth century, who brought with them glass workers as well as some of the wares of the East. Much of the glass made in Spain subsequent to this date is in imitation of the shapes of

Fig. 303.—Spanish Glass ; Sixteenth Century. (S. K. M.)

Arabian pottery, and this is still the case in much of the modern Spanish glass. Spanish glass of the Renaissance was similar in form and in material to the Venetian work of the same period, and during the seventeenth and eighteenth centuries the work was in imitation more or less of the contemporary Dutch and Flemish glass (Fig. 303).

In Holland, glassware seems to have been made by Murano artificers, who from time to time settled in that country and brought the secrets of their trade with them. The objects made were naturally imitations of the Venetian glass, and many of the Dutch drinking-glasses were very graceful in design.

In Amsterdam, Antwerp, Brussels, and throughout the Low Countries generally Venetian glass had been imported in great quantities in the time of and prior to the seventeenth century, and it is difficult to say how much of the old glass found at those places is Dutch, Flemish, or Venetian.

Engraving on glass was much practised in Holland, and many Dutch goblets have well executed portraits of kings, queens, and other persons.

Glass making has been practised in Germany, like in most European countries, from the days of the Romans downwards, especially in the Rhenish Provinces, but German examples dating from the Middle Ages are very rare.

There is documentary evidence which proves that glass

Fig. 304.—German Glasses. (S. K. M.)

was made at Mainz as early as the beginning of the eighth century.

The earliest example of German glass in this country is a *wiederkom*, or cylindrical drinking-vessel, which bears the date of 1571, but an older one, of the date of 1553, is preserved in the Künstkammer at Berlin.

A favourite decoration on the German Wiederkoms is the arms of the emperor or electors, those of the different states of the empire, and of private owners (Fig. 304).

The colour of this kind of glass is usually green and the

decorations are enamelled or painted in grisaille; as a
rule the German cups and wine glasses of the seventeenth
century are richly decorated (Fig. 305). In the German
wine-glasses known as "flügelglässer" is seen an imitation
of the Venetian "winged glasses" (Fig. 301).

Fig. 305.—Decorated German Vases; Seventeenth Century. (S. K. M.)

Bohemian glass of the seventeenth century is noted for
its clearness and good quality, and illustrates the advancement made in the art of engraving on glass. The engraved
work was done with a diamond point as in etching, with
the lapidary's wheel, and by means of biting the glass with
fluoric acid; the latter method is said to have been dis-

covered by Henry Schwanhard of Nüremberg in 1670. John Schäper was a very clever glass engraver and decorator of this period.

A beautiful kind of German glass is known as Kunckel's ruby glass, the originator of which was the director of the Potsdam glass works, where he produced this variety about 1680.

Many relics of glass vessels and beads have been found in Roman tombs, and in various parts of England, of a greenish or blue colour. These may have been imported or may have been made in England, but there is no certain evidence of this. Glass vessels for drinking purposes have been found which are believed to have belonged to the Anglo-Saxon period (Fig. 306).

The material of these is thin, the colour is generally of a pale straw tint, and strips of thickened glass ornament the outside, arranged in the nature of parallel lines, or wound spirally to produce a kind of network decoration.

Venetian glass found its way to England in the sixteenth century; in the inventories of Henry VIII. (1529) and of Robert, Earl of

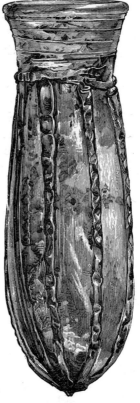

Fig. 306.—Anglo-Saxon Drinking Cup. (S. K. M.)

Leicester (1588), large quantities of Venetian glasses are mentioned as belonging to the above.

Some Muranese glass workers were engaged at this time (1550) in the service of the King of England. The name of an Italian—Jacob Vessaline—is mentioned as a glass maker who worked at Crutched Friars in the beginning of Elizabeth's reign (1557), and in the year 1589 there were supposed to be fifteen glass houses in England.

Sir Robert Mansel was a prominent glass maker of the seventeenth century; he obtained patents in the year 1616 for the making of window glass and all kinds of vessels, and from the remains of glass objects that were found on the site of Princes Hall, in Broad Street, London, it is believed that his works were on that spot.

Mansel employed Italian workmen in the first instance, and it appears that prior to 1623 he had set up works in Milford Haven, at Newcastle-on-Tyne, in Scotland, and other places. The Newcastle furnaces were the most successful, the others being practically failures. Mr. Nesbitt thinks that the success of the Newcastle-on-Tyne works was due to the new system of flint-glass making, which must be credited as an English invention.

Flint or crystal glass is made of a mixture of silicate of potash and lead. It was known but imperfectly made by the Romans in their clear glass variety, which contained a small portion of lead. In the Middle Ages the glass which contained lead was called "Jewish glass," and was generally used for painting on, as it was more fusible than other varieties which did not contain lead. But all authorities agree that the English invented a new product in their flint glass, which was made after many experiments at Lambeth in 1673, as "clear, ponderous, and thick as crystal."

Mr. Nesbitt infers that it was the use of coal in the furnaces instead of wood that led to the development of the process. When using coal the melting-pots had to be covered in the furnace, which lessened the heating powers and thus made the fusing more difficult. To put more alkali in the mixture would have helped it to fuse at a much lower heat, but it would have injured the colour and quality of the glass, so lead was added in certain proportions, which gave the requisite clearness and strength.

All kinds of glass vessels and plate glass for carriage windows were made at Lambeth, under the management or patronage of the Duke of Buckingham.

Though there are no records of glass making in Ireland of a very early date, the glass beads and glass bosses which decorate the objects of Irish art, such as the crosses, croziers, brooches, book-covers, and the celebrated

Fig. 307.—Stained Glass; Fifteenth Century.

Ardagh Chalice, prove that the art was known in Ireland at least in the ninth century, if not earlier. Mention has also been made in old writings of this period of glass vessels for use in Irish churches.

Painted or stained window glass is the glory of our Mediæval churches. The earliest coloured windows were doubtless made from mosaic-like arrangements of different bits of coloured glass. The mosaic window led to the representation of pictorial subjects in stained glass, the latter being formed of pieces of self-coloured glass, or that kind having each piece stained in one colour throughout, cut in the requisite shapes, and fastened together by an arrangement of lead lines which form the main lines of the design; to help out the drawing and expression the stained glass is shaded in hatchings, stippling, and bold lines, usually in a brown colour. Painted glass, as distin-

Fig. 308.—Window Glass; English, Fifteenth Century.

guished from stained glass, is that which is painted on clear or tinted grounds with various enamel colours made from metallic oxides. After the painting is finished the piece of glass is fired, and the enamel colours become fused with the glass surface, and really become part of the glass itself. More finish, a wider range of colouring, greater detail, and generally a more pictorial effect is produced by the artist being able to use freely the enamel colours; but a corresponding loss of depth and brilliancy of colour and of bold decorative effect which belonged to older examples of stained glass must be set against any advantages the painted variety may possess from its pictorial point of view.

The earliest instance in the use of stained glass for church windows is supposed to have been in those that were given by Count Arnold to the Abbey of Tegernsee in Bavaria in the year 999. The thirteenth and fourteenth century were the finest periods for the stained-glass windows of the Gothic cathedrals both in England and on the Continent. About the middle of the sixteenth century

Fig. 309.—Chinese Glass Bowl. (S. K. M.)

enamel colours began to be used, and, as before observed, the designs showed a striving after pictorial effects.

The revival of classic art in the Renaissance period has also a great deal to do with this change in the style and method of execution in painted glass, and we find that the greatest painters — but not always the greatest decorators—of the period supplied cartoons and designs for this class of work.

Glass making has been known in China and Japan from very early times, but it appears to be difficult to obtain anything like authentic information as to its history from our present imperfect knowledge or acquaintance with the native records.

There are stories of ancient Chinese glass vessels that are said to have been seen by the French missionaries of the last century, one of which vessels was so large that "a mule could have been put into it," and that the Chinese made a kind of glass called "lieou-li" that was sufficiently elastic as to bend easily.

The vitreous enamels of the Chinese were of course used as glazes on their porcelain wares and pottery, but it seems that formerly they only made glass objects in the imitation of precious stones, gems, and in their enamels. Chinese glass is often made to simulate rock crystal and jade carvings; their glass snuff-boxes and other small objects are usually well coloured, and are decorated with relief work of ornament, landscapes or figure subjects, the objects generally being of a massive character (Fig. 309).

CHAPTER IX.

THE DECORATION OF BOOKS.

BOOKS may be illustrated in a more or less pictorial manner without any particular regard to the decoration of the page, or with due regard to its ornamentation. In the latter case the designer of the decoration will be the illustrator and decorator in one.

The great majority of modern illustrated books are not decorated in the true sense of the word, but have their illustrations inserted as pictures, or scraps of pictures, without borders or frames, and with little or no relation to the distribution of the printed matter or to the boundary lines of the page. In this respect the modern practice is different from that observed in the Mediæval and Renaissance book illustration, for in the two periods named, when a purely literal or pictorial scene was inserted, it had usually borders like mouldings, or borders of rich decoration, or sometimes bands and lines only, which separated the picture from the printed or written text, and harmonized with any other decoration that might be on the page. Thus an artistic unity was usually preserved in the book decoration of earlier times, which, generally speaking, is the exception in the present day, and not the rule.

The modern practice was brought about by the invention of copper-plate engraving—about 1477—when the copper-plate illustration became, in a great measure, the substitute for wood-engraved blocks of a former period. The plates were usually engraved with copies of pictures, and the

book decorator was superseded by the painter; the art
and practice of the former declined, while the work of
the latter became fashionable, and has remained so ever
since.

Photography has been a considerable aid to the pictorial
side of book illustration, and has, on the other hand, been
a great help to designers of decorative illustration, for by
the use of photography the designer is enabled to have the
work of his hand reproduced in facsimile, as in the process
block method, which has been such a powerful rival and
competitor to all kinds of engraving that it has now
almost crushed them out of existence.

Before the invention of printing books were very scarce,
as they were written in manuscript, and were mostly of
a devotional character, made for the use of the clergy and
others in monastic establishments or religious houses.

The writers and decorators of these missals or illuminated
books were chiefly the brothers or monks of the several
religious orders.

Some of the earliest and best decorated books are those
belonging to the Irish Celtic art of the seventh and eighth
centuries. The remarkable designs of illuminated initials
and capitals, and the intricate geometric patterns, spirals,
and involved interlacings of many varieties, all executed
with astonishing skill, were not excelled or equalled by
the scribes and designers of similar work in England or
on the Continent.

Foremost in importance among the many remaining
monuments of Irish art in book decoration is the celebrated
" Book of Kells," now preserved in Trinity College, Dublin.
It was formerly supposed to have been brought to the
Columban Monastery of Kells, or Kenlis, the ancient
Cennanas, by St. Columba, the founder of that Christian
house, whose death is said to have taken place in the year
597; but this is likely to be only tradition, for it would
appear, according to some later authorities, that the
character of the lettering and the style of the ornamen-

tation fixes the date of its execution about the end of the
seventh century.

Although the native Irish phase of Celtic art possesses
many characteristics of its own, it is a development in
some degree of the more Eastern Romanesque ornament,
and symbolic Byzantine, or even the more primitive
Greek. It is also mixed with a few geometric forms and
symbols that had existed in Ireland before the introduction of Christianity in the fifth century.

In the " Book of Kells," for instance, there are several
illustrations which show in some parts a Greek influence,
and in one page the Greek monogram of Christ appears.

The initial letters in square or rectilineal capitals usually
occupy large portions of the illuminated page, and are
often embedded in rectangular panels with borders, the
latter being filled with elaborate interlacings and spirals,
&c. (Fig. 310).

The smaller text used by the Irish scribes was founded
on the round or uncial Roman variety of lettering, but
in the Irish variety there is a distinct improvement on the
Roman in its beautiful and restrained quality of artistic
simplicity, combined with its perfect legibility. In some
Irish manuscripts an angular cursive or running hand was
also used.

An illustration given at Fig. 311 of the frontispiece from
the " Epistle of Jerome," in the Irish missal known as the
" Book of Durrow," is a fine example of Celtic ornamentation. This and the previous illustration are from Miss
M. Stokes' handbook on "Early Christian Art in Ireland."

The influence and art work of the Irish scribes and missal
decorators in England and on the Continent has been much
greater than was formerly believed. Missionaries were
sent to England, Scotland, and to the Continent, from the
great monastic establishments in Ireland during the period
from the seventh to the eleventh centuries, and carried
with them " Gospels," " Psalters," and other missals,
besides making many other religious books for the use of

the monasteries they had founded in foreign countries. These Irish scribes also taught their art of book illumination to the monks who lived at such places where they set up their missions, or where they had become recluses in

Fig. 310.—Portion of Illuminated Monogram; Book of Kells. (S.)

the foreign monasteries already established. This accounts for the number of Irish manuscripts that have been found in such monastic houses as that of St. Gall in Switzerland, Bobio in Piedmont, at Mentz (Mayence), at Ratisbon in

Fig. 311.—From the Epistle of Jerome; " Book of Durrow." (S.)

Bavaria, at Honau on the Rhine, and at many other places on the Continent. The style of art in all the manuscripts found at these places, though introduced at the inception of Christianity into Ireland from Italy through Gaul, had died out in the latter countries during the fourth and fifth centuries, and was re-introduced, as we have seen, under a modified phase into the Continent by the Irish missionary scribes.

The majority of the Anglo-Saxon manuscripts, if not written by Irish scribes in England, were either decorated or copied closely from the work of the latter. This is supported by some written testimony, but the ornamentation of the pages themselves are distinctly of Irish design.

A common feature in the illuminated pages of the books of the Middle Ages was the dividing of the pages into four compartments with ornamental borders, and each compartment holding the figure of a saint or symbols of the Evangelists, or having a miniature on the top half of the page and two small columns of text below.

Anglo-Saxon manuscripts, with classical treatment of the figure designs, may be seen in the King's Library at the British Museum. The figures have the attenuated Byzantine character, with the linear treatment of the draperies, and with the long lobe-like forms which strongly mark the intended position of the limbs under the drapery; while others show the influence of the early Christian paintings of the catacombs at Rome and Naples.

The " Charter " of the foundation of Newminster at Winchester (966) and several " Gospels " in Latin of the eleventh century in the British Museum, are examples of the best kind of Anglo-Saxon illuminated manuscripts.

" Psalteries," " Gospels," and botanical works known as " Herbals " were among the principal kinds of illustrated books, which were executed in considerable numbers during the thirteenth and fourteenth centuries. The text in these books was usually in solid columns, neatly written in a kind of half-uncial letter in Latin, with large initials and surrounded by broad borders, having little scrolls and trefoil leaves or flowers in which four or six miniatures were placed at intervals. Some pages had the upper half or more occupied by a miniature and had less text, but nearly always there were the accompanying delicate borders designed with great spirit and freedom, and consisting of ornament made up of leaves, flowers, fruit, stems, lines, and spirals, executed on the vellum ground in bright colours and burnished gold.

A characteristic of some of the missals of the fourteenth and fifteenth centuries was the calendar pages at the beginning of the book. The pages which contained the calendar had also, in some cases, miniatures in the borders representing the seasons.

The Bedford Missal (1442), in the British Museum, is a good example of the best French book decoration of that period. It contains a calendar, and was the work of a French artist, though executed in England.

Towards the end of the fifteenth century the miniature began to assume more importance and to occupy the whole of the page. The borders had become more realistic in treatment; foliage, flowers, and insects were rendered almost naturally on gold or coloured grounds, with cast shadows, so as to give the utmost relief.

This treatment was not an improvement on the former flat Gothic style, as it tended to lead to shadowy and meretricious work.

Two of the very finest books of this period are the " Romance of the Rose," in the British Museum, and the Grimani " Breviary " in St. Mark's, Venice. In the latter magnificent book some of the miniatures are ascribed to the Flemish artist Memling.

The miniatures of the splendid choir books of Siena Cathedral are the masterly designs of Girolamo da Cremona and Liberale da Verona, who were famous at this kind of work. The quantity, variety, and purely Italian character of the decoration of these books would almost be sufficient to form a school of Renaissance art in itself.

With the invention of printing a great change came about in the production of decorated books; but it is curious to note that, for a long time after, in order to produce a book it was thought necessary by the means of woodcuts and type to imitate the illuminated missals of the former times.

A good illustration of this may be seen in the woodcut blocks from the recently discovered Sarum Missal (Figs. 312, 313). This very important acquisition to the list of Caxton's works was found in 1893, in Lord Newton's library at Lyme Hall, Cheshire, and is one of the works which Caxton sent to be printed in France. It contains some additions to the text in Caxton's handwriting and has an impression of his peculiar mark at the end of the book.

The illustrations have been printed from wood blocks, and coloured by hand afterwards, according to the practice which obtained at the latter end of the fifteenth century.

Another interesting survival of the practice of placing a cross at the bottom of the page, on which was represented the crucifixion, is seen underneath the latter illustration (Fig. 313) in the Lyme Missal. In the earlier illuminated missals this device was resorted to in order to keep the picture of the crucifixion from being damaged by the frequent kissing of the cross; and so a small cross was placed at the bottom of the picture to enable the piously inclined to still perform this act of piety without damage to the book.

The custom of engraving blocks for book illustration in outline, to be filled in afterwards in colour, led the way to line engraving on wood, where the pure line work was left uncoloured, and soon after became a style by itself, which ultimately, as the art of black and white, was sought after and prized for its own sake.

The invention of printing from type may be traced from the woodcuts, as we have remarked above, some of the earliest of which were those cut for playing cards at the beginning of the fifteenth century.

Fig. 312.—Page from the Caxton "Lyme Missal."

The invention was soon after applied to the production of the xylographic or block-printed books, which were printed in colour from the block. The colour was spread on the block, a sheet of paper was placed on the top, and then rubbed over by the hand to get the impression. The early block-books printed in this way had more pictorial or decorative work in their pages than text or literary matter, and therefore appealed more directly to the great uneducated masses of the people of the times for whom they were compiled. By means of the block printing, many proofs could also be taken to supply the increasing demand for general knowledge which was springing up everywhere in the fifteenth century. Letters, whole words, and legends were now also cut for the printing of literary matter in the block-books. Book blocks were cut in Germany, Holland, and Flanders; the period of their production was from the year 1420 to 1510.

The invention of printing by movable type has been ascribed to various people, but it is now pretty certain that the one name most entitled to this honour is that of John Gutenberg, a native of Mentz (Mainz), who set up a printing establishment in that city in the year 1455, and who worked in connection with Fust, another German printer. The invention, therefore, may date about 1450.

It was about 1455 that the Mazarin Bible was issued from the press of Fust and Gutenberg at Mentz. Lord Ashburnham's copy of the Mazarin Bible, printed on vellum, has been sold this year (1897) for the sum of £4,000.

Peter Schœffer was in partnership some years later with Fust, and in the year 1457 they issued the famous Mentz Psalter (now in the British Museum), the first book printed in different colours from the same block, and the first printed book with a date. This book is a triumph of technical skill, and is unique in its beauty among printed books of the earliest period.

There are few, if any, of the early printed books that

Fig. 313.—Page with the Crucifixion from the Caxton "Lyme Missal."

cannot lay a great claim to artistic merit, but this would hardly have been possible if the designers of the type and ornament for the decoration of the pages, at the advent of printing, had not had before their eyes the splendid models left them by the caligraphers and illuminators of the preceding centuries.

It will be convenient here to say a few words concerning early English printing, which is associated with the name of its great founder, William Caxton (1423-1491). He was a merchant and a diplomatist, but a man of strong literary tastes. He learned the art of printing from Colard Mansion, at Bruges, where he had set up as a merchant ; but leaving his business, he entered the household of the Duchess of Burgundy, sister of Edward IV., where he was engaged in literary pursuits, and for her he made a translation of Le Fevre's " Recueil des Histoires de Troyes." It was in order to multiply copies of this work that he learned the art of printing, and it is said that this was the first English book ever printed, which was probably printed by Mansion at Bruges, under the literary direction of Caxton, in the year 1476.

Caxton came back to England in 1477, and set up a printing press at Westminster, from which he issued a great many books during the last fourteen years of his life. His first book printed at Westminster was a work called "Dictes and Sayings of the Philosophers," which is known to be the first English book printed in England. It is now shown in Case VIII., King's Library, in the British Museum. Among Caxton's other books may be mentioned several editions of the poets Chaucer, Lydgate, and Gower, Malory's " Morte d'Arthur," &c. He evidently sent books of his own composition to be printed on the Continent, as witness the Sarum Missal before mentioned.

The early printed books did not have title-pages. The slow development of this feature after the invention of printing is accounted for by the reason that in this respect, as in others, the first printed books were modelled in imitation of the illuminated missals, and it was not deemed necessary in the mediæval books and manuscripts to have a title-page, the scribe of the olden time merely recording in a note or label fastened to the end of the volume the name and description of his work; so this habit was continued for a long time by the early printers. This note or ending was called a *Colophon.*

Title-pages began to come into use about 1490, but it was not until about forty years later that they became general.

Printers' devices, which were generally of an heraldic character, were commonly seen on the title-pages, some of which were very elaborate and finely designed. The famous printing house of Aldus at Venice had a device of an anchor with a dolphin twined around it, and the motto " Propera tarde," or " Festina lente " (hasten slowly). It was from the printing press of Aldus, in 1499, that the celebrated book called *Poliphili Hypnerotomachia,* " The Dream of Poliphilus," was issued. It is a finely illustrated book, consisting of classical compositions of figures and processions, many architectural designs, ornamental letters, emblems, and devices, all of which are executed in outline and printed from wood blocks.

The illustrations have a fine quality of line, somewhat in the spirit and style of Mantegna's processional designs, or like those great woodcuts in the " Triumph of Maximilian " by Hans Burgmair and Albert Dürer; they are supposed—without, however, any definite proof—to be the work of Gentile or Giovanni Bellini. The book is a romance written and illustrated in the spirit of classical antiquity that so deeply coloured the art and literature of the early Renaissance epoch. A reproduction of the illustrations of this book in photo-lithography by Mr. W. Griggs, with notes by Dr. Appell, was issued by the Science and Art Department in 1888.

Somewhat in the style of " The Dream of Poliphilus " is

Fig. 314.—Illustration from Woodcut of Dante's "Inferno;" Fifteenth Century.

the illustration (Fig. 314) from an edition of Dante's "Inferno" of the same period.

A reduced specimen of the flat treatment of a Renaissance border, from a woodcut which appeared in an edition of "Herodotus" printed at Venice in 1470, is shown as the Frontispiece of this volume. This rich and delicate design is extremely effective in white on a black ground, and is artistically appropriate to the decoration of the page, much more so than the later French and German work in borders and title-pages, which was usually of an extremely heavy character.

Shaded designs of an architectural kind, such as friezes, columns, bases, and pediments, with corpulent figure decoration and heavy mouldings, were compositions which in the latter end of the sixteenth and during the seventeenth centuries took the place of the earlier light arabesque scroll-work of the Italian school, which revelled in the beauty of purer outline and in flat treatment of black and white.

Jean Goujon, Jean Cousin, Virgil Solis, Ducerceau, Stimmer, Jost Amman, and others, though versatile and vigorous to the highest degree, and clever French and German draughtsmen of the sixteenth century, their work in book decoration was more like designs for stone carving and sculpture than legitimate decoration for books. At the end of the century, however, a more correct appreciation of book-cover decoration was manifested. This was due to the happy influence of Arabian design when mixed with the prevailing Renaissance forms. The Oriental craftsmen who came to Italy, and the great commerce of Venice and Europe generally with the East, served to colour in a marked degree the design of the ornamental arts, and nowhere do we see the purely Arabian strap-work and peculiar Saracen leafage used to such advantage as in the tooled and stamped book-cover designs of this period. The Henri Deux book-cover design (Fig. 315) is Arabian in its details, but Renaissance in its general

Fig. 315.—Cover of a Book, Henri-Deux Style; Sixteenth Century.

arrangement. It might have been designed by Ducerceau, but perhaps more likely by Solomon Bernard of Lyons— known as "Le Petit Bernard"—who was a prolific designer of small pictures for wood-engraved book illustrations. He died at Lyons in 1570.

Both of these designers, as well as another famous designer of book decoration, Geoffry Tory, were very partial to the use of strap-work and Arab foliation. The latter artist was also a scholar and author, and produced many fine designs for book-covers. Fig. 316 is a very delicate and rich design for the cover of a "Book of the Hours," by Tory, and is a good example of the Franco-Renaissance of the sixteenth century.

Jean Grolier, Viscount d'Aguisy, was one of the earliest and greatest bibliophiles of France. Though of Italian origin he adopted France as his country, and was Treasurer-General of France when he died, in 1565, at the age of eighty-six. He was appointed ambassador to Clement VII. in the year 1534, and at this time had begun to collect valuable books, that had been chiefly printed in Venice and at Basle. These books were generally unbound copies, but were printed with great care on beautiful paper. On his return to France he employed Geoffry Tory and other designers as well as the best craftsmen in bookbinding to decorate and clothe his precious works. The illustrations we have given are such as are usually found on the Grolier bindings, which nearly always consist of designs composed of strap-work or interlacings and delicate tracery, clothed with Arabian foliage, worked on prepared costly leathers in various colours, and often heightened with gold.

Grolier's bindings usually bore in addition to the title of the book the inscription "Jo Grolierii Et Amicorum," indicating that they belonged to Grolier and his friends, at the same time adding a testimony to the unselfish spirit of the great book-lover.

The strap-work and Oriental foliage designs, which had

Fig. 316.—Cover for a "Book of the Hours," designed by Geoffry Tory; French, Sixteenth Century.

developed so much in France, went even further in Germany, not only in bookbinding decoration, but in gold and silversmiths' work, and in architecture—as we have noticed before in this volume—and nearly all the German, Flemish, and Dutch artists of the sixteenth and following century, who designed for book decoration, adopted the above features in their ornament. Great masters like Albert Dürer, Holbein the younger, Lucas Cranach, and Hans Burgmair, and the "little masters"—Jost Amman, Hans Sebald Beham, Aldegrever, Virgil Solis, Jerome Bang, Peter Flötner of Liége, the Collærts and Janssens of Antwerp, and Lucas Kilian of Augsburg—were the principal designers and engravers for book decoration and illustrations, in which work they were engaged among their varied and prolific labours in other branches of decorative art.

During the seventeenth century the power of design was growing rapidly weaker, the ornament became coarser in feeling and imitated the cumbersome and heavy traditions of classical art. Headpieces, tailpieces, and printers' devices or marks were now more in fashion, rather than the consideration of the design of the page as a whole decorative scheme.

Title-pages with heavy architectural pretensions and pictorial views began to be very common at the end of the century and throughout the eighteenth century.

The pictorial illustration in black and white was due to the development of copper-plate first, and steel engraving afterwards, as new methods for book illustration. These processes were developed very much in Italy and France at the beginning of the eighteenth century, and in England their use in book illustration might be said to extend from about the middle of the eighteenth to the middle of the present century. This period embraced that of the publication of a type of English books of essays, poems, and short stories, known as Anniversaries, Amulets, Annuals, Keepsakes, Souvenirs, &c. These books were filled with beautifully executed line engravings of landscapes and figure subjects, and most of them were of the highest order of technical skill. The period of their existence was from 1780 to 1830.

Book decoration had become more and more pictorial and less decorative when the method employed was line engraving, for, generally speaking, pictures in oil or water-colour were copied with great fidelity and skill by the engraver for use in book illustration, and thus through the agency of the burin or engraver's tool the painter supplanted the book decorator.

Many of the line engravings in the books of the above period show a mixture, on the same plate, of pure line engraving and etching, the latter being a process in which the lines of the design are scratched into the metal plate, which had been previously covered with a wax prepara-tion, and the lines thus exposed are bitten deeper by an acid solution into which the plate is immersed.

Three artists of great talents—Prout, Stothard, and Turner—supplied designs and water-colour drawings of landscapes, figures, and decorative compositions, that were engraved as book illustrations. The illustrations, though on a small scale, to Rogers's "Poems," were very beauti-fully engraved by William Finden, after the designs of Stothard, who made the figure compositions, and of Turner, who did the landscapes. Finden was the great interpreter of Stothard's figure designs, but was equally successful in his engraving of Turner's landscapes.

Stothard has designed many illustrations for books which are characterized by a fine sense of decorative value ; his figures were, as a rule, clothed in light classical costumes, and were graceful in pose and in drawing. The best engravers of the day, such as Finden, Heath, Allen, Fox, Goodyear, Robinson, and Humphreys, were engaged for the publishers in translating his designs for book illustration.

Steel-engraved frontispieces to books on science, history,

travels, architecture, and philosophy had become very common in the eighteenth century. The designs of these were more or less of a heavy classical type of architectural framing and allegorical figures, sometimes enclosing portraits or landscape views. Hogarth's engraved designs and the work of Flaxman may be said to be at the opposite poles of art; the dramatic realism of the former is in strong opposition to the classic idealism of the latter. The works of both have been used as book illustrations, but neither of them can be called book decorators, their engraved works being produced as plates, or as a series of pictures, and the text of the books written merely in explanation of the plates.

The poet and highly imaginative artist, William Blake, in his designs for his "Songs of Innocence" (1789), and in his "Book of Job," reverts to the old missal-painters' manner of embodying together the text, ornament, and miniatures, in one decorative scheme of unity, in the artistic treatment of the page. Blake engraved his own designs, and printed them off in black and white, or sometimes in colour.

During the later years in which steel engravings for books were in fashion, the revived art of wood-engraving was making a slow headway towards recognition and favour in England, and its complete revival was owing to the persistent efforts and genius of Thomas Bewick (1753-1828). Bewick was not only a wood-engraver and a craftsman of the highest order, but was an artist gifted with a fine feeling for humour and pathos, and many of his small compositions are characterized by a good deal of pictorial effect. His best works, from a technical point of view, are his illustrations of natural history, the finest of which are the illustrations in his book, the "History of British Birds," which show Bewick at his best in the rendering of bird form and feather texture. He also designed and executed many dainty little compositions of landscapes with figures and animals as tailpieces.

The school of Bewick, formed of his pupils and others, served to keep alive the art of wood-engraving until the revival was assured, for Bewick had a difficult task to get the public to appreciate his work during his lifetime.

The names of his principal pupils were Luke Clennel, who was the most celebrated, and who was also a good water-colour painter; Charlton Nesbitt, Robert Johnson, and William Harvey.

A self-educated engraver of some note was Robert Branston, of Lynn, Norfolk (1778-1827).

John Thompson was a pupil of Branston, who excelled his master, and was the best engraver of his time in England.

A great name among English wood-engravers is that of William J. Linton, who has done more by his work and pen to advance the art than any one. His best work was executed about the middle of this century, particularly in the engravings of Rossetti's designs for Tennyson's poems (1857-59). He is also known as a writer and designer of considerable power.

A pupil of his—Mr. Walter Crane—whose work is so well known and admired in the present day, has designed some fine decorative work for book illustration. His children's books are good examples of colour and design, but perhaps his own poem, "The Sirens Three," where he has designed and executed the lettering and beautiful decoration, best fulfils the conditions of what a decorated page ought to be, and may be ranked as one of his greatest efforts in book decoration.

The late Randolph Caldecott, whose characteristic humour appears in every line of his work, was another great designer of children's books. His colouring is very harmonious and refined, and though his work is mostly of a pictorial character, yet in his larger pages he displays a true feeling for the decoration of the page.

Children's illustrated books of fairy tales have multiplied very much of late years, and in many of them is seen some of the old decorative feeling, where the text and illustrations are considered in an artistic relation to each other. This will also be noticed in many illustrations to poems which often appear in the monthly magazines of the present day.

On the other hand, picture illustrations and scrappy designs of the vignette order are very common.

These are generally inserted, without any apparent order, on any part of the page, and the type matter filled into the vacant spaces. This picture-screen method of book, newspaper, and magazine illustration has no doubt been developed by our recent acquaintance and infection with Japanese art, which, though highly artistic and decorative in many senses, is wanting in balance of mass, and is only occasionally right in arrangement of line. Japanese decoration as such is generally charming, but when the Western designer copies the Japanese ideas without the style and methods of execution, the result may have novelty to recommend it, but otherwise it is a failure.

It is hardly necessary to say that the reign of wood-engraving is almost now at an end as far as book illustration is concerned, and, like steel engraving, has nearly become an art of the past, owing to the great advance made in recent years in the many methods of black and white reproduction, which is mainly due to the powerful help and agency of photography.

END.

PRINTED BY J. S. VIRTUE AND CO., LIMITED, CITY ROAD, LONDON.

CHAPMAN & HALL'S
ART PUBLICATIONS.

◆◆◆◆◆◆◆◆◆◆◆◆◆◆

STUDIES IN PLANT FORM AND DESIGN. By W.
MIDGLEY and A. E. V. LILLEY. With numerous Illustrations. Second
Edition. Demy 8vo, 4s.

WOOD CARVING. By Jos. PHILLIPS. A Carefully Graduated
and Educational Course of Wood Carving, specially adapted for Schools
and Technical Classes. With 13 Illustrations, 3s. 6d. ; 15 Full-size Shaded
Working Drawings, 5s.

RAPHAEL: HIS LIFE, WORKS, AND TIMES. By
EUGENE MUNTZ. A New and Cheap Edition, condensed from the original
work. Royal 8vo, 7s. 6d.

A PRACTICAL HANDBOOK OF DRAWING: For Modern
Methods of Reproduction. By CHARLES G. HARPER. With many Illustrations showing comparative results. Crown 8vo, 7s. 6d.

EGYPTIAN ART. By C. RYAN. With 56 Illustrations. Crown
8vo, 2s. 6d.

PRINCIPLES OF ORNAMENT. By J. WARD. Edited by
G. AITCHISON, A.R.A. Fully Illustrated. New and Enlarged Edition.
Crown 8vo, 7s. 6d.

DECORATIVE DESIGN. An Elementary Text-Book of Principles and Practice. By F. G. JACKSON. Fully Illustrated. Third Edition.
Large crown 8vo, 7s. 6d.

THE DECORATION OF METALS: Chasing, Repoussé, and
Saw Piercing. By JOHN HARRISON. With 180 Illustrations. Crown 8vo,
3s. 6d.

WOOD-CARVING IN THEORY AND PRACTICE, AS
APPLIED TO HOME ARTS, with Notes on Design. By F. L.
SCHAUERMANN. 124 Illustrations. Second Edition. Imp. 8vo, 5s.

SCIOGRAPHY: or, Parallel and Radial Projection of Shadows.
Being a Course of Exercises for the use of Students in Architectural and
Engineering Drawing. By R. PRATT. With numerous plates. Oblong
4to, 7s. 6d.

THE SCULPTOR AND ART STUDENTS' GUIDE TO
THE PROPORTIONS OF THE HUMAN FORM. With measure-
ments in feet and inches of Full-grown Figures of Both Sexes and of
Various Ages. By Dr. G. SCHADOW. Oblong folio, 31s. 6d.

ELEMENTARY PRINCIPLES OF ORNAMENT. By
JAMES WARD. Illustrated. 8vo, 5s.

LONDON: CHAPMAN & HALL, LTD.,
Agents to the Science and Art Department.

DIAGRAMS FOR CLASS TEACHING.

(Adapted to the Requirements of the Science and Art Department.)

THE PRINCIPLES OF MINING. Arranged by E. T. HOWARD, M.A., F.G.S , and E. W. SMALL, M.A., B.Sc., F.G.S. These Diagrams have been arranged in accordance with the list given in the Directory of Science and Art (1895). The object has been to supply a really useful selection at a very moderate cost. Twelve sheets, size 30 in. by 40 in. Price 21s. net; on rollers and varnished, £2 2s. net.

TERRESTRIAL AND ASTRONOMICAL PHENOMENA AND OBJECTS. By R. A. GREGORY, F.R.A.S., author of "Elementary Physiography," "The Planet Earth," &c. These diagrams have been prepared to illustrate Phenomena and Objects which cannot be experimentally demonstrated or easily observed. It is believed that they will not only be of value in Departmental Classes, but also in Elementary Schools where Physical Geography is taught. Twelve sheets, size 30 in. by 40 in. Price 21s. net; on rollers and varnished, £2 2s. net.

BOTANICAL.

ILLUSTRATING A PRACTICAL METHOD OF TEACHING BOTANY. By Professor HENSLOW, F.L.S. Nine sheets coloured, 42 in. by 31 in , £2; on rollers and varnished, £3 3s.

MACHINE DETAILS.

SIXTEEN COLOURED DIAGRAMS. By Professor UNWIN. 31 in. by 23 in., £2 2s. ; on rollers and varnished, £3 14s.

MODELS.

SYLLABUS OF ART EXAMINATIONS.

Minute by Science and Art Department.

MODEL DRAWING,

ELEMENTARY AND ADVANCED STAGES.

Models and Vases prescribed by the Science and Art Department for the use at the above Art Examinations. These Models and Vases have been duly approved by the Authorities, and specially manufactured for CHAPMAN & HALL, LIMITED.

The Entire Collection consists of—

1. VASE—Bottle.	8. HEXAGONAL PRISM.
2. VASE—Majolica Vase.	9. TRIANGULAR PRISM.
3. VASE—Large Earthenware Vase.	10. SQUARE PRISM.
4. CUBE—Large.	11. SQUARE PYRAMID.
CUBE—Small.	12. SKELETON CUBE.
6. CONE.	13. SPHERE.
7. CYLINDER.	14. RING.

Price in box, complete, £4 net.
Set for Elementary Stage (Subject 3A—First Figure), £2 16s. net.
Set for Advanced Stage (Subject 3A—Second Figure), £1 4s. net.

CASTS.

A CATALOGUE OF CASTS,

Especially selected for the use of Schools of Art, Art Classes, Technical Schools and Public and Elementary Schools. Price 1s.

This Catalogue contains Illustrations of 423 different Casts, a great number of which are made by Messrs. Chapman & Hall from original and copyright designs, and from exhibits in the South Kensington Museum. The selection and manufacture are under the personal supervision of the Art Master of one of the largest Art Schools of England.

NOTICE.—The above diagrams, models, &c., can be inspected in the Show Room of Messrs. Chapman and Hall's premises, together with a vast assortment of mechanical and other models, vases, diagrams, and drawing examples. Catalogues post free.

LONDON : CHAPMAN & HALL, LTD.,

Agents to the Science and Art Department.